AMERICAN AUTHORS
AND CRITICS SERIES

GENERAL EDITOR

JOHN MAHONEY

University of Detroit

THEODORE DREISER AT 45—SPOKESMAN OF AN AGE

THEODORE
DREISER

An Introduction and Interpretation

JOHN J. McALEER
Boston College

Hard-bound edition distributed by
BARNES & NOBLE, INC.
Publishers · Booksellers · New York

*Holt, Rinehart and Winston, Inc. is the
publisher of this title and the exclusive
distributor of the paper-bound edition.*

813.52
M 11 t
64344   January 1969

Permission has been granted by The World Publishing Company to
quote from the following works by Theodore Dreiser: *A Hoosier
Holiday* (Copyright 1916 by John Lane Co. Copyright 1943 by
Theodore Dreiser); *Hey, Rub-A-Dub-Dub* (Copyright 1920 by Boni
& Liveright. Copyright 1926 by Theodore Dreiser. Copyright 1947
by Mrs. Theodore Dreiser); *An American Tragedy* (Copyright 1925
by Horace Liveright, Inc. Copyright 1926 by Theodore Dreiser.
Copyright 1953 by Helen Dreiser); *The Financier* (Copyright 1912
by Harper & Bros. Copyright 1927, 1940 by Theodore Dreiser); *The
Titan* (Copyright 1914 by John Lane Co. Copyright 1925 by Horace
Liveright, Inc.); *Jennie Gerhardt* (Copyright 1911 by Harper & Bros.
Copyright 1923 by Horace Liveright, Inc. Copyright 1926 by
Theodore Dreiser); *Dawn* (Copyright 1931 by Theodore Dreiser);
The 'Genius' (Copyright 1915 by John Lane Co. Copyright 1923 by
Horace Liveright, Inc. Copyright 1943 by Theodore Dreiser); *News-
paper Days* (Copyright 1922 by Boni & Liveright. Copyright 1949
by Helen Dreiser).

Permission has been granted by Doubleday & Company, Inc., to
quote selections from the following works by Theodore Dreiser: *The
Stoic* (Copyright 1947 by Helen Dreiser); *The Bulwark* (Copyright
1946 by Doubleday & Company, Inc.).

Permission has been granted by David McKay Company, Inc. to
quote from *The Living Thoughts of Thoreau*, Ed. Theodore Dreiser.

Permission has been granted by the University of Pennsylvania Press to quote from the *Letters of Theodore Dreiser*, Ed. Robert H. Elias.

The author deeply appreciates Mrs. Frank E. Hudson's kind permission to include in this study her heretofore unpublished pencil sketch of Theodore Dreiser. Grateful acknowledgment is also made to Mrs. Louise Campbell, Dreiser's long-time editor-typist, and to Mrs. Neda Westlake, curator of the Dreiser Collection at the University of Pennsylvania Library, for their invaluable assistance. Others who gave help and encouragement include Walter Harding, Frank Edward Manual, John L. Mahoney, George Smith, John Sullivan, Edward Hirsh, James T. Farrell, Albert Mordell, and William Alton Dickson.

ABOUT THE AUTHOR

JOHN J. MCALEER, professor of English at Boston College, is the author of more than a hundred articles and numerous short stories and poems. Among his contributions are a series of bio-critiques on eminent Shakespeareans, including Pope, Theobold, Kean, and Dowden, which have appeared in the *Shakespeare Newsletter*. Professor McAleer is the editor of *Ballads and Songs Loyal to the Hanoverian Succession* and a contributor to the *New Catholic Encyclopedia*. In addition, he serves on the reviewing staffs of *Drama Survey, America,* and *Commonweal,* and is with the editorial department of the Boston *Globe*.

To Ruth, my wife

PREFACE

THEODORE DREISER's life and art have been closely assessed in several book-length studies. Shorter critical pieces, undertaking parallel inquiries, have multiplied into the hundreds. Dreiser has been called "the Mount Everest of American fiction," "the Hindenburg of the novel," "a many-sided monolith," "the wheelhorse of American naturalism," "bellwether of modern fiction," "high romantic," "the peasant of our literature," "a Flemish artist," and "a belated Victorian." He has been acclaimed "chief spokesman for the realistic novel," "one of the great folk writers," and even "one of the great moral leaders of mankind." His merits have been compared favorably with those of Dr. Johnson, Michelangelo, Balzac, Goethe, Wagner, Dostoevski, Tolstoi, and with those of a thoroughbred horse. He has been deplored as "the Caliban of American fiction," "one of the last berserkers," "a Man of Ice," and "the worst writer of his eminence in the entire history of literature," not excepting Richardson. Although many of the commentaries on Dreiser contain forceful insights both into his personal history and into his achievements as a writer, taken in aggregate they are disappointing. Like the swords of an illusionist, which penetrate a cabinet only at fixed points, they adhere to a pattern which leaves vital zones untouched.

The present study, mindful of the voids in Dreiser scholarship, seeks to elucidate the total conception which Dreiser rendered as a man and an artist. As the first step toward this goal, we fixed the character of Dreiser's thought by a chronological reading of his complete works. This hitherto untried approach surprisingly affirms Dreiser's consistency and, to a large extent, takes him out of the arena of controversy. Working from this bedrock, the study conducts a clinical investigation into the common indictments brought against Dreiser, and brings them into new perspective. It shows how his personal history molded his vigorous spirit of inquiry. It distinguishes, in a blend of influences that extend from crises which bruised his psyche in boyhood, to his systematic pursuit, in his adult years, of philosophical maturity and spiritual integrity, the genesis of his major works. It traces the connection between plot, image, and idea in his novels and reveals how his interests and experience relate to, and even explain, his form, his style, and his art. It offers definitive assessment of his extensive use of symbols, and explains how certain symbols—notably, his abundant motion symbols—are tied, in their recurrence and interaction, to a functional purpose. The moving world of Theodore Dreiser did not rest on an effervescent compassion, but on a dynamic theory of flux. Finally, the study gives account of Dreiser's architectonic genius and of those lurking currents of transcendentalism which, throughout his works, are a sustaining force.

Chestnut Hill, Mass.   J. J. McA.
December 1967

CONTENTS

ILLUSTRATIONS

CHRONOLOGY

1871 Herman Theodore Dreiser born August 27, in Terre Haute, Indiana, to John Paul Dreiser, a German immigrant, and Sarah Maria Schänäb Dreiser.

1879–1884 Lived with family, in grinding poverty, in Vincennes, Sullivan, and Evansville, Indiana; in Chicago and, finally, in Warsaw, Indiana.

1886–1887 Attended high school in Warsaw. In the summer of 1887 broke off his education to seek work in Chicago.

1889 Entered Indiana University in September.

1890 Sarah Dreiser died, in Chicago.

1892 Joined the staff of the Chicago *Globe* in the spring. In November went to St. Louis to work for the *Globe-Democrat*.

1893 Became drama critic of *Globe-Democrat*. Transferred to staff of St. Louis *Republic*. Fell in love with a country schoolteacher, Sara Osborne White, twenty-seven months his senior.

1894 Set out for New York. Formed fast friendship with Arthur Henry, city editor of the Toledo *Blade*. Joined staff of the Pittsburgh *Dispatch*. Read Balzac's *Human Comedy*, Spencer's *First Principles*, and Huxley's *Science and Christianity*, and abandoned Catholicism in favor of mechanistic determinism. In November found employment with the *New York World*.

1895–1897 Edited *Ev'ry Month* under aegis of his brother, the song writer Paul Dresser.

1898 Served as consulting editor for *Ainslee's* and *Success* magazines. Married to Sara White.

1899 Began writing short stories at Arthur Henry's home in Maumee, Ohio, in July. In September began *Sister Carrie*.

1900 *Sister Carrie* given token publication by Doubleday, Page and Company. John Paul Dreiser died.

1901–1903 Began *Jennie Gerhardt*. Suffered mental breakdown. Started comeback as assistant feature editor, New York *Daily News*.

1904–1905 Joined Street & Smith, editing dime novels. Named editor of *Smith's Magazine*.

1906 Edited *Broadway Magazine*. Paul Dresser died.

1907 Became editor of Butterick "Trio." (*Delineator, Designer, New Idea Woman's Magazine*) with a combined circulation of nearly one million.

1908 Friendship with H. L. Mencken began when Mencken became a contributor to the *Delineator*. Conferred with Theodore Roosevelt, at the White House, on founding the National Child Rescue League.

1910 Dismissed from Butterick editorships in October.

1911 *Jennie Gerhardt* published. Departed in November for six-month stay in Europe.

1912 *The Financier* published.

1913 *A Traveler at Forty* published.

1914 *The Titan* published. Final separation from Sara White Dreiser.

1915 Traveled in August and September on two-thousand-mile automobile tour through Indiana and adjacent states. *The 'Genius'* published.

1916 *Plays of the Natural and Supernatural* published. *The 'Genius'*, attacked by the New York Society for the Suppression of Vice, became a *cause célèbre*.

1918 *Free and Other Stories* and *The Hand of the Potter* published.

1919 *Twelve Men* published. Took as his mistress Helen Patges Richardson, his mother's grand-niece. Settled with her in California.

1920 *Hey, Rub-A-Dub-Dub* published. *An American Tragedy* begun the following summer.

1922 *A Book About Myself* (*Newspaper Days*) published.

1923 *The Color of a Great City* published. Returned to New York to research *An American Tragedy*.

1925 *An American Tragedy* published in two volumes.

1926 From June to October toured Scandinavia, Germany, France, and England, with Helen.

1927–1928 Departed on eleven-week visit to U.S.S.R. Sole meeting with Hemingway, in Paris. Published *Chains* and *Moods, Cadenced and Declaimed*. Published *Dreiser Looks at Russia*.

1929 *A Gallery of Women* published. Settled at Mt. Kisco, New York, at "Iroki."

1931 *Dawn* published. In November led Dreiser Committee to Kentucky to inquire into labor unrest in Harlan County.

1932–1934 *Tragic America* published. Served as co-editor of *American Spectator* with James Branch Cabell, George Jean Nathan, and Eugene O'Neill.

1938 Attended International Peace Conference in Paris in July. Visited Barcelona to witness last week of the siege. In September conferred with Franklin Roosevelt, on Spanish Relief. In December settled in Glendale, California, with Helen.

1939 *The Living Thoughts of Thoreau* published.

1941 *America Is Worth Saving* published.

1942 Agreed to send papers to University of Pennsylvania. Barred from speaking in Toronto, in September, by Ontario's Attorney General. Suffered a coronary occlusion. Sara White Dreiser died in St. Louis.

1944 Presented Award of Merit Medal by American Academy of Arts & Letters. Married Helen Richardson in Stevenson, Washington on June 13.

1945 Applied for membership in Communist Party, July 20. Completed *The Bulwark* in May; a week later began work on *The Stoic*. Died of heart failure, December 28, in Hollywood.

1946 *The Bulwark* published.

1947 *The Stoic* published.

1955 Helen Dreiser died, September 22; buried beside Dreiser at Forest Lawn. University of Pennsylvania received *Notes on Life*, the huge, unfinished philosophic-scientific treatise which had held Dreiser's attention during the last fifteen years of his life.

INTRODUCTION

THEODORE DREISER believed that the American Dream, and the precepts that safeguarded it, put before Americans false goals which estranged them from Nature and left them unfulfilled; the passion with which he wrote from that conviction dominated all his work. Not surprisingly, therefore, his strongest partisans have been those whom his courage and ideals engaged; his strongest foes those who opposed them. Accordingly, in the storm of controversy that has ever swirled around Dreiser, his stature as artist has been uncertainly considered.

Fault was found with Dreiser's work in three principal areas. He was said to be a willful despoiler of public and private morality, a tawdry thinker, and an egregiously bad stylist. The first charge, though it plagued Dreiser through much of his lifetime, rarely is heard today. Ironically, modern writers have exercised with such liberality the freedom Dreiser procured for them that his transgressions now seem puny. As to the second criticism, Dreiser's thinking was much less tawdry than has been supposed, even by his admirers. A systematic inquiry into the growth of his thought shows that he seemed inconsistent merely because his quest for philosophic ultimates was constant and he never hesitated to abandon a position when he found it untenable. Throughout his life Dreiser experienced steady intellectual growth.

As to the allegation that his style was bad, lately there has been a shift away from this view from which his reputation has benefited. In point of fact his weaknesses as a stylist often were overemphasized by those whose disapproval found its genesis in matters unrelated to his style. His earliest detractors were alienated by his brutal frontal assault on the Protestant ethic, and by the realization that a Teuton-Slav had challenged Anglo-Saxon dominion over American letters. Later critics were stirred by his adoption of a chemicomechanistic theory of life. After 1930, his open advocacy of communist causes inspired attempts to diminish his stature as an artist in order to lessen the consequence of his political affirmations.

1

From the start Dreiser was at war with much more than the gen-
teel tradition in America. He saw American social thought and romantic idealism as no longer germane to emerging conditions in the
modern world. He sought, at first, to reshape American values within
the existing political system; eventually, he concluded that the political system itself must yield place to something new. Dreiser's assumption that communism would give Americans the paradise the
American Dream could not provide, rested more on a fond hope than
on sober understanding of political realities. He himself owned that
his hope was not deep rooted. But his belief that the idealism of the
American Dream had been betrayed, that the values from which it
had taken its substance had lost relevance, merits respectful consideration.

In young manhood Dreiser concluded change was the basic law
of Nature and then, appropriately, committed himself to a pattern of
life physically, philosophically, and spiritually nomadic. Hence his
repugnance for the anchoring stabilities that religion, society, and
the state, proffer man. Dreiser's quest for ultimate realities often
made him ridiculous in the eyes of his fellow men: it brought him
under censure and even sharp attack. Yet when satisfied that he was
expressing truth as he saw it, he was impervious to criticism. A
villager by upbringing, by instinct a pastoral poet, Dreiser turned
to the city because he found in it the raw materials he needed to
know life. More than once he was found by friends convulsively sob-
bing on street corners as he observed poor, struggling humanity en
masse. Dreiser's preface to *The Living Thoughts of Thoreau* speaks
of humanity's "orphaned ache." Earlier, in 1920, in *Hey, Rub-
A-Dub-Dub,* pondering man's role in the universe, he decided
man would act most wisely if he came "to think of himself rather as
a waif, an unloved orphan in space, who must nevertheless and by
his own effort make his pathetic way in the world." Throughout his works, the orphanhood of every major character is, at some
point, dwelt upon with tender solicitude.

Dreiser's works have been scrutinized with less critical acuity
than the works of any other major American writer. Seldom has he
been evaluated dispassionately. In survey accounts he is passed
over hastily because no one quite knows how to supply him relevance. His achievements tend to be redistributed among writers who
went to him for apprenticeship—Anderson, Lewis, Faulkner, Masters, Fitzgerald, Farrell, Dos Passos. Who sees that the revolt of the
village began with Dreiser? Who sees him as master chronicler of
the dissolution of the American Dream? Dreiser was the first novel-

ist to recognize that Emersonian self-reliance had been perverted by predators into an astonishing complacency and indifference to the moving course of history. He should stop being pilloried for his political, social, and moral views, and be evaluated instead as a force in American literature second in fecundity only to Emerson himself, and, at that, truer to the mark. He should be reverenced as a moralist because he makes his readers think about the meaning of human existence, the shabbiness of material goals, the plight of the unfortunate, the necessity of loving truth more than one's self, the factors that intervene to obstruct man's free expression of Nature. The present age applauds his views on the deadening effect of outmoded conformities, pious hypocrisy, crippling conventions, and a romantic idealism which renders inert the will to action. But it does not acknowledge his precedence in proclaiming these views. Nor will it own that his animosity toward religion itself is directed less against honest faith than that narrow dogmatism which can make religion an exercise in mental and physical inertia. Dreiser should be cherished also as the most ample of social historians, for he is the one writer of his age to whom man today can turn to explore in depth the genesis and development of the twentieth-century world. To posterity he gave his whole mind, giving us a chance to know him, the things he held to be true, and the times he lived in and challenged.

A "MOTHERY" BOY

A T SEVENTEEN, Sarah Maria Schänäb,[1] a farm girl living near Dayton, Ohio, fell in love with John Paul Dreiser, an itinerant weaver who had left Germany six years before, in 1844, to escape military conscription and a waspish stepmother. John Paul, who was twenty-nine, was a fervent Roman Catholic. Sarah, a Mennonite, was sure her family would disown her if she married him. Nevertheless, on New Year's Day, 1851, four months before her eighteenth birthday, she did slip away to marry him and embrace his religion. Although Sarah's father eventually deeded her five acres of land, he never consented to see her again after her marriage.

Before she was twenty-one Sarah had given birth to three sons. One night she wished vehemently that the boys were dead so she could be free to enjoy herself. When they sickened and died, shortly thereafter, Sarah was certain their deaths were a judgment on her, and vowed she would give herself completely to her children, henceforth, if only she had more. She spent the rest of her life making good her promise—bearing five sons and five daughters in the twenty years that followed. All ten children, taxing their mother's strength with almost constant cares and demands, lived to survive her.

Sarah's twelfth child was Herman Theodore Dreiser. In the days before he was born, spirits were seen in the house on Ninth Street, in Terre Haute, Indiana, and the anxious father brought in a priest to perform minor rites of exorcism. At the time of Theodore's birth, at 8:30 in the morning of August 27, 1871, Sarah saw the three Graces, in moods unmistakably convivial, pass through her bedchamber. Yet the new child was without favor—puny, listless, and nearly sightless in his right eye. The psychic gifts of an ancient German crone were then invoked. Under her direction, on three successive nights the infant was carried outdoors where an incantation—

---

[1] Schänäb was eventually corrupted to Snepp or Schnepp. *See* Theodore Dreiser, *Dawn* (New York, 1931), p. 253.

"Wass ich hab, nehm ab; wass ich thu, nehm zu!" [2]—was read over him under the light of the full moon. Six weeks after his birth, by the time the great Chicago fire was raging, Theodore Dreiser was showing a tenacious will to live.

John Paul Dreiser, "a thin grasshopper of a man," was already fifty when he became a father for the twelfth time. Dreiser once described him as "honest, worthy, and defiant." Regrettably, his days of defiance had ended before Theodore was born. In 1869, a mill in which he had a heavy investment had burned in Sullivan, Indiana. Bound by conscience, John Paul reduced his family to penury in his efforts to compensate neighboring farmers for the loss of tons of fleece that had been stored at the mill.

In 1878, after a succession of removals to smaller and shabbier quarters here and there in Terre Haute, the home was broken up so that John Paul and the older children could look for work in one direction while Sarah, with Claire, Theodore, and Edward—the younger three—could go in another and seek some kind of homely service to maintain them till better days.

Sarah went first to Vincennes, Indiana, where Susan Bellette, a young woman she once befriended, had promised her a home. But Sue was keeping a house of assignation for firefighters, so after three months Sarah moved her fascinated brood on to Sullivan. Presently they were joined there by Mary Frances, who tearfully confessed she was pregnant by a Terre Haute lawyer who refused to marry her. During the remaining months of her pregnancy, Sarah shielded her daughter from prying eyes, and in April 1879, Mary Frances gave birth to a stillborn boy. At midnight, Sarah herself dug a grave near the house and buried the baby. From this episode Dreiser later drew details for his portrait of Jennie Gerhardt.

Sarah and her children stayed four years at Sullivan, receiving periodic visits from John Paul. Sullivan, his "mother's home region" appealed to Dreiser. There he saw at every hand evidence that Sarah's family had been free from want, a circumstance which contrasted meaningfully with his own situation. At times he ate cornmeal mush fried because there was no milk for it. Once he was put out of school because he lacked shoes. Often, to keep the fire going, he gathered coal along the railroad tracks. Until he was forty a memory of childhood sufferings made him dread the approach of winter.

---

[2] "What I have, diminish [wane]; what I shall do, flourish [wax]." *See Dawn,* p. 8.

Still later, as a poet, he would reflect sadly on "the shadowland of childhood/Through which I darkly stumbled. . . ." [3]

Dreiser's relationship with his mother was the most significant he ever knew. He describes her as "a dreamy, poetic, impractical soul," who had neither social training nor moral bias. All her children adored her and kept coming back to her, even the married ones. Primarily, Sarah was loving, tolerant, and understanding, whereas John Paul habitually chided his children for wayward behavior—though certainly with ample cause. Paul, the oldest son, was arrested three times before he ran away from home while yet in his teens. Marcus Romanus early showed potential (later abundantly realized) as a ne'er-do-well, and the three oldest girls all became mothers before they became wives. Yet to Dreiser, John Paul seemed a narrow rigorist who turned up periodically to disturb an easygoing household with demands for reform and discipline which he had no apparent right to make. In contrast, his wife was a marvel of understanding. She was a big, rawboned woman, but neat, cheerful, tender, resourceful, and occasionally, though with little reason, even rhapsodic. Wherever she lived Sarah set out a flower bed and a vegetable garden. She took in washing and boarders; she went out to scrub when necessity required. She ministered to dying neighbors, sheltered unwed mothers, fed itinerant priests, and took in little farm girls to ready them for First Communion. Above all Sarah was compliant to the flow of Nature. What Nature willed for her, she accepted with wise complacency. When Nature and the social code conflicted, she took her stand with Nature.

To Dreiser, Sarah was security. Years later he spoke of himself frankly as a "mothery" boy. "I was always a 'mother child,' hanging to her skirts as much as I was permitted until I was seven or eight years old." Sometimes, when her children taxed her patience too much, Sarah would pack a basket, draw on the Mennonite shawl and bonnet which had survived her conversion to Catholicism, and announce she was leaving. Once, to make it seem that she had made good her threat, she hid in a cornfield. Seized with hysteria, Dreiser fell unconscious. He wrote later: "Long after I had passed my thirtieth birthday . . . I still used to dream of her as being alive but threatening to go off and leave me, and would awake to find myself in tears. Even to this day, dreams of her invariably evoke in me a great sadness and longing, the result, I presume of the psychic

---

[3] "Where?" in *Moods, Cadenced and Declaimed.*

impact of those terrors of long ago." At sixty Dreiser would say, "It always seemed to me that no one ever wanted me *enough,* unless it was my mother."

In the spring of 1881, the key turned in the lock of a door in Evansville, Indiana, and Sarah Dreiser was shown into a comfortable, newly furnished home. At her side stood John Paul, Jr., her runaway son who, as Paul Dresser, was now a famous Broadway song writer. The American Dream had come to pass for the Dreisers. Paul was thirteen years Theodore's senior, a huge, impressive man with many of his mother's traits. Dreiser thought to himself at the time, "Was this not my own brother, strong and rich, a veritable bulwark . . . against further misfortune?" To Dreiser, Paul was an irrefutable negation of all his father's strict preachments. Nevertheless, in the summer of 1884 the Evansville interlude ended when Paul went back to New York after quarreling with Sallie Walker, his mistress (and the guiding spirit of his munificence), whom he later immortalized as "My Gal Sal."

Led by Sarah, the brave matriarch, the family now set forth for Chicago. There Theodore took a job as cashboy in a dry goods store, but his mother quickly ended the experiment when he became frightened and mentally confused. In a few months, pursued by easy-payment collectors, the family fled back to Indiana, to Warsaw. Thus ended Dreiser's first encounter with the American Dream.

In Warsaw, John Paul rejoined the family and once again they stood united. Moreover, their new neighbors knew nothing of their past history so they were taken up as respectable. Especially important to Dreiser was John Paul's decision, made here, that his children could attend public school. The Teutonic severity of the German priests and nuns at the schools Dreiser had gone to up to this time had always terrified him. But problems persisted. Already stretching out toward his full height of six feet, one and a half inches, Dreiser was unusually thin; his large upper teeth were crowded and bucked, his mouth twisted, and his right eye lower than his left and slightly turned out from the line of vision. He was shy and unsure of himself, and his classmates thought him a "gawk." He welcomed, therefore, an escape route pointed out to him by his teacher, May Calvert. With Miss Calvert's encouragement, Dreiser fled into the world of books—Shakespeare, Herrick, Dryden, Defoe, Fielding, Pope, Goldsmith, Scott, Dickens, Thackeray, Irving, Hawthorne, Cooper, Emerson, and Kingsley all fed his imagination. Irving's *Alhambra,* with its Aladdin fantasies, particularly enticed him. It was while reading *The Alhambra* that Dreiser had a typical clash with his father. "What is all this trash, Dorsch?" John Paul had asked. Dreiser made his scorn quickly felt and a few days later, in a gesture he could ill afford, John Paul paid seven dollars to an itinerant peddler for a full set of Irving's works.

Dreiser owns that he found his father mild, intelligent, and apt at characterizing people, when religion was not his topic. But John Paul saw mostly everything in terms of religion, and religion, as he saw it, was a system enjoining an inexorable order. Years later, when Dreiser visited Mayen-am-Moselle, John Paul's birthplace in Germany, and found it to be a little, walled-in Catholic town, he could not forbear comparing it to his father's mentality. A much-cited passage sums up his grievances:

> My dogmatic father . . . was a Catholic and a bigot. I never knew a narrower, more hidebound religionist, nor one more tender and loving in his narrow way. He was a crank, a tenth rate . . . Francis of Assisi, and yet a charming person if it had been possible to get his mind off the subject of religion for more than three seconds at a time. He worked, ate, played, slept, and dreamed religion. . . . he was constantly attempting to drive a decidedly recalcitrant family into a similar point of view.[4]

Sometimes Dreiser blames the church for his father's narrowness; at other times he concedes a part to disappointments John Paul had had in America, and to the Teutonic strain—stern, prideful, domineering. His conflicts with his son were not the only troubles John Paul's return to his family produced. Sylvia and Emma insisted on dating boys they picked up on the streets. John Paul correctly surmised no good could come of such adventures. Bitter harangues ensued, and the house bristled with accusations, threats, and tearful protestations. The girls saw their father's anxieties as typical old-fashioned notions of a foreign-born parent. Their defiance persisted, and in due time Warsaw buzzed with the news that Sylvia was pregnant by a seducer who refused to marry her. Word of the scandal was everywhere, and Dreiser thought himself permanently discredited socially. Books became more than ever his refuge and, unexpectedly, he received sympathetic understanding from a most unlikely source—Mildred Fielding, a Yankee spinster from Malden, Massachusetts, his teacher at the Warsaw high school. That Dreiser's life should be blighted by scandalmongers outraged Miss Fielding. She told him to "think high thoughts and not bother about ma-

[4] *A Hoosier Holiday.*

terial joys." But the storm of gossip proved too much and he decided
to break off his schooling and turn elsewhere to life.

With his mother's blessing Dreiser set off for Chicago. There he
saw a dazzling material prospect which put before him the goals of
the American Dream: "In my life-hungry, love-hungry state, this
new rich prosperity with its ease, its pretty women and its efforts at
refinement . . . set me to riotous dreaming and longing. . . ." Enticed though he was by the American Dream when he reached Chicago, Dreiser was poorly outfitted to pursue it. He was not eligible
for some jobs by reason of inexperience; timidity made him dis-
qualify himself for others. In desperation, he took a job as dishwasher
in a squalid Greek restaurant run by a grubby sensualist named
John Paradiso. In 1920, with consummate irony, Dreiser cited this
same Paradiso as source of the philosophical musings published as
Hey, Rub-A-Dub-Dub.

Settled after this fashion, Dreiser at once arranged to bring his
mother to Chicago, feeling "life would be nothing without her, so
close had I always been held by the strong cord, the silver tether of
her affection, understanding, sweetness, sacrifice." Mame, Sylvia,
and Al fell in with his plans, and Sarah, with Claire and Ed, returned
a final time to Chicago to an apartment they had made ready for
her on Ogden Avenue. Presently Dreiser found work in the stockroom
of Hibbard, Spencer, Bartlett & Company, a wholesale hardware
house. There he met Christian Aaberg, a bitter Dane, who assured
him that "mind" was the key to success. Under Aaberg's prodding,
Dreiser began to believe attainment of the American Dream was
possible for him after all. And help came unexpectedly to give
his new goals an assist. Still troubled about Dreiser's interrupted
education, early in August 1888 Mildred Fielding sought him out
at the hardware house. Clad in drab work clothes, wan, racked with
a cough from a developing lung lesion, Dreiser was a forlorn spec-
tacle. Mildred Fielding came to a prompt decision: she herself
would send him to college. Her resourcefulness as good as her resolve, she made arrangements with Indiana University and, in the fall
of 1888, Dreiser was admitted as a special student.

New vistas shown him in college put Dreiser in a quandary. He
began to reflect: "Here was this great, flashing, extended, mysterious world, as I saw it, and it was these commonplaces of living and
salary and some little reputation that interested almost all." When
college ended for him after one year—his grades were fair, but his
benefactress had other responsibilities, and his family had need of
his earning power—he had gained back his health and, once more,

had set his footsteps in the direction of self-realization. Four years later, Mildred Fielding, who had married in her mid-thirties, died in childbed, without seeing her faith in Dreiser vindicated. To the end of his days he spoke of her with a tenderness he showed otherwise only for his mother. Although he believed his stay at college had diminished his dependency on his family, Dreiser did not find his mother of less importance to him. She was and remained, "the central, centripetal star" of his world. He concludes, writing more than forty years later: "Nothing since has ever altered her peculiar emotional and vital relationship to me, however numerous the years."

But the pastimes of prosperous college classmates had quickened in Dreiser also an interest in the sexual promise of women. From the age of fifteen he had found the feminine form alluring. In Warsaw, a baker's daughter had enticed him into a packing case in the bakery yard and there, in that floury bower, initiated him into the mysteries of sex. But the contact was fumbling and he became convinced that self-abuse had cost him his manhood. This obsession made him self-conscious in the presence of women for years to come. In after years he believed these early inhibitions had served him a good turn. Had sexual conquests come easily, he would never have cultivated his intellect.

Dreiser's fictional accounts of his later amours—a constant succession of affairs, particularly between the ages of thirty and fifty —earned him a reputation as a great libertine. But lack of diversity among these accounts suggests his experiences varied little from one to another and that he sought from women companionship even more than carnal pleasure. Indeed, most of the women who loved him cited as his first attribute, not his skill at love-making, but his ability to make them think well of themselves. Over and over again in Dreiser's books, a middle-aged man, who feels that he is losing that vital urgency of spirit that allies him to the flux of Nature, renews himself in a love affair with a girl of eighteen. At sixty Dreiser owned he had felt the *grande passion* just five times in his life, and that three of the five women he loved passed from his ken unaware of the fires they had lighted. The remaining two he married. Dreiser saw sex as "the great, the dominating force!"—as a kind of power which stirred an inward sense of flux that drew one to Nature. He finds sex, "not only the warp and woof of life as we know it, but obviously the will of the Creator, whether he is divine or supremely evil and contemptible." Even so, he found "controlling sensuousness" as repelling as repressiveness. Sex for Cowperwood is never an escape. Through it is expressed his participation in the flux of Nature and his quest for an unknown goal within Nature, adumbrated in the beauty of woman but incomparably greater than her beauty. This point of view supplies relevancy to the priority Dreiser gives to the quest for sexual gratification over its actual attainment: "Via sex gratification—or perhaps better, its ardent and often defeated pursuit—comes most of all that is most distinguished in art, letters, and our social economy and progress generally." Dreiser dealt with sex to show its function as the force which energizes man, and compels his quest for spiritual fulfillment within Nature.

Dreiser's friends spoke of his fine, domed forehead, his well-shaped nose, of a face "fine, groping, pathetic," and even of "curiously long, beautiful hands." But in familiar moments, they said his mouth looked like "an ill-healed wound," or was "cut like a scallop out of a pie," or even that his whole countenance resembled "a pith-stricken radish." The arresting feature of his face, however, was his right eye. Even when Dreiser was in good humor, this eye kept a look of discouragement that made him seem incapable of enjoying himself. He appeared to be glancing to one side as though trying to escape whatever company he might be with. He admitted, ultimately, that through life this afflicted eye was worthless to him. He could see with it only by holding something up close, but could not read with it at all. In college, moreover, he passed through an anxious interval when his left eye temporarily failed him as well. In the light of this handicap, Dreiser's many references in his fiction to eye magnetism as a power establishing sexual contact between men and women have special significance. In both men and women, blindness commonly is attended by a sense of castration. The man feels deprived of his manhood, the woman feels ugly and unwanted. Thus often the blind are incapable of sexual intercourse. Dreiser's own consciousness of a disfigured, useless eye surely contributed to his emotional inhibitions in adolescence. It is worth pondering, therefore, how he came to develop a theory of purposeful sexual behavior dependent upon eye action which enabled him to utilize his own eyes as an actual asset. His personal compensation, indeed, was so complete that Frank Harris saw Dreiser's eyes as "*the* feature of his face," and Dreiser attributed to his most forceful lotharios his own eye color—gray blue. Dreiser's acquisition of eye power was achieved suddenly and dramatically. When he came home from college he found his mother in declining health. Although Sarah was only fifty-seven, she had fallen into a lethargy and kept to the house. Understandably, his concern was great and he gave her every mo-

PATTERNS OF DESTINY

CARICATURE BY DAVID LEVINE

13

ment he could spare. Twice weekly, in what was perhaps an unconscious effort to draw her again into the flux of Nature, Dreiser took her riding in a buggy belonging to a real estate agency he worked for. But her strength waned steadily and, in the autumn of 1890, she took to her bed. One morning in November he was alone with her when she asked to be helped to the bathroom. He had his arms about her, supporting her, when suddenly she sank to the floor by the bed. Dreiser knelt by her. Sarah said nothing, but looked steadily into her son's eyes. Caught up in what he believed later to have been a mystical experience, Dreiser felt the magnetism of her eyes (like his own, gray blue) infusing his. It was as though some legacy of power had passed to him. Then suddenly there was a glazing over of Sarah's vision and Dreiser saw that she was dead. Feeling strangely altered, he called other members of the family into the room. With some new resource of vision he watched as they came into the bedchamber to gaze at Sarah's body. None of them, he was convinced, had been bound to Sarah as he had been.

Sarah's death held for Dreiser a further trauma, even more far-reaching in its consequences. A priest was summoned, a literal-minded Bavarian, who raged because Sarah had died without the last rites. He insisted she was entitled neither to a funeral mass nor burial in consecrated ground. Although his brother Paul was able to arrange both for a mass and Catholic burial at St. Boniface's Cemetery, on the North Side, Dreiser fumed. He dispised the Church that considered itself too good to receive his mother.

In the days following Sarah's burial Dreiser little resembled the person he had been before. His mother had grappled him to Nature with a mystical gift of force; his ties with organized religion were all but severed. In the void left, a disposition to seek affinities in Nature asserted itself in the easy manner of his mother, vaguely contending with a strange sense of "the diaphanous nothingness of things."

His mother's death launched Dreiser upon a lifelong quest for the security taken from him when she died. Forty years later he still spoke of his dependency on Sarah in the present tense: "This lone woman who was my mother is of strange import to me." For much of his life he was a cosmic wanderer, wary of accepting the spiritual solace he found eventually in Nature. The Church had rejected his mother; acceptance of spiritual values would make him accomplice to that rejection. Inasmuch as the security he craved was objectified for him in his memory of his mother, he could accept nothing that would put distance between them. "There is in me the spirit of a lonely child somewhere and it clings pitifully to the hand of its big mamma, Life, and cries when it is frightened. . . ."

In *Hoosier Holiday,* which he dedicated to his mother, Dreiser hails Sarah as one uncommitted to the restrictive codes of Church and society, but allied to Nature:

> One of the most perfect mothers ever a man had. . . . An open, uneducated, wondering, dreamy mind, none of the customary, conscious principles with which so many conventional souls are afflicted. . . . A great poet mother. . . . She loved the trees and the flowers and the clouds and the sound of the wind. . . . A great-hearted mother—loving, tender, charitable, who loved the ne'er-do-well a little better than those staid favorites of society who keep all laws . . . I always say I know how great some souls can be because I know how splendid that of my mother was.

The pursuit of women which Dreiser began soon after his mother's death probably was basically compensatory, and, in one sense, is to be viewed apart from his commendation of sex as "warp and woof of life." He sought somewhere a woman to take up Sarah's role. Even in his choice of wives Dreiser seems to have been influenced by his Oedipal longings. His first wife was named Sara. Helen, his second wife, was his cousin, raised by her grandmother, Sarah Dreiser's blood sister and veritable twin. Helen's emotional referents were almost identical to his own.

In 1963, Margaret Szekely, a Dreiser confidante in the late 1920s, told William Swanberg: "He needed a mother and I supplied the need." Elsewhere Swanberg notes, "Dreiser . . . liked to be babied. . . ." And again, "He needed a woman—a mother—to pet and pamper him." When Dreiser met Mrs. Lion Feuchtwanger in Berlin, in 1927, he reported: "She explains that I need someone to *mother* me. I heartily agree!" Throughout his fiction, Dreiser's Oedipal attachment is readily in view. A favorite figure is an eighteen-year-old girl—Jennie Gerhardt, Aileen Butler, Etta Barnes, Esther Norn, Emanuela—emotionally drawn to her father, yet more often than not disguising the attraction by forming an attachment for one of his contemporaries. In *The Stoic* the intimacy is deepened when Cowperwood, at sixty, makes his eighteen-year-old mistress his legal ward and shortly, also, makes a mistress of his teen-age "grandniece." *The Titan* suggests that both he and Berenice, his future ward, viewed her role less as mistress than as mother. He saw her, "in the way of a large, kindly, mothering intelligence which could see, feel, and understand." When she looked at him, "she could not help being moved by a kind of tenderness, sympathy, mothering affection." In *An American Tragedy,* Clyde Griffiths responds with cooing contentment to Sondra Finchley's baby talk, a device Dreiser uses earlier in "Will You Walk Into My Parlor?" to undo a strong-willed male. Even Solon Barnes is no bulwark on his wedding night: "His ardor was tempered by a yearning, voiceless desire to be mothered by this girl whom he loved so fervently."

The mother as protective haven is a commonplace of Dreiser's works. Jeff Ingalls, protagonist in "Nigger Jeff," is caught and lynched because he slips home to see his mother instead of taking flight. When Hurstwood sinks into vagrancy after Sister Carrie leaves him, he is received at the Sisters of Mercy mission by "a big, motherly looking woman." In "Sanctuary" the spurned wife returns to the orphanage of her girlhood to ask the Mother Superior to take her in and protect her forever from the world outside. When Eugene Witla loses both Angela and Suzanne he turns to a Christian Science reader, Mrs. Johns—"a motherly soul"—and comes "to lean on her in his misery quite as a boy might on his mother." Mrs. Johns even sings to him "in a sweet motherly way." It is to his mother that Clyde Griffiths turns when every other recourse fails him. The last words Stewart Barnes writes before his suicide are "Mother, forgive me." Dreiser's idealization of his mother finds further acknowledgment in many of his female characterizations. Sarah is the archetype of Mrs. Gerhardt, Mrs. Johns, Mrs. Berchansky, Mrs. Griffiths, and Mrs. Barnes, and, in some aspects, of Jennie Gerhardt and Berenice Fleming as well.

Criticism has duly noted the rocking-chair allusions in *Sister Carrie* but has not remarked their over-all relevance to Dreiser's work. Rocking is a surrogate sexual activity. For the child the rocker can be a womb surrogate. Dreiser's nonfictional as well as fictional works abound with references to rocking chairs and related mechanisms which serve both his philosophical and psychological needs. He says of one of his early homes in Terre Haute: "There was a swing in a basement where I used to swing all alone by the hour, enjoying my own moods." In Sullivan, he recalls: "Sitting by one of the windows of our living room . . . I used to rock and sing by the hour, enjoying the morning sun." And in Warsaw: "In a swing, a hammock, a rocking chair, I thought, reading and dreaming to carve out something for myself in the future. . . ." In Chicago, he set aside a few minutes after breakfast each morning, "and these I would spend in a rocking chair on the back porch . . . singing and thinking of the mystery of life and of my future." As a cub reporter in St. Louis he would seek out hotel lobbies "with comfortable rocking chairs where one might sit and dream." Marguerite Tjader Harris states that while writing *The Bulwark* he rocked constantly, and adds: "This slight, rhythmic movement seemed to soothe the restlessness that was ever in his body and mind, perhaps a part of his creative energy itself." This observation brings to mind Dreiser's own description of life as "a mere idle rocking of force in one direction or another at times."

The rocking-chair references involve a further Dreiserian idiosyncrasy. Louise Campbell wrote in 1933: "In the country or any quiet place he will 'set and rock' by the hour, humming a monotonous tune and staring into space while pleating and repleating his large white handkerchief." Even with a houseful of guests, Dreiser was noted for taking up his rocker abode, spreading open his handkerchief, then folding and refolding it into squares while he listened alertly to others talk. In his early days as editor, his handkerchief manipulations mesmerized visitors. Abraham Brill, with whom he was on intimate terms, thought the habit of sexual significance. Psychology might explain it also as a security surrogate, kindred to the cuddle-blanket toddlers carry, or the diaper which, with its comfort and warmth, the infant mind equates with the mother who supplies it. Dreiser's own intense sense of orphanhood argues the inevitability of such a compulsion.

In *An American Tragedy,* Roberta Alden's mother tells the court that Roberta, on her last visit home, placed her arms about her neck and said, "I wish I were a little girl again, mamma, and that you would take me in your arms and rock me like you used to." Concurrent with his quest for fulfillment within the flux of Nature, Dreiser seems then to have retained, via rocker and handkerchief, a link with the only protective haven he had ever known—his mother. At the same time, as flux activities, they emblemized his quest externally. Helen Dreiser's summary of the uncompleted portion of *The Stoic* says that after Cowperwood's death, Berenice Fleming's special concern was to have been a little blind girl whose parents had neglected her, allowing her "to sit for hours and hours in a little rocking chair in a corner, with no least stimuli or interest. . . ." By love and understanding this unhappy child eventually was to be coaxed out of her state of withdrawal to the point where she would spend hours sliding down a children's playslide! This solution to her dilemma was meant to suggest, apparently, that identification with the flux of Nature restored her to well-being. It stands as a curious reminder that the half-blind Dreiser shed his own early inhibitions by forging an alliance with Nature.

Sarah Dreiser's magnetic spirit had held the family together during her lifetime. After her death quarrels were constant. Finally, longing for "the creature comforts and pleasures of life," Dreiser decided to join Edward and Sylvia who wished to go out on their own. "You're going, are you?" said the sorrowful John Paul when the time came for Theodore to say good-by. "I'm sorry, Dorsch, I done the best I could. . . . I have prayed these last few days. . . . I hope you don't ever feel sorry." The move was made and the family scattered for what was to be its final breakup.

2

A SEEKING PROMETHEUS

EVEN BEFORE his mother's death, impressed by the success of a Mennonite cousin who edited country weeklies, Dreiser had wanted to be a newspaperman. In 1892, after an interval of small jobs, he sought work with the *Daily Globe*, Chicago's least consequential newspaper. Tall, gangling, eager, his hair combed in a pompadour, his treacherous vision bolstered by gold-rimmed eyeglasses, Dreiser could not have seemed to promise much to the *Globe*'s city editor, John McEnnis, but he was allowed to join the paper on a trial basis. Real help came from a copy reader, John Milo Maxwell, who liked Dreiser's earnestness. Although Maxwell was a cynic, he found himself, against his practice, putting Dreiser's copy into shape for him. When Dreiser turned up some information presaging Cleveland's nomination at the Democratic Convention that year, Maxwell helped him with a presentation of it that got him a permanent berth on the paper.

For some time Dreiser had been attending free lectures by nonsectarian ministers who preached the Emersonian gospel of self-realization through self-trust and hard work. Moreover, through the initial impetus given by Miss Fielding, he had read Thoreau and Emerson avidly and had become enthralled by such transcendental showpieces as William Ellery Channing's "A Poet's Hope" which bade him "soar unlimited" over the "infinitest sea." In the news office the rule was, "Cheat and win and you were all right; be honest and lose and you were fired." And what was true there, Dreiser found out, was true of the world in general. Bit by bit these perceptions began to modify his idealism. When McEnnis got him a transfer to the St. Louis *Globe-Democrat* to give his talents greater range, Dreiser set forth, his mind seething with grandiose ideas of himself as an historian or philosopher, but with his eye on the main chance.

The friends Dreiser made in St. Louis were as important to his mental growth as were his reportorial experiences. The *Globe-Democrat*'s brilliant editor, Joseph B. McCullagh, was wrapped in an aura of remoteness that allowed no familiarities, but the example he offered as a man of force held the young reporter in awe. More immediately instructive were Dreiser's friendships with two of his colleagues, Robert Hazard and Peter McCord. Hazard had written a novel modeled on Balzac and Zola. Dreiser found it quite the most powerful book he had ever read and was amazed to be told America was not ready for it. McCord's influence was even more far-reaching; though fundamentally as wholesome as a circuit rider, he was as intolerant of restrictive conventions as the most resolute voluptuary. Dreiser records his indebtedness to McCord in *Twelve Men*: "I was a moral coward, and he was not losing his life and desires through fear—which the majority of us do. He was strong, vital, unafraid, and he made me so."

Impelled by a fear that he might lose his job and not be able to get another, Dreiser developed the instincts of a bullying competitor. At twenty-one he became the *Globe-Democrat's* drama critic. But he soon made the fatal misstep of covering three play openings in absentia while chasing down another news lead. Since a storm forced cancellation of all three plays, Dreiser's reviews gave *Globe-Democrat* rivals a field day. Without waiting to be fired, he cleaned out his desk and went to work for a smaller paper, the St. Louis *Republic*, at a considerable cut in salary.

At the *Republic* Dreiser was eager to oblige, and full advantage was taken of his pliancy. He was asked to cover, in a comic vein, a baseball series being staged for a summer charity; for five weeks his articles regaled *Republic* readers. To reward this yeomanly service the paper sent him to the World's Fair in Chicago, as cicerone to a group of young school teachers, winners of a contest the paper had sponsored. By the time the group got to Chicago, Dreiser was surreptitiously courting two of his charges—one, a titian-haired country girl, proper and maidenly in her reserve; the other, a forward, sensuous brunette. In due course prudence prevailed, and he gave full attention to the demure redhead—Sara Osborne White. So began an attachment which led to marriage six years later, and to some of the stormiest days Dreiser would ever endure. Here, too, was born an ideal commemorated in the auburn hair of Aileen Butler, Berenice Fleming, and of the second Mrs. Dreiser, Helen Patges Richardson.

Although John Paul lived until 1900, the Fair trip brought Dreiser into his last contact with his father. The experience Dreiser by then had had of the world made the older man seem more abject than ever: "I could see him then as he really was, a warm, generous and yet bigoted and ignorant soul, led captive in his childhood to a brain-less theory and having no power within himself to break that chain. . . ."

Dreiser already was weary of St. Louis when his brother Paul came to town, in December 1893, as the star of a road company melodrama, *The Danger Signal*. Paul urged him to move on to New York, insisting he would never reach his true zenith otherwise. Mindful of this advice, Dreiser resigned from the *Republic* in February and headed east, stopping first at Grand Rapids, Ohio, to investigate the prospects of running a country newspaper. But country editors were notoriously beholden to their advertisers, and the thought of giving voice to their "clock-work motions and notions" was more than Dreiser could bear. He took a train to Toledo. There his quest for work led him to the man who was to shape his final destiny—Arthur Henry, city editor of the Toledo *Blade*. At first glance, the two young men (Henry was twenty-six at the time, four years older than Dreiser) recognized themselves as intellectual af-finities. Nevertheless, there was no opening on the paper for Dreiser and, needing money badly, he went on to Cleveland with the under-standing that he could return to Toledo if a job came up on the *Blade*.

It was in Pittsburgh, however, that Dreiser's cross-country prog-ress came to an abrupt halt. There he got a job with the *Dispatch* and had fair success writing light pieces intended for reader en-tertainment. There, too, he was gripped by the appalling evidence of social injustice which he found in the great steel city, and formed his first suspicions that the American Dream was antagonistic to Na-ture. If, as he later said, he had left his youth behind him when he left St. Louis, certainly, in Pittsburgh he found maturity, and dis-carded romanticism. In keeping with this change in social outlook, Dreiser's reading helped to remold his personal ambitions. At the Allegheny Carnegie Library he read Balzac's *Human Comedy*, and with such a tutelary divinity there was no chance of overlooking the lesson Pittsburgh had to teach him. The following summer, thwarted in his efforts to write about the conditions around him, he decided to move on to New York. Before taking this step, however, in July he went back to Montgomery City, Missouri, to see Sara White. Sara, or "Jug," as her family called her, personified the attitudes Dreiser was rapidly discarding. But by its seeming success in calling the American ideal into existence, the family, ruled over by Jug's fa-ther, Arch Herndon White (a patriarch whom even Dreiser adored), gave him renewed hope of escaping into the life he had often dreamed about. By the time he left Montgomery City, Dreiser was firmly committed to marry Jug. Yet, back in Pittsburgh for a final inventory of his resources before entering the lists in New York, the gap that separated him from true compatibility with Jug at once widened. He read Herbert Spencer's *First Principles* and Thomas Huxley's *Science and Christianity* and *Science and Hebrew Tradition*. Their impact on him was overwhelming. Huxley assisted him to a formal dismissal of organized religion; Spencer won him to a belief in mechanism. Here, at last, was an explanation of man's place in Nature, though not a comfortable one, for while mechanism reaffirmed his alliance with Nature, it stripped Nature of its kindly aspect. Nature's golden process was not designed to benefit man; it was a thing of caprice. Dreiser relates: "Up to this time there had been in me a blazing and unchecked desire to get on and the feeling that in doing so we did get somewhere; now in its place was the definite conviction that spiritually one got nowhere, that there was no hereafter. . . . Man was a mechanism, undevised and uncreated, and a badly and carelessly driven one at that." It was a theme with which he long would conjure. In *Hoosier Holiday*, reflecting on "life and change, and the driving, destroying urge of things," he protests: "We talk about the hardness and cruelty of men! Contrast their sharpest, most brutal connivings with the slow, indifferent sapping of strength and hope and joy which nature practices upon each and every one of us." This belief in Nature's indifference to man's ultimate well-being was to color Dreiser's thinking for many years and perhaps accounts for the "touch of the eternal Weltschmerz" Mencken found there. Part of the pleasure Dreiser found in Arthur Henry's friendship, he himself puts down to an "invariable optimism and gayety" in Henry which counterbalanced his own "all too solemn and personally disquieting contemplation of the fate of man." At forty-five Dreiser described it as a fault of his temperament that, at a moment's notice, while "having the best time in the world," he would find himself thinking suddenly, "I am getting old . . . Life is slipping on and away . . . Nothing endures." In *The Stoic* Dreiser was to suggest that man's pursuit of beauty in the feminine form constitutes a groping toward harmony with the cosmic consciousness, the ultimate refuge from dissolution. There is a link between the sense of transiency and sexual pleasure—the desire perhaps to escape the bonds of mortality through the procreative act. These paired feelings intrigued Dreiser and more persistently and openly than most men do, he groped toward an understanding of them, believing that if he could understand what implanted these feelings within him, he could approach an understanding of the mystery of existence itself.

Dreiser felt he had a particular claim on New York, where he at last arrived in November 1894. Paul had gone there and conquered the American Dream. But soon Dreiser saw that New York was filled with able young men who could not find work. In desperation, he pushed his way into the city room of the *New York World* and accosted Arthur Brisbane. Amused by his brashness, Brisbane put him to work. By every expectation the Alger myth fostered, Dreiser now should have risen rapidly in the world of journalism. Instead he was given a further chance to see how broad was the chasm separating the American Dream from actuality. He found he was not even on the *World*'s payroll but merely assigned to reportorial piece work. Rancorously he announced his resignation only to learn that the *World* had not found him of much use anyway. He now resolved to become a freelance writer—quite possibly to guard his ego against further hurt. In his struggle to make good his intention, he entered a period of hardship bordering on major need, and was reduced to sleeping in flophouses. He was nearly convinced he had no future in New York when Paul, who had been on the road with a new show, returned to Broadway, and intervened in his usual role of deus ex machina. It was decided that Howley, Haviland, and Company, a music publishing house in which Paul owned a third interest, should publish *Ev'ry Month*, a journal to promote the sale of sheet music, and that Dreiser would edit it.

As *Ev'ry Month*'s editor, Dreiser assured his readers that "To walk in virtue and simplicity blessed on every hand, is better than riches and great honor, and more to be desired than power and great place." Paradoxically, such Thoreauvian sentiments, coupled with his own natural gifts for editorship, brought him quick material returns. *Munsey's, Harper's, Metropolitan,* and *Cosmopolitan* welcomed his articles. Prior to November 1900, when *Sister Carrie* was published, Dreiser had close to eighty articles in print. By 1897, when he ceased to edit *Ev'ry Month*, he held consulting editorships on both *Ainslee's* and *Success*. For the latter magazine he interviewed Edison, Carnegie, Armour, Howells, Depew, Stieglitz, Marshall Field, Madame Nordica, and Anthony Hope, building a series of success stories around the Algerine theme, "Unceasing struggle in adversity brings ultimate triumph."

Dreiser's role as interviewer of notables actually had begun in St. Louis when he interviewed John L. Sullivan and Annie Besant for the *Globe-Democrat*. Then his favorite question had been, "What

do you think of life, its meaning?" As a writer for *Success* he continued to ask this question of the great and near-great. Surely these
men of force could provide some help in sounding the depths of this
mystery that never ceased to intrigue him. When they did not, he
was undiscouraged. He sought out originals—local celebrities in
odd corners of the world, not for material feats but for their moral
worth—to put the same question to them. Such pieces as "A Doer
of the Word," "A Country Doctor," "A Mayor and His People,"
"A True Patriarch," are the record of these inquiries. Each man
had his answer but Dreiser could be sure of none; each seemed in
some way flawed and, hence, not something he himself could adopt.

In 1898, Dreiser's successes made him think his career was developing promisingly. Then a letter came from Jug's sister, Rose,
who told him Jug was pining away while waiting for him to send for
her. Making sentiment stand muster for a love that had waned,
Dreiser arranged a rendezvous in Washington, D. C. There on December 28 (a date that forty-seven years later would be recorded
also as the day of his death), he and Jug were married. Within six
months Dreiser was certain his marriage had been a disaster.

In *The 'Genius'* Dreiser fictionalized the breakup of his marriage.
In this work, when matters came to the final crisis, Eugene Witla
turned upon his wife and told her: "You have always insisted on
holding me down to the little, cheap conventions as you have understood them." The complaint was Dreiser's own. He believed Nature was actively hostile to social convention and to the view of
morality propagated by organized religion. In *Hoosier Holiday* he
states: "As yet we do not understand life, what the laws are that
govern it. . . . we do not know what life is—not nearly enough to
set forth a fixed code of any kind, religious or otherwise." In *Dawn*,
he recalls how, as a youngster, he himself had suffered under "the
heavy pressure of those moral and religious standards which then
dominated the Middle West and which exacted the last jot and
tithe in the matter of exterior conformity and mental preciseness."
In difficulties men have in adhering to religious precepts, and in the
insincerity of some avowed religionists, Dreiser found proof of the
powerful compulsions of Nature: "How earnestly is the Sunday
School and the precept and the maxim invoked, and how persistently
so many of them go their own way. They do not know what it is all
about, all this talk about religion and morality and duty. In their
blood is a certain something which responds to the light of the sun
and the blue of the sky."

Despite his attacks upon organized religion, Dreiser, as an un-committed inquirer into man's spiritual destiny, never really closed any door. In 1912, he wrote: "In a way, blind adherence to principle is justifiable, for we have not yet solved the riddle of the uni-verse. . . ." In *Hoosier Holiday* he reveals: "I have no deadly op-position to religion . . . It is only when in the form of priestcraft and ministerial conniving it becomes puffed up and arrogant and decides that all the world must think as it thinks, and do as it does, and that if one does not one is a heretic and an outcast, that I re-sent it."

American social thought, an amalgam of Anglo-Saxon mores and what Mencken calls "mellowed Methodism," ran a strong second, after religious arrogance, in the order of Dreiser's dislikes. He thought of it as attaining to its most flourishing state in the region of his boyhood and accordingly talks reprovingly of "midwestern social conceptions" and "the great lock-step of the middle and far west." Anglo-Saxon frigidity, of course, was responsible for mak-ing "a sin of sex" in America. The sanctions of Anglo-Saxon middle-class Protestant morality dominated the world of Dreiser's boyhood and he learned to hate them because they bore so heavily upon him. His assimilation had been blocked not because his was a foreign household and his creed an alien creed, but by successive breaches of social thought made by members of his immediate family. He at-tacked social thought as one who found it obstructing man's har-monious participation in the flux of Nature.

Just as he believed social thought to be dependent upon the town for its continuance, he saw the town in turn dependent upon an idealistic concept of a well-ordered home and family life, which in turn rested upon an idealistic concept of marriage. By marrying Jug he believed he was acquiring a well-ordered family of the very kind to which he wished to be allied. Later, from the vantage point of his broken marriage, he has Eugene Witla ruminate on the home-life of his in-laws, the Blues: "Any form or order of society which hoped to endure must have individuals like Mrs. Blue, who would conform to the highest standards and theories of that society . . . but they meant nothing in the shifting, subtle forces of nature. They were just accidental harmonies blossoming out of something which meant everything here to this order, nothing to the universe at large."

Even so, Eugene's conditioning momentarily checks his promiscu-ous activities: "Did not the decencies and the sanities of life depend

on right moral conduct? Was not the world dependent on how the
homes were run?"

In *Hoosier Holiday* Dreiser shows how he himself resolved this
dilemma:

> There was a time not long ago when Americans felt that the be-
> ginning and end of all things was the home . . . a comfortable home
> in which to grow and vegetate. Everything had to be sacrificed to
> it. . . . We have seen several generations go by since they were
> built. Have they been any better than their sires, if as good? . . .
> I myself have witnessed a great revolt against all the binding perfec-
> tion which these lovely homes represented.

As the failure of his marriage led Dreiser to think of the "ideal
home" as a device contrived by moralists to keep restrictive social
thought in force, he came to take a similar view of marriage itself.
Marriage assures: "the death of affectional and social experience
. . . it is absolutely inimical to the roving and free soul . . . the
spectacles which entertain the sober and stationary in art, literature,
science, indeed every phase of life, would never be if all maintained
the order and quiet which monogamy suggests." Pinpointing its basic incompatibility with the flux of Nature, Dreiser says: "The trouble with marriage is that in its extreme interpretation it conflicts
with the law of change, or balance and equation, and hence suffers
a severe and seemingly destructive defeat."

As a contrivance through which conventions were held in force,
marriage gave Dreiser a theme to which he returned again and again
in his fiction. In "Free," Haymaker is held to a loveless marriage
because of "respect . . . for convention, moral order, the duty of
keeping society on an even keel. . . ." In *Jennie Gerhardt*, Lester
Kane succumbs to societal pressures to enter into a conventional
marriage only, on his deathbed, to repent it. *The 'Genius'* is Dreiser's
most elaborate exploration of the theme that marriage countermands
Nature. "The grasping legality of established matrimony" found
in Dreiser an implacable foe. He believed most men had little capacity for cerebration and that this fact enabled conventions to
prosper. In *The Financier*, he says:

> The conventional mind is at best a petty piece of machinery. . . .
> It has its little siphon of thought-processes forced up or down into
> the mighty ocean of fact and circumstance; but it uses so little,
> pumps so faintly, that the immediate contiguity of the vast mass is
> not disturbed. Nothing of the subtlety of life is perceived. . . . When

some crude, suggestive fact . . . suddenly manifests itself in the placid flow of events, there is great agony or disturbance and clogging of the so-called normal processes . . . and life . . . ceases or goes lamely ever after.

By showing the law to be infinitely malleable in the hands of the people committed to upholding it, Dreiser concludes that social thought is not practically applicable—as with organized religion, Nature actively disputes it. Yet Dreiser did not deny that social thought could draw honorable men to its standards. His Governor Swanson, in *The Titan*, portrays one such man. The mayor, in "A Mayor and His People," portrays another. In *A Traveler at Forty*, Dreiser says "I like the man who takes society and social forms seriously, though I would not be that man for all the world." Many of his stories are concerned with the struggle that goes on between "those content to be slowly put to death by custom," and those who defy it. Frequently, this struggle occurs within one individual— Hurstwood, or Lester Kane—as in a series of what Dreiser calls "approaches and recessions" he is drawn to the flux of Nature, but pulled back by social pressures in a contest that finally destroys him. Grandiose dreams led Dreiser into journalism and kept him there for several years. Even Pittsburgh did not disenchant him wholly. He arrived in New York determined to succeed as a journalist, and his job on the *World* held promise of such success. But he gave up the job and resolved to direct his aspirations to higher goals. It was not mere chance that in the last decade of his life he found in the transcendentalism of Thoreau a philosophy that most nearly matched his own. Romantic idealism, truly, was the one aspect of Dreiser's early conditioning that he was unable to renounce when he repudiated the stabilities which held society in place. His emotional ties to his mother had been the fulcrum which had pried him loose from these other commitments. But romanticism, in its glorification of womanhood, provided the very context in which idealization of his mother developed. Eventually he found an outlet for his capacity for romantic idealism in social and political reform.

Dreiser knew sentimentalism was a pitfall. Summerfield, in *The 'Genius'*, believed: "Mercy was a joke to be eliminated from business. Sentiment was silly twaddle." In *An American Tragedy*, Clyde's sentimental desire not to hurt Roberta leads to her pregnancy and his undoing. In *The Stoic*, he says of Cowperwood: "He knew only too well that out of sentiment came nothing that was sufficient in any crisis to warrant its preservation. If life had taught him anything, it had taught him that." While the theory, then, was clear to Dreiser, he never could master the practice; so far as he could see, the only ones who could were grasping men of affairs. In *The Titan* he reveals his dilemma: "Woe to him who places his faith in illusion —the only reality—and woe to him who does not. In one way lies disillusion with its pain, in the other way regret."

Dreiser saw that romanticism in America had made woman the keeper of morality. In this role she refused to acknowledge reality and relentlessly persecuted those who did. As a result, many women found themselves either torn by natural passions which they were compelled to suppress or shunned by society for not repressing them. Dreiser's *Twelve Men* profiles twelve liberated men; but his *Gallery of Women* portrays fifteen ensnared women, each in her own way struggling to be free, yet thwarted by inhibitions or social obstacles. Some, like Esther Norn, fling themselves with blind trust into the flux of Nature and suffer painfully for lack of preparedness. Dreiser believed women to be "temperamental rather than intellectual," so inevitably, as they strive to escape a dilemma not truly of their own making, they fare badly.

An inevitable adjunct of Dreiser's indictment of the social stabilities was his dismissal of all formal systems of education. He believed they were devised to perpetuate a specific approach to life to which their organizers were committed. He denounced the Catholic parochial school system as a type of schooling exacting "faith and blind obedience." If this was the goal of Catholic education in Dreiser's boyhood, its methods, if they may be judged from the mildness of their impact on him, must have been so imperfect as to have offered little cause for concern to him or anyone else. To Dreiser even the public school system, with its bias toward democracy, offered no true alliance with Nature. Emerging from its "sheltering confines and precepts," ninety-nine percent of those educated under the system are seen to "end in the most humdrum fashion—not desperately or dramatically—just humdrum and nothing at all."

In his preface to *The Living Thoughts of Thoreau,* Dreiser acclaims Thoreau's opinion that education turns men into "prejudiced observers." Dreiser relates: "The most important thing for all men, and for each man, as he saw it, was to sweep aside all that has been imposed on him, unverified by his own existence, and so to live unprejudiced by socially evolved theories." In commending Thoreau, Dreiser reaffirmed his own reliance on Nature.

3

THE WELLSPRINGS OF LIFE
AND HUMAN ACTIONS

EVERY GREAT culture has had a myth to concretize its goals and give it momentum. In ancient Egypt a national myth was built up in consonance with the Nile. In the United States, the frontier gave the national myth its context. This energizing myth, the Mosaic myth, took shape first in the hearts of the Puritan settlers of New England and was an extension of the belief that they were a chosen people, ordained by Divine Providence, under a new covenant, to found in the new world a second Israel. Since this belief was sustained by the practical view that material prosperity was an earnest of Election, the New England settlements grew and prospered. Although the myth lost definition as its practical aspects were communicated to later Americans, essential features—the conviction of destiny and the desire for material prosperity—persisted in a form which came to be called the American Dream. It is this attenuated myth that Dreiser speaks of when he alludes to "that American pseudo-morality which combines a pirate-like acquisitiveness with an inward and absolute conviction of righteousness."

Growing up in the midwest, Dreiser was given every chance to observe the scope and manner of the American Dream. Yet social isolation kept him at a sufficient remove from it so that he could sense its inadequacies as well as its grandeur. His predilection for protagonists who are pursuing the American Dream, and the compassion which he extends to them in their failure to find happiness, often are mistaken for a vote of confidence in materialism. Quite otherwise, he sought consistently, through his tragic protagonists, to condemn the American Dream as a destructive illusion.

Dreiser's faith in the American Dream was not seriously challenged until he went to Pittsburgh. Going from Pittsburgh to Missouri to see Jug he found his outlook had altered: "The very soil smacked of American idealism and faith, a fixedness in sentimental and purely imaginative American tradition, in which, I, alas! could

not share. I was enraptured . . . but I could not believe that it was
more than a frail flower of romance. I had seen Pittsburgh." Accordingly, when he began to write fiction it was not as an eager petitioner
of riches and fame but as a polemicist who saw it as his first duty
to bring under assault the false standards upon which American society was reared. *Sister Carrie* is not a defense of the compromises
which country girls make to win their way in the big city, but a bitter indictment of the success goals Carrie Meeber pursues under the
spell of the American Dream. *Jennie Gerhardt* affirms the superiority of Nature to arbitrary material goals which man sets for himself in a society oriented toward worldly success. Even Frank Cowperwood is not envisaged by Dreiser as a hero of the American
Dream. Cowperwood, Dreiser says, lacks a first-class speculative
mind. He pursues material goals but the unfulfilled part of his spirit
reaches out to love, art, beauty, and to a shadowland beyond—to an
imperfectly understood desire to be fulfilled in Nature. Only a for-
tuitous turning back to Nature saves Eugene Witla from destructive
absorption in the pursuit of the American Dream, just as later it
will intervene to save Solon Barnes and Berenice Fleming. For
Clyde Griffiths there is no timely intervention of Nature. In his
pursuit of the American Dream, Clyde alienates Nature past all possibility of rapprochement.

For many years Dreiser construed hopefully "the morning vigor"
of Americans. At the same time he saw this energetic spirit thwarted
by the American Dream. *Hoosier Holiday* sounds an emotional
warning:

> Dear, dear, darling Yankee land—'my country tis'—when I think of
> you and all your ills and all your dreams and all your courage and
> your faith—I could cry over you, wringing my hands. But you, you
> great men of brains . . . beware! These be simple souls . . . dream-
> ing sweet dreams of life and love and hope. Don't awake them! . . .
> let them now know their faith is nothing, their hope is nothing, their
> love nothing—or you may set the bonfires of wrath alight. . . .

Good will toward America persists but the rapacious have spoiled
all: "I am in favor of the dream of democracy, on whatever basis it
can be worked out. It is an ideal. But how, I should like to ask, is a
proletariat such as this . . . to hold its own against the keen, resourceful oligarchs at the top?" To illustrate the folly of the American Dream, Dreiser undertook to portray the unequipped individual
adopting the recognized goals of American life and struggling fu-
tilely to attain them. Clyde Griffiths is Dreiser's most complete study

of such an individual. In the Steiners and Slusses whom Cowperwood leaves in his wake, Dreiser portrays a score of others.

Although Dreiser scorned materialism, he did not condemn all businessmen. Financiers at least were not dupes; they defied the fixed codes of society; they were thinkers and organizers; they were likely to be men of force, impelled by a strong sex drive that allied them to the flux of Nature. Dreiser respected the businessman, like Archibald Kane, who attains prosperity by hard work and conscientious service. But behind him Dreiser sees invariably a seeking son whose passion for riches is obsessive. Even Solon Barnes has such a son. From Joseph G. Robin, the "X" of " 'Vanity, Vanity,' Saith the Preacher," Dreiser learned that the rich man, by questing beauty, can maintain his link with Nature and so escape the general taint of avarice. To both Phil Millerton, in "Albertine," and Frank Cowperwood, by way of exempting them from the general indictment he imposes on money-makers, Dreiser gives a commitment to the quest for beauty. *The Titan* explains: "Life rises to a high plane of the dramatic, and hence of the artistic, whenever and wherever in the conflict regarding material possession there enters a conception of the ideal." Inasmuch as Dreiser saw sex as an avenue to appreciation of the beautiful, a voice of Nature summoning man, the financier who, beyond wealth, quested beauty, inevitably had to be a man of force. In support of this thesis Dreiser's trilogy alternates back and forth between accounts of Cowperwood's business and boudoir prowess. His sex drive compels Cowperwood to succeed as a man of business and, as well, to see success as a step to a higher end sought in Nature. At the conclusion of *The Titan*, Cowperwood loses mastery of events in Chicago, but gains Berenice Fleming. Business recedes as beauty moves to the fore. The significance of this exchange should not be lost. Dreiser scores it as a gain for Cowperwood.

The one person upon whom Dreiser expends no compassion is the man motivated by greed. His works abound in indictments. The son-inheritor who abandons the ideals of a high-principled father is "money-centered." Robert Kane is representative: "Cold and conventional in character . . . neither warm-hearted nor generous . . . he would turn any trick which could be speciously, or at best necessitously recommended to his conscience." Gilbert Griffiths is Dreiser's definitive portrayal of the type. In the Dreiserian utopia, as in that of More, every generation would have to prove itself, all prospects of inheritance being rigidly disallowed.

When in 1929 Dreiser received a request for biographical information from the Jewish Biographical Bureau, he replied, "I have not the honor to be a member of your distinguished race. The loss is mine." The following year he told an interviewer from *The Jewish Journal,* "The Jews are one of the greatest races which ever stood on earth." Yet he insisted further, "You Jews want to be a race which envelops the earth. You'd like to have your fingers in every pie." In September 1933, in *The Spectator,* Dreiser stated, "The world's quarrel with the Jew is not that he is inferior, but that he is superior." He went on then to suggest that Jewish prowess in commerce and certain practical professions was so marked that Jews should voluntarily limit their participation in such professions. He advocated further the establishment of a national homeland for the Jews to which they might be deported forceably from America. A race "as gifted, as definite, as religious in its predilections," he wrote in 1935, should want its own homeland. Such views would not have gone unprotested in an open democracy at any time. Coinciding as they did with Hitler's fanatic persecution of Jews in Germany, they met with bitter protest. Even an OWI broadcast, beamed to Germany in 1944, in which Dreiser denounced Nazi persecution of the Jews, could not purge him of the charge of anti-Semitism.

In his fiction, Dreiser's references to Jews follow a pattern. In *Sister Carrie,* Drouet boasts of outwitting a rival businessman, "a regular hook-nosed sheeny." In "Will You Walk Into My Parlor?" Mr. Diamondberg, "a smug, dressy, crafty Jew," a dealer in "cloaks and suits," joins the team of those trying to undermine Gregory, the lofty reformer. In *An American Tragedy,* Hortense Briggs meets her match in Isadore Rubenstein, a lewd and greedy Jewish clothing dealer. Anti-Semitic references in Dreiser's fiction, then, were directed against the Jew as businessman. References to the Jew in his autobiographical works and personal correspondence show a similar bias. In his early days in Chicago, Dreiser worked for a Jewish laundry and was used badly by his employers. In St. Louis he was scooped regularly by an aggressive rival newsman whom he believed to be Jewish. His experiences on Pulitzer's *New York World,* his battles with Horace Liveright, and with motion picture colossi, brought added antagonisms. In *Dawn,* he dismissed his early anti-Semitism with this observation: "I was not then aware, as I am today, of the possible beauty of the individual soul in any race, Jew as well as Gentile." But even here, he seems willing merely to concede the possibility of exceptions among the general run of Jews.

Dreiser's conditioning disposed him to believe Jews were, to a man, rapacious. Thus it was natural for him to seize on every indication of this without giving equal weight to exceptions. In indulging this false emphasis, Dreiser had fallen into a trap which has worked injury to the Jews through the centuries. A man opposed to so many shibboleths of the established order should have known better.

Although Dreiser's encounter with Huxley and Spencer emboldened him to turn away from organized religion, social thought, and the American Dream, it did not in any way abate his interest in man's origins, significance, and destiny. Throughout his life he kept these matters under scrutiny and revised his views in the light of what his inquiries taught him. When he first read Spencer, he saw man as the product of accidental, indifferent, and cruel forces. By 1911, we are told of Jennie Gerhardt's musings: "Was it all blind chance, or was there some guiding intelligence—a God? Almost in spite of herself she felt there must be something—a higher power which produced all the beautiful things—the flowers, the stars, the trees, the grass. Nature was so beautiful! If at times life seemed cruel, yet this beauty still persisted. The thought comforted her. . . ." Clearly, Dreiser's faith in Nature persists. In 1913 he could write: "I trust the universe is not mechanical, but mystically blind." With *Hoosier Holiday*, Dreiser emphatically moves beyond strict mechanism: "I once believed . . . that nature was a blind, stumbling force or combination of forces which knew not what or whither. . . . Of late years I have inclined to think just the reverse, i.e., that nature is merely dark to us because of her tremendous subtlety and our own very limited powers of comprehension. . . ." In 1918 Dreiser wrote Frank Harris: "My God if I have one, is dual—a compendium of so called *evil* as well as 'good' and a use of both for purposes which man as yet may not comprehend." Presently, he takes a view broad enough to re-encompass strict mechanism: "We do not as yet know what Nature is seeking through man, if anything —certainly not his immortality. . . . One thing we do know: our impulses do not always accord with moral or religious law . . . yet our impulses are assuredly provided us by a Creator, if no more than the mechanistic one of the chemists and physicists. We do not compound ourselves."

At the time he began *An American Tragedy* Dreiser had come to no fixed conclusions about man's origins. The years during which he moved from a belief in an accidental origin for man to tentative belief in a cosmic intelligence that had called man into existence for some purpose, also found him pondering the significance of man. Spencer himself had held for an inevitable and controlled progress for mankind; Dreiser long discounted it. Even after he began to favor grander conceptions of man's origin and destiny than mechanism could sustain, the belief that human behavior was governed by the chemical make-up of individuals (a viewpoint tentatively explored in *Sister Carrie*) gained favor with him. Certain attractions and repulsions, chemical in origin, determined success or failure. These processes were, in turn, under the control of some unknown force.⟩

In the last twenty-five years of his life, Dreiser would consider increasingly the question of man's ultimate destiny. Prior to that time, as mechanist or near mechanist, he could foresee for man no destiny other than annihilation. Spencer saw all existence as an equilibrium between rival forces, and believed this process evolutionary. Spencer's speculations concerning evolution at first had no appeal for Dreiser. As late as 1911 he told an interviewer he did not believe in progress—only change. Yet the equilibrium theory interested him. Hitherto he had been oppressed by his sense of transiency. Here was someone who said change was the axis on which Nature turned. He concluded: "[there is an] inherent necessity for difference which exists in Nature itself . . . it is not man or his laws but Nature itself which set[s] up astounding and pathetic differences between men and things, and so provides that variety and those contrasts . . . which . . . move or irritate and flagellate us into action and so more life . . . [and] are essential to life itself."

In young manhood Dreiser was unwilling to concede to man the power to control change or even to believe that responsiveness to change would dispose him for some higher destiny. Change was mechanistic. It happened to man whether he willed it or no. He could either comply with it or protest it. To protest it was to go against the flux of Nature. To accept it was to be taken into Nature's harmony. Change gave Dreiser a goad with which to prod organized society: "The caution, sprung from somewhere, to keep an open mind is well-grounded in Nature's tendency to change. Not to cling too pathetically to a religion or a system of government or a theory of morals or a method of living, but to be ready to abandon at a moment's notice is the apparent teaching of the ages—to be able to step out free and willing to accept new and radically different conditions. This apparently is the ideal state for the human mind." He conceives of a "vast, universal sea of motion, where change and decay are laws . . ." *Hey, Rub-A-Dub-Dub* takes up the same thought, in a patiently apocalyptic vein:

> If I were to preach any doctrine to the world it would be love of change, or at least lack of fear of it. . . . The most inartistic and discouraging phase of the visible scene, in so far as it relates to humanity, is its tendency to stratification, stagnation and rigidity. Yet from somewhere, fortunately, out of the demiurge there blows ever and anon a new breath, quite as though humanity were an instrument through which a force were calling for freshness and change. . . . By this same thing which brings man into being is he ended before he becomes inelastic and unpliable. Indeed, Nature constantly replaces her handiwork . . . creating newer, greener, sappier things. This is just as true of religions, theories, arts and philosophies as it is of animals, races and individuals. Nothing is fixed.

Inevitably, Dreiser's most forceful characters are those who understand that change manifests the flux of Nature, and cooperate with it. In "Chains," Dreiser calls age eighteen "The wonderyear!" It is his preferred age for his heroines—Carrie, Jennie, Aileen, Berenice, Suzanne, Etta. The men who love them, who are often twice their age, are in love with the idea of youth itself. To Dreiser, youth is the fullness of Nature. To be caught up in it is to be caught in the flux of Nature and exempted, for a time, from the phenomenon of dissolution: "Let us erect to youth an altar. . . . youth, like spring, is ever with the world . . . youth and beauty abide where all is change!" Here the pulse of Nature beats strongest: "Youth will not believe that the end of life is death. Life must go on. Beauty must reign eternal. Hope must be justified. . . . So cries youth, and well it may, for the unending vibration of life is its justification." Youth is the perfect goad. Its whips of want, hope, and dreams impel men to churn with the peristalsis of Nature.

A longing to repossess youth is a fixed trait of Dreiser's forceful characters. Cowperwood needs "some one with youth and beauty and force." Habitually he "turned his face to that dawn which is forever breaking where youth is. . . ." "Life is so short," Eugene Witla tells Christina, as they ride together in a light trap on a country road. And Dreiser continues: "She felt what he felt, the need of persistent youth and persistent beauty to keep it as it should be, and these things would not stay."

The quest for contentment is at the core of every Dreiser novel and each ends with the offer to his protagonist of an adventure essentially spiritual. Even in his most carping days Dreiser maintained an opening to the infinite. The emphasis on religion in his two posthumous books ascribed not to a sudden turnabout on Dreiser's part but to a lack of the skepticism that hitherto accompanied his spiritual probings. In his preface to *Living Thoughts of Thoreau*, Dreiser finds all the great sages of the world from Diogenes to Woolman, "Each seeking . . . to solve the orphaned ache of one who is not ready to believe that for all his ills or grievances or longings, he is to be dismissed at death, with death." Through all his years of public skepticism, Dreiser was a waif wandering in the cosmos, seeking something to assuage for good and always his "orphaned ache."

No aspect of Dreiser's quest for philosophical ultimates was more consistently held to than his effort to comprehend the meaning of beauty. Predictably, his reverence for the mystery of sex led him to approach beauty through woman. He saw the relationship of man and woman as the "key to the mystery of existence," and beauty as the force which turned that key. Of the youth he was, he says, in a phrase allying sex and beauty with the flux of Nature: "He was definitely enthusiastic about girls or beauty in the female form, and what was more, about beauty in all forms, natural and otherwise. What clouds meant to him! . . . What the murmur of the wind, the beauty of small sails on our lakes, birds a-wing, the color and flaunt and rhythm of things!"

Cowperwood's pursuit of beauty parallels Dreiser's own. *The Financier* discloses: "Wealth, in the beginning, had seemed the only goal, to which had been added the beauty of women. And now art, for art's sake—the first faint radiance of a rosy dawn—had begun to shine in upon him, and to the beauty of womanhood he was beginning to see how, in fact, the only background for great beauty was great art." Dreiser confides: "[Cowperwood] revered the sincere artist. Existence was a mystery, but these souls who set themselves to quiet tasks of beauty had caught something of which he was dimly conscious . . . their hearts and souls were attuned to sweet harmonies of which the common world knew nothing." At length, to stress that the farthest reach of his mind has been into the spiritual, not the material, Cowperwood's search for beauty is cast in Grail-quest context: "At last he saw clearly, as within a chalice-like nimbus, that the ultimate end of fame, power, vigor was beauty. . . . That was it: that *was* IT. And beyond was nothing save crumbling age, darkness, silence." In *The Stoic* Cowperwood at last realizes that in women he has sought not fleshly delirium but spiritual exaltation: "Alone among women, she [Berenice] had brought . . .

something sensitively involved with beauty and creative thought." Cowperwood's ruminations take him no further, but Dreiser's own keen consciousness of beauty and his attempts to probe to the heart of its mystery carried him finally far beyond these thoughts into a region where answers sought through a lifetime seemed to repose.

4

THE GRAIL IMPULSE

WHILE VISITING Arthur Henry at his home in Maumee, Ohio, in July 1899, Dreiser, at Henry's urging, began to write short stories. In September he returned to New York, accompanied by Henry, who had decided that they both should write novels. Dutifully Dreiser jotted down the words "Sister Carrie." He relates: "My mind was a blank except for the name. I had no idea who or what she was to be. I have often thought there was something mystic about it, as if I were being used, like a medium." By October 15, Dreiser had reached the point in his story where Carrie learned Hurstwood was married and broke off with him. Hurstwood's frustration (or was it Carrie's?) became Dreiser's own and he could not go on. In mid-December, under pressure from Henry, he began writing again and carried the narrative through to the scene in which Hurstwood debates rifling the safe. At this point, on January 25, work stopped again. Dreiser felt he had lost the thread of his story. In February, Henry read the manuscript and pressed him to continue. He went to work again, but as he approached Hurstwood's decline he stopped. "Somehow I felt unworthy to write all that. It seemed too big, too baffling. . . ." Nonetheless he *did* return to it, and by May had completed all but the last few pages. Toting pad and pencil, he took a trip to the Palisades alongside the Hudson. There, stretching out on a broad ledge overlooking the flowing river, he lost himself in the flux of Nature, and within a few hours was able to finish off the last ten paragraphs of the book. During the next month, with the help of Henry, Jug, and Mary Annabel Fanton, he cut the manuscript by 40,000 words.

Sister Carrie, up through Carrie's flight with Hurstwood, is based on the history of Dreiser's sister, Emma. A study of newspaper accounts, baggage records, and other materials has led Steinbrecher to the following conclusions: In mid-February 1886, L. A. Hopkins, "a trusted clerk" at Chapin & Gore, a smart downtown Chicago saloon, stole $3500 and some jewelry from his employers and, leaving behind a wife and daughter, eloped with a "dashing blonde" to Toronto. The blonde was Dreiser's sister, Emma Wilhelmina. She went willingly with Hopkins, first to Toronto, then to New York. There Hopkins failed to prosper.[1] In February 1895, Emma, with Theodore's connivance, moved permanently out of Hopkins' life. Dreiser says that the idea for Hurstwood came to him in New York, in 1894, when he was wandering about looking for a job. The characterization was sharpened by Dreiser's own experiences but Hopkins unquestionably was Hurstwood's prototype.

In June 1900, Dreiser gave the manuscript of *Sister Carrie* to a friend, Henry Mills Arden, editor of *Harper's Magazine*. After six weeks, Harper's returned the manuscript. Then Arden told Dreiser to offer it to Doubleday, Page, & Company, and Dreiser personally took the manuscript to the Doubleday offices and gave it to Frank Doubleday himself. Doubleday, about to leave for Europe, passed it along to novelist Frank Norris, whom he retained as a reader. Henry Lanier, a junior partner of the firm and son of Sidney Lanier, later recalled that Norris thought the book "of almost epochal importance" and insisted it be published. Doubleday's senior partner, Walter Hines Page, later ambassador to England, capitulated. Congratulations poured in. The Player's Club invited Dreiser to lecture. In high spirits, he and Jug went to Montgomery City at the end of June to visit Jug's parents. On July 19, Page wrote to Dreiser; he had now decided that the choice of characters in *Sister Carrie* would not interest most readers—and that Dreiser would have a hard time "living down this sort of material." But the book was already in page proofs.

The full facts about Doubleday, Page's change of heart may never be known. Common lore has it that Frank Doubleday passed the book along to his wife, Neltje De Graff Doubleday, and that she was appalled by it. In a preface to a later edition of the book, in which he blames Mrs. Doubleday for *Sister Carrie*'s difficulties, Dreiser says tellingly, "She was a social worker and active in moral reform." What a sermon lost, then, if she was not the actual censor of the book.

A different account of the book's suppression is given by Henry Lanier: "It was Frank who made the trouble. He hated it enough without other influence, called it 'indecent,' and begged us at once to

[1] George Steinbrecher, Jr., "Inaccurate Accounts of *Sister Carrie*," *American Literature*, XXIII (January 1952), pp. 490–493.

break the contract. If we went ahead with it, although he couldn't stop us, he warned us he would do all in his power to ruin the sale." Yet Lanier concedes that Neltje Doubleday "was one of those deceptively beautiful characters who loved to dominate in the name of virtue."

Although Doubleday and Page offered to find another publisher, Dreiser stubbornly—and unwisely—held them to their agreement. Got up in cheap red binding, *Sister Carrie* was published, without fanfare, on November 8, 1900. The edition consisted of 1008 copies. Of these, 129 were sent out to reviewers by Norris. Of the rest, stored in a subbasement without any attempt to market them, 465 were sold. Much later the other 414 copies reached the stalls of J. F. Taylor & Co., a remainder house. Dreiser's royalties, all told, came to $68.40. The reviewers, taking their cue from the indifference of the publishers, found little to praise.

The suppression of *Sister Carrie* almost finished Dreiser both as an artist and as a man. Magazines for which he had written previously now refused to accept his articles. His spirit itself was nearly annihilated. He had two new novels underway, "The Rake," an anticipatory version of *An American Tragedy*, and "The Transgressor," forerunner of *Jennie Gerhardt*. But as he wrote he grew restive. In a fit of despair he destroyed the thirty chapters he had written of "The Rake." In November 1901, he headed south with Jug. The following March, Jug returned to her family in Missouri. In May, with only ten chapters of *Jennie Gerhardt* to show for the six months he had been away from New York, Dreiser set out on a walking tour. From Roanoke, Virginia, he walked to Philadelphia. There, in the summer, Jug joined him. In December, however, she went back to Missouri, and in February Dreiser returned to New York.

Alone, he took a $1.25-a-week room and lived on bread and milk. His weight dropped to 130 pounds; a delirium of malnutrition, of possible pellagra, seized him. He imagined an intruder in his room, saw everything crooked, and felt he had to keep turning to the right, in a circle, to bring his environment back into alignment. He thought he had become two people. In desperation he sought the East River, meaning to drown himself. There he met, not Charon, but a whimsical canal boatman ferrying potatoes to the Wallabout Market in Brooklyn. The fellow's blundering good-heartedness altered Dreiser's mood. He went back to his room. A short while later, Paul found him and dispatched him to a Westchester sanitarium, run by an ex-wrestler, William Muldoon—the "Mighty Culhane" of *Twelve Men*. Dreiser remained with Muldoon from April 21 to June 2, 1903.

Brown Brothers

THE COMPLETE EDITOR

41

From him Dreiser learned, with a certainty he had lacked before, that man, to endure, must bind himself to Nature.

In June, believing rude work would restore his stamina, Dreiser got a job as a manual laborer with the New York Central Railroad. In September, Jug rejoined him. At Christmas he took a post as assistant feature-section editor of the New York *Daily News*. He was resolved now to be a practical business success and his work went forward. In the fall of 1904 he left the *Daily News* to become editor of *Smith's Magazine,* and within two years he had increased the circulation to 125,000. He then became editor of the *Broadway Magazine.* Its circulation, under Dreiser's editorship, quickly jumped over the 100,000 mark.

Paul had died on January 30, 1906. Dreiser was now truly on his own and, for the moment, not making a bad job of it. In 1907 Dreiser bought a one-third interest in the B. W. Dodge Company and arranged for *Sister Carrie*'s reissue. The *New York Press* noticed it now as "a minor curiosity of literature" but Agnes Repplier and Harrison Rhodes praised it liberally. By 1917, even copies of the ignominious first edition sold at $25.00.

Unknown to Dreiser, Thomas H. McKee, one of the owners of the *Broadway Magazine,* had been Doubleday's attorney at the time *Sister Carrie* was suppressed and had played a major part in that suppression. He now used his new association with Dreiser as a chance for further harassment. He complained "You do not dig up writers that I want." Yet Dreiser had enlisted for the magazine the services of such reputable writers as Channing Pollock, O. Henry, and Rudyard Kipling. In the summer of 1907 he left the *Broadway Magazine* to become managing editor of three magazines published by the Butterick Publishing Company. Soon he was earning a salary of $14,000 a year. At Butterick's Dreiser organized a staff of thirty-two, and in four years pushed circulation up from 400,000 to 1,200,000. Dreiser's fitness to be an editor is shown in the opinions of some of this staff. Arthur Sullivant Hoffman, managing editor of the *Delineator,* said: "He was a damn good editor." Charles Hanson Towne insisted, "Every department of the organization was under the control of Mr. Dreiser. Not a detail escaped his vigilant eye. He O.K.'d every manuscript that we accepted—read them all, in fact, and continuously gave out ideas to the entire staff, and saw that they bore fruit."

The principal Butterick magazine was the *Delineator.* To prospective contributors, Dreiser offered this statement of policy:

In fiction the *Delineator* buys things of an idealistic turn. . . . we like realism, but it must be tinged with sufficient idealism to make it all of a truly uplifting character. Our field in this respect is limited by the same limitations which govern the well regulated home.

One wonders how even a munificent salary could have kept Dreiser content with his lot. The truth is, it did not. In 1909 he secretly took over editorship of the *Bohemian,* a new magazine planned to depict life as it is. Yet writing to Mencken, Dreiser makes it clear that even here he drew a sharp line between truth of Nature and mere pornography; "I don't want any tainted fiction or cheap sex-struck articles, but I do want . . . an apt realistic perception of things as they are." To Dreiser, realism never meant crudeness. Thus in 1928 he wrote Philip Wylie: "Why do you insist so upon a certain frankness about life: even the cat covers up after herself. . . ."

Publication of the *Bohemian* began in September 1909, and ended in December, when it ran out of advertisers and subscribers. As a more orthodox diversion Dreiser launched, through the *Delineator,* his extensive Child-Rescue Campaign, designed to find proper homes for orphans—a concern that reflected Dreiser's obsessive interest in the waifs of the world, among whom he never ceased to count himself. With the backing of Theodore Roosevelt, he was successful in setting up the National Child Rescue League.

Meanwhile, Dreiser found still other recreations. In 1909 he fell in love with an eighteen-year-old girl, Thelma Cudlipp. Thelma's mother, a Butterick employee, arranged for her to go abroad for a year to think things over. Dreiser left Jug and moved into a furnished room. His persistent emotional needs are illustrated in one of his late letters to Thelma, "I am a little pleading boy now in need of your love, your mother love, won't you help me?"

On October 1, 1910 Butterick's fired Dreiser and gave out a face-saving report that he had taken a year's leave of absence. Dreiser then resumed work on *Jennie Gerhardt.* Nothing more came of the Cudlipp affair—Thelma presently married an ex-governor of New York and, in later years, resumed her correspondence with Dreiser. It did bring an end to Dreiser's career as editor, however, as well as to his marriage. Presently, Jug went home to her family, but from time to time she returned to him. Their final separation did not come until 1914.

Jennie Gerhardt (1911) was both a critical and popular success. Like *Sister Carrie,* the story is based on family history, on events that had befallen Mame and Sylvia. Always a businessman after having been an editor, Dreiser sensed the power and prospects of the book even before the public rendered its verdict. He began yet another novel, *The Financier*, announced as the first volume of a trilogy, and had it half drafted before *Jennie Gerhardt* saw print.

In the autumn of 1911, urged by the English publisher Grant Richards, Dreiser sailed for England. A record of his five-month European tour appears in *A Traveler at Forty* (1913). Here appears Theodore Dreiser, sojourner in English country houses, solemn witness to the rural funeral of a young girl, awed onlooker at "the Houses of Parliament, that noble pile," and potential guest-in-residence at the Franciscan monastery at Spello. Less Irvingesque is an account of an evening spent with a London prostitute, given over, Dreiser alleges, to a discussion of the private woes of her profession. To assure Dreiser an agreeable voyage home, Richards booked passage for him on the *Titanic*. Dreiser, short of funds, transferred his booking to the *Kroonland*. The third day out, word of the *Titanic*'s sinking passed among the male passengers. When he arrived back in New York, Dreiser's mind was swarming with new impressions and new awe at the mystery of existence.

By November 1912, *The Financier* was in print. Where before he had been content to deal with the deranging effect social thought and the American Dream had on individuals, now Dreiser sought to show how the American people, lulled into moods of complacency by pious preachments, were being exploited by a greedy minority of bankers, politicians, and businessmen.

The year 1913 brought Dreiser to Chicago to gather facts about Charles Tyson Yerkes, prototype of Frank Cowperwood, the protagonist of his trilogy. In 1914 the second volume appeared—*The Titan*. Before the book saw print Harper's, touching Dreiser in a sensitive spot, had withdrawn as publisher and John Lane had to step in in their stead. Swanberg makes much of Dreiser's reluctance to trust his publishers; so often had his trust been betrayed by them however, that it would have been strange had he not been wary. Even Swanberg concedes that over the years, following the *Sister Carrie* fiasco, there existed virtually "a national conspiracy" determined "to scuttle Dreiser."

In August 1915, after finishing his next novel, *The 'Genius'*, Dreiser set out with a friend on a 2000-mile motor trip through Indiana and adjacent states. From this experience came his next book, *Hoosier Holiday*. Nothing in all his works more evokes pathos than the account of this veteran newsman and novelist seeking everywhere memories of his mother, the one dependable sanctuary of his nomandic childhood. *Hoosier Holiday* is, in fact, one of Dreiser's major works. *Hey, Rub-A-Dub-Dub* alone more conspicuously records his philosophical impressions and the quest for values which was his ruling passion.

The 'Genius' was published in October 1915. Its first year in print it just got by. Then, in the summer of 1916, John S. Sumner, executive secretary of the New York Society for the Suppression of Vice, received in his mail a selection of pages torn from the book, on which seventy-five lewd and seventeen profane passages were noted. Sumner ordered the publisher to either delete the offending passages or destroy the plates from which the book was printed. Alarmed, the Lane Company withdrew the book from public sale, and Dreiser determined to put up a fight. Mencken, who saw the incident as a potential *cause célèbre* around which battle could be joined for freedom of the arts, put in circulation a petition signed eventually by 485 prominent writers—including Ezra Pound, William Rose Benet, Jack London, Sinclair Lewis, Willa Cather, Booth Tarkington, Ida Tarbell (then speech writing for Woodrow Wilson), Edgar Lee Masters, and Robert Frost. Even the venerable Howells wrote to a friend: "I have no doubt that half literature, prose and poetry, could as reasonably be suppressed as Mr. Dreiser's book. . . ."

Since Sumner had achieved his purpose merely with a threat, Dreiser had to bring suit against the Lane Company itself for failing to honor its contract. Although the case was ably argued by John B. Stanchfield, the five judges appointed to review the matter ruled in favor of Lane. As a result, *The 'Genius'* stayed out of print for five years. In 1923, Horace Liveright reissued it without excisions, its jacket blurb proudly trumpeting the objections the Vice Society had brought against it.

The *succès de scandale* of *The 'Genius'* made Dreiser's name a naughty word to a whole generation scarcely aware of the vicissitudes of *Sister Carrie*. And in the short run, it cost Dreiser heavily. In early 1917 he had to make do on an income of ten dollars a week. In 1918 he received seventy-six rejection slips for various short pieces submitted to a wide selection of magazines. And the University of Michigan placed a "For Faculty Only" restriction on his works. That same year the *New York Tribune* fired Burton Kline, editor of its Sunday edition, for printing Dreiser's "Love." But if *The 'Genius'* fixed Dreiser in the minds of one portion of the public as a scoundrel and sapper of morals, in another it gained him

status as champion of freedom of the arts. The battle for freedom of
the literary artist was fought after all not around *Sister Carrie* but
The 'Genius'. Within a few years, Americans were reading books that
in 1915 seemed a century in the future.

In 1917, Dreiser put himself under contract to Liveright, beginning the only publishing relationship that ever truly provided
security while he wrote. *Twelve Men* (1919), the first major book
he did for Liveright, was a reprise of those moving, often magnetic
relationships that had awakened and redirected Dreiser's spirit in
those troubled years when he was realigning himself with the flux of
Nature. It was also a farewell to the phase of his life that began with
his arrival in New York twenty-five years before. In 1919 Dreiser
could feel he had stood up to New York, its newspapers, magazines,
publishers, and censors and given no quarter. Then, too, the let-
down that followed his recent battles pointed to a need for change.
He traveled that summer in Indiana, visiting his old school teacher,
May Calvert, and John Maxwell, mentor of his early days in journalism. Characteristically, Dreiser was checking his guidelines. As
fall drew near he made up his mind to resettle in California.

Dreiser always associated a change in thinking with a change in
physical locale. Appropriately then, his decision to go to California
paralleled a new intellectual phase. By late 1919, in *Hey, Rub-A-
Dub-Dub*, he was scheming openly for social reforms which were a
blanket negation of mechanism and social Darwinism:

> He [man] should reject vain theory, especially that which relates
> to a mythical reward hereafter, and cling only to those methods
> and forms of procedure which give promise or hope of a larger re-
> ward here, tending to strengthen his capacity for living here and now.
> . . . If he is to extract any joy out of his span he must think and
> plan to make things better not only for himself but for others, since
> joy for himself depends upon his joy in others and they in him.

Hey, Rub-A-Dub-Dub was written after Dreiser read George W.
Crile's *Man: an Adaptive Mechanism*, H. W. Frink's *Morbid Fears
and Compulsions*, John B. Watson's *Psychology from the Point of
View of the Behaviorist*, and Jacques Loeb's *The Organism as a
Whole*. Now that he had dismissed with thanks his "twelve men,"
these were his new mentors. He does not claim to have effected a
synthesis of their ideas, merely to have reinforced his own thought
where he recognized they had dealt with ideas that already appealed
to him.

Dreiser's decision to go to California late in 1919 was not motivated solely by his desire to court change. Late in September of that
year he was visited in his New York studio by a cousin he had
never met before, Helen Patges Richardson. Helen had been raised
by her grandmother, Esther Schänäb, Sarah's sister. At the time of
her visit to Dreiser she was twenty-five, and fleeing from an unhappy
marriage. Dreiser was instantly in love again. He offered marriage;
Helen hesitated. He offered love; Helen accepted. And the two set
out together for California, tempestuously united in blood, in temperament, in the young girl's desire for a protector, in the man of
forty-eight's desire to shelter himself in the arms of someone half
his age. Within his own family Dreiser had at last found sanctuary,
bound not by terms of church or society—those terrifying fetters
—but by beauty, youth, force, the promise of haven, alliance with
the flux of Nature, and the kinship of identical emotional referents
—"mothers" whose adored traits had been "quick energy, strength,
humanitarian warmth, bohemian vivacity." The relationship begun
at this time ended only with Dreiser's death.

Dreiser's Los Angeles years were productive. There he completed
Newspaper Days (1922), a record of the years in which he was learning his profession and acquiring maturity. Its candor impelled even
Dreiser's most stringent critics to concede that his fiction had not
been written, after all, simply to shock his readers. The man explained
the books.

While in California, Dreiser also worked on *Moods,* a selection
of poems, and readied for publication *The Color of a Great City*
(1923), sketches of New York written between 1898 and 1910. Here
also twenty chapters of *An American Tragedy* were completed before he returned to New York in October 1922. Helen states that as
he wrote *An American Tragedy,* Dreiser was under terrible pressure,
fearful that he would be unable to finish. Part of the time he lived on
gin to stimulate his creativity, a habit he leaned on increasingly as
he grew older. Yet he proceeded with relentless thoroughness. With
Abraham Brill he discussed the psychology of murder; with Clar-
ence Darrow, the subtleties of the law courts. With Helen, in June
1923, he traveled to Cortland and South Otselic, through the Adiron-
dacks, and rowed with her to the cove known as the South Bay inlet
of Big Moose Lake, where Chester Gillette had drowned Grace
Brown. At Troy he visited Cluett, Peabody & Company to observe
shirt collars being made so he could describe accurately Clyde's
duties in his uncle's shirt factory. He pored over the official records
of the Gillette trial, absorbing every detail with his marvelous eye.

He visited the death house at Sing Sing, and talked with a condemned murderer to be sure the final scenes of his book would have no note of falsity. When he wrote the murder scene he wept copiously.

An American Tragedy came out in December 1925 and met with general critical acclaim. Indeed, within a year it went into its seventh printing. Ironically, not until he had written the definitive refutation of the American Dream, did the American Dream come true for Dreiser. Magazines now clamored for his stories and articles, and he received an invitation to visit the Soviet Union as guest of the Russian government. The greatest excitement attending publication of *An American Tragedy* involved the sale of the movie rights. Dreiser's share came to $135,000, up to that time the largest sum any author had ever received from Hollywood for a single novel. But Dreiser had too much integrity to offer himself as a foe of the American Dream if secretly he coveted its fruits. He contributed liberally to the support of his family, in sums approaching half his income. In 1942 he wrote to a government office: "No show or vainglorious spending has ever been connected with my life. I have had too many dependents to aid. And besides, show or display has never interested me. A writing table, bed and a chair in even so little as a hall bedroom was, for the major part of my early years, my total equipment. If we lose this war it may be that such will again be my total equipment. Even so, what of it? I fancy I can take it."

The cordiality of Dreiser's first dealings with Hollywood did not last. The 1931 film version of *An American Tragedy* outraged him. The social message of the book had been discarded. He brought suit to keep the movie from being shown. The studio argued that the material was not Dreiser's to control, that he had taken it from court records. The obvious question then was why did the studio pay nearly $150,000 for the screen rights when it could have had the same material for nothing merely by plundering the court records? The ruling, nonetheless, went against Dreiser. When Hollywood made a second version of *An American Tragedy* in 1951 ("A Place in the Sun"), Dreiser's point of view prevailed, though he was six years in his grave. A superior film resulted.

In June 1926, Dreiser set out with Helen on a tour of Scandinavia. Before returning to New York late in October, they visited Prague as guests of President Masaryk at the presidential palace (Masaryk, possibly mindful of Dreiser's Czech ancestry, counted himself among Dreiser's enthusiastic admirers), and England, where Dreiser visited Shaw whom he found "flashing with ideas." On their arrival home Dreiser met further fame: *An American Tragedy*, adapted for the stage by Patrick Kearney, had become a box office success. But now his restiveness asserted itself anew. He developed a passion for twenty-five-mile hikes—and for another woman. Lonely, forbidden by Dreiser to pursue an infatuation of the kind he allowed himself, Helen took up the study of Hindu thought. Out of this incident grew Dreiser's final development of Berenice Fleming in *The Stoic.*

Dreiser's own philosophical growth during his mature years as a novelist, though capricious, was decisive. His early concessions to mechanism had contended against contrary dispositions. In *The Financier* he wrote: "It would seem as though the physical substance of life . . . were shot through with some vast subtlety that loves order, that is order. The atoms of our so-called *being,* in spite of our so-called *reason* . . . know where to go and what to do. They represent an order, a wisdom, a willing that is not of us. They build orderly in spite of us."

A Traveler at Forty advances this speculative position:

> I, for one, would be the last person in the world to deny that everywhere I find boundless evidence of an intelligence or intelligences far superior to my own. I have always innately presumed the existence of a force or forces that, possibly ordered in some noble way, maintain a mathematical, chemical, and mechanical parity and order in visible things. I have always felt, in spite of all my carpings, that somehow in a large way there is a rude justice done under the sun, and that a balance for, I will not say right, but for happiness is maintained.

Hoosier Holiday shows a wavering certitude: "We race atoms are being driven to do something, construct something. . . . I do believe that these atoms are not toiling for exactly nothing. . . . There is something back of man." *Hey, Rub-A-Dub-Dub* renews these speculations: "Where there is so much order and love of order in every one and everywhere there must be some great elemental spirit holding for order of sorts, at any rate. Stars do not swing in given orbits for nothing, surely, or at least I might have faith to that extent."

At sixty, though he no longer posited speculations of man's origins on mechanism, Dreiser still was not convinced that the supreme ordering intelligence was benevolent. During this period his gropings for an understanding of man's significance in the scheme of the

universe were similarly cautious. In *Jennie Gerhardt* man's thrall-
dom to fate is all but complete. Of Bass Gerhardt, Dreiser says, he
was "arrested and fined for what fate was practically driving him
to do." As he came to acknowledge a higher intelligence, Dreiser had
to reconcile it with his concept of the flux of Nature, for which, obviously, it was responsible. He was unable to say whether or not the
flux was benevolent, he knew only that man was drawn to it, and
belonged in it. *The Color of a Great City* produces a mood of acquiescence: "I am not morbid. I know that men must make good. I
know that to be useful to the world they must have a spark of divine
fire. But who is to provide the fire? . . . Nature? God? Very likely,
although there is room for much discussion and much illumination
here." In *Dawn* a note of resignation shows itself. Man can strive to
bring harmony into society but his efforts do not mean much: "While
I am one who believes that it is certainly advisable to try to or-
ganize life . . . I am not one who now sees this visible scheme of
things as enormously important. . . . It is some form of titillating
illusion with about as much import to the superior forces that bring
it all about as the functions and gyrations of a fly."

Hoosier Holiday had averred: "Life was intended . . . to sting
and hurt so that songs and dreams might come forth." It is a curiosity of Dreiser's thought in his middle years that he had a Kantian
understanding of pain as a motive principle. The poem "Life" actually asks, "Who would be happy and there were no pain?" Full
rapprochement is effected in the preface to *Living Thoughts of
Thoreau*. Thoreau had defended cruelty, injustice, and evil as the
Cosmic Being's "seeming and yet not necessarily real hurry and disorder" (a matter laid bare to the marrow, of course, in Emerson's
remarkable poem "Brahma"). Dreiser continues: "For at no point
in connection with all this is he willing to imply, let alone admit,
the absence, even for any fraction of time, of a universal and apparently beneficent control, which, however dark and savage its
results or expressions may seem to us at times, is nonetheless, in
some larger and realer sense, the substance of something that in its
infinite breadth and allness and duration is good—and more, artis-
tically beautiful and satisfying, and so, well intended for all." By
the time Dreiser came to set down this statement, his own views
on the creator and man's significance and destiny were moving into
alignment with views concerning pain and suffering to which he long
had been partial.

Dreiser seems early to have concluded that the ultimate experience which beauty has to reveal is essentially spiritual. Sometimes

he illustrates the need men have for fulfillment through beauty by detailing their pitiable gropings toward beauty—Mrs. John's pedestrian home, which so repels Eugene Witla, or Opal Broderson's "fine furniture." In "Ida Hauchawout" he relates: "I recognize too well the formless and untutored impulses toward beauty which struggles all too feebly in the most of us, animals and men. . . . Beauty, as each interprets it for himself, must certainly be the anodyne that resolves all our pains." In *Dawn* first appears a view—boldly linking beauty to the flux of Nature—which impels Dreiser far toward his final convictions: "The vast creative impulses of life, or in the phrase of the world, God himself, are on the move, and the fixed envies the unstable and the unstable the fixed. Only a love of beauty endures: that strange taste for joy and delight in mental and material harmonies. . . ."

Although his notions of pain, beauty, and the flux of Nature impelled Dreiser toward eventual revision of his views concerning man's origin, significance, and destiny, through middle life he continued to visualize no high destiny for man. *Hoosier Holiday* has one insistent emphasis: "Man is a slave . . . toiling with forces and by aid of forces which he does not understand, and effecting results the ultimate use of which he cannot possibly grasp."

In "Esther Norn," Dreiser decides in a marine metaphor which emphasizes man's orphaned condition: "Men are forever launching little cockleshell craft upon a limitless and troubled sea that comes to nowhere, faring forth early in search of . . . the blessed isles of happiness, and never finding them." He believed his quest for ultimate answers would continue to progress so long as he kept himself responsive to the flux of Nature. He dreaded fixity as the foe of all creative accomplishment. *Hey, Rub-A-Dub-Dub* states: "If I were to preach any doctrine to the world it would be love of change, or at least lack of fear of it. . . . There is something controlling, of which we are a part and not a part. . . . What is He or It like? . . . all names and fames and blames by which we qualify it are as nothing, save that they brighten the face of its one outstanding tendency, which we must accept whether we will or not—change."

Speaking of his mother, Dreiser once said, "Mysticism? Thy name is Slav." Sarah was much given to experiences Dreiser understood as "mystical," and he fully shared such interests. During the years in which he scoffed at the possibility of a higher intelligence interested in man's welfare, he maintained an opening to the infinite which acknowledged no distinction among crude superstition, pseudo-mysticism, and genuine psychic phenomenon. As early as 1909 he advocated serious scientific inquiry into seances. *The Financier* endorses mental telepathy. This same period saw his passion develop for Charles Fort's mystical writings, and friendships with men like John Cowper Powys, who were "receptive" to the arcane. The winter of 1915–1916 found him experimenting with a Ouija board. *The 'Genius'* abounds in evidence of Dreiser's interest in the occult. Eugene consults an astrologer who gives him a correct forecast of his future life. To Eugene, finding a penny means he will sell one of his paintings, a squeaking door means sickness in the house, a howling dog, death. Angela's opportune scrutiny of the contents of Eugene's pockets is not coincidence, it follows a psychic impulse. *Plays of the Natural and Supernatural* (1916) likewise is suffused with inquiries into the occult.

Dreiser early sought to confer respectability upon his interest in the occult by describing it as scientific inquiry. In 1909 he tried to convince Mencken that science, in its pursuit of truth, is a religious work, that it is in the direction of science that the religious spirit of man has turned. In *The 'Genius'* Eugene finds science remiss in not investigating the occult: "Why didn't chemistry or physics throw some light . . . on the truthful prediction of the astrologer, on the signs and portents which he had come to observe for himself as foretelling trouble or good fortune for himself." In 1928 Dreiser began making systematic inquiries into science in an attempt to fathom the Unknowable, starting in July of that year with a three-week visit to the Marine Oceanographic Institute at Wood's Hole, Massachusetts. There he questioned researchers repeatedly as to whether or not there was a God. He came away convinced that men of science were unwilling to recognize and investigate psychic phenomena. By 1930 he was ready to affirm total disillusionment in science: "I am through with scientists. They don't see mysticism. . . ." Science receives its final dismissal from Dreiser in the preface to *Living Thoughts:* "Nowadays, the scientists insist that philosophical generalizations must be founded on scientific results. All talk of any supreme regulating and hence, legal or directing force or spirit is *out*. There is no known God or Spirit. . . . It is at this point that the *why-asking,* scientifically informed but mentally non-creative philosopher, parts company with the *how-limited* scientists of the laboratories. . . ."

No fundamentalist churchman could match Dreiser's contempt for science once it became clear to him that science did not maintain an earnest responsiveness toward the mysterious forces ordering existence. His thinking may have been confused, Swanberg concedes, but "it was never shallow."

In October 1927, Dreiser sailed for France. From Paris he went on to Moscow, in November, to begin a visit that lasted eleven weeks. On his return journey he passed through England, pausing long enough to lunch with Winston Churchill, who assured him Soviet power shortly would crumble.

On first arriving in Russia, Dreiser showed no disposition for quick conversion. In his diary he wrote: "As opposed to communism and its enforced equality I offered international, benevolent capitalism as very likely to achieve the same results." The journal of this visit, *Dreiser Looks at Russia* (1928) begins with an assurance that he had not been bought up by his free trip to Russia: "I am an incorrigible individualist—therefore opposed to Communism. . . ." But the chance to tongue-lash capitalism was not to be missed: "It is a mistake to imagine that any true distinction for man is to be derived from material possessions. . . . Man's true distinction is mental. . . . In Russia one senses that so clearly." Presently he reveals that his thinking, indeed, has been affected: "Via communism . . . it is possible to remove the dreadful sense of social misery . . . which has so afflicted me in my own life in America and ever since I have been old enough to know what social misery was." This conviction deepened when Dreiser surmised that communism was mounting an offensive against the very injustices he long had deplored. The next year Ernita, one of the women in his *Gallery,* affirms: "In my youth and zealotry I had imagined that communism could and would change the very nature of man—make him better, kinder, a real brother to his fellows. Now I am not sure that communism can do that. But at any rate it can improve the social organization of man some and for that I am still willing to work." By the spring of 1930 Dreiser was openly active in behalf of the radical left. A visit to Tom Mooney in San Quentin prison was followed by an appeal to the Governor of California for Mooney's release. In 1931 Dreiser accepted chairmanship of the National Committee for the Defense of Political Prisoners, and in *Dawn,* he ruminated: "While I see no change in the ratio of those who must die unfed in the west as well as the east, in Russia at least, is there not a light feebly beginning to glow? I wait to see it flame brightly, illuminating a stubborn, selfish, greedy world." The year 1931 also saw publication of *Tragic America* which excoriates the whole capitalistic system and calls for a change of government. In November of that year Dreiser formed the Dreiser Committee to conduct an on-the-spot investigation of conditions in the Harlan County coal fields, in Kentucky. John Dos Passos, a member of the committee, recalls Dreiser on this occasion as "shy, opinionated, sensitive as an old bull elephant," but continues, "there was a sort of massive humaneness about him, a self-dedicated disregard of consequences, a sly sort of dignity that earned him the respect of friend and foe alike." Following the visit to Kentucky, Dreiser and his committee were indicted by the Bell County Grand Jury for criminal syndicalism—a charge subsequently dropped. The pattern of Dreiser's activities in the years immediately following was such that in July 1934 he wrote to a Soviet official:

> I have been called upon by the militant communists of this country to perform every known service from writing and speaking to entering dangerous areas in order to bring about favorable results for mistreated and injured American workers, and always at my expense. . . . I am constantly being called upon by Russian newspapers and various organizations to submit opinions, articles, and whatnot to their publications and causes without any return to me whatsoever. Accordingly now I feel that if further material of mine is to be used, it should be paid for in order that I might recapture at least a fraction of the money that I have expended on Russia's behalf here and in Russia.

But a letter to Bruce Crawford the following year emphasizes how tenuous were the ties binding Dreiser to communism at this time: "Recently I have been interested in technocracy as a way out, really a better way for American purposes I think than the various isms we have been following. . . . Personally, I despair of communistic efforts in this country. . . ."

In December 1937 Dreiser told Dos Passos: "I was strong for Russia and for Stalin and the whole program, but in the last year, I have begun to think that maybe it won't be any better than anything else." The next year, the communist-dominated League of American Writers invited Dreiser to attend an international peace conference in Paris. Shortly before he sailed, league members arranged a dinner in his honor and had Ralph Bates give "the old dope a great harangue about Spain." He was urged again to join the league, but "the old dope" refused to budge. At the conference, Dreiser averred, without espousing any political system, "we should find ways and means of sharing peacefully what has been given us by nature. . . ." Now followed a visit to Barcelona, to witness the last week of the siege. On his return to America he determined to persuade President Roosevelt to authorize formation of a committee to aid Spanish civilians of both political factions, Loyalists and Insurgents. Roosevelt, engrossed by the Munich crisis then building, reluctantly granted Dreiser a fifteen-minute appointment at Hyde Park, on the morning of September 8, 1938. Beguiled, however, by Dreiser's earnestness and zeal, Roosevelt extended the interview to luncheon aboard the yacht *Potomac*. There, while cruising the Hudson, the two men worked out details for establishing the relief committee. Presently, when Dreiser found he lacked necessary backing, Roosevelt personally intervened to bring the plan to completion. Surely the gossipers of Warsaw, Indiana, in 1886 would have been astounded could they have known that Dreiser, fifty years later, would be counseling a president. Characteristically, Dreiser used the occasion not to ask for anything for himself but to speak for all mankind.

5

"I WAS AN ISHMAEL . . .
A WANDERER"

THE YEARS in which Dreiser awakened to the possibilities of bringing about social reform through political action brought other involvements also. From January 1929 through the spring of 1931, with Helen as chatelaine, Dreiser's suite at the Rodin Studios became the mecca of intellectual and artistic society. During this period *A Gallery of Women* was published, a book nicely apposite to his new interests, for the women of his "gallery" are struggling to free themselves from age-old conventions limiting woman's role in society. Dreiser adjudged his *Gallery* a bolder book than *Twelve Men* and rightly so; here his protagonists do not merely ignore convention, they defy it. In the spring of 1930 Dreiser toured the southwest. Anyone seeking a way to push him further into the socialist camp could not have been better advised than to have sent him on this journey. What Dreiser saw left him aghast at America's social needs, and eager to find some panacea for them. In May 1931, *Dawn*, chronologically the first volume of his autobiography and the work of many years, was published. In the twentieth century perhaps Gandhi's autobiography alone is a work of comparable candor. A third autobiographical volume, "A Literary Apprenticeship," was long projected but never written.

In 1931 Helen persuaded Dreiser to move from New York City to Iroki, a house he had built at Mt. Kisco, New York, on a thirty-seven-acre estate overlooking Croton Lake. This polyglot domicile, which looked like parts of several houses joined together, architecturally was the perfect expression of Dreiser's passion for change— a visible, functional statement of transition. Iroki was Dreiser's principal residence until December 1938, when after some stormy estrangements from Helen he suggested they make a fresh start together in California, simplifying their lives "to the bare necessities." This was much in the spirit of Thoreau, under whose influence he lately had fallen.

Tragic America was published in January 1932. *The Living Thoughts of Thoreau,* a selection of quotations from Thoreau for which Dreiser completed his preface in November 1938, came out early in 1939. In the interval he published no other books. From 1935, the task of gathering material for *Notes on Life*—a massive evaluation of scientific, religious, and philosophical thought, and the emotional, economic, and social condition of mankind—had gone forward, but he was too caught up in world problems to discipline himself for creative effort.

Dreiser was amazed to see how kindred his own thinking was to Thoreau's. A letter to Edgar Lee Masters, in March 1940, confides, "I felt . . . after condensing Thoreau—that I had gotten together a body of real thought most valuable to me if no other." With Thoreau, Dreiser rejects institutions because of their tolerance for unverified opinions, and scorns formal education as inimical to intellectual growth; with him he frowns on science for its cautious empiricism; he acknowledges the existence of a superior ordering intelligence, which is benevolent; he sees Nature as the means through which man can be brought into harmony with this spiritual intelligence; he sees work as a means of bringing man into harmony with Nature; he concedes that change is essential to Nature; he concedes that things which seem evil or cruel to man may be a necessary part of Nature's plan for creation; he grants the creative evolution of mankind and owns to being optimistic concerning man's ultimate end; he sees Beauty as the embodiment of the Cosmic Being. Manifestly Dreiser's fallow period as a fiction writer had been, intellectually, a period of broad change.

In March 1934, writing on "The Myth of Individuality," Dreiser had prescinded from strict mechanism: "Since by reason of creation, man is not only made but controlled by nature or creation, his thought is its thought; his reactions its reactions." In the summer of 1937, he spent three months at the Long Island Biological Association laboratories hoping to observe microscopically fundamental units of protoplasm. Appropriately, the advance in understanding vouchsafed him here, while it began in the laboratory, found its confirmation in the world of Nature. Leaving the laboratory one afternoon, he saw outside the door, some yellow flowers growing beside the path. Plucking one to examine it, he was amazed to find the same wonderful detail he had been looking at all day. He wept, then, at the realization that everything in Nature has loving care bestowed on it.

With publication of *Living Thoughts* the direction in which Dreiser's ruminations were carrying him became evident. He insists that Thoreau, "far from looking upon himself as a will-less, thought-less machine," saw himself "rather, possibly, as the inhabitant *in part* of a machine or instrument built by another. . . ." He decides, approvingly, that Thoreau "reached the very definite conclusion . . . that underlying all is a universal, artistic, constructive genius." He allows, further, that Thoreau's over-all views have impressed him more than "all of my philosophic and scientific reading of re-cent years from Democritus to Einstein. . . ."

In July 1940 a query came to Dreiser's desk from a college stu-dent asking him to clarify his philosophic position. Dreiser used the occasion to prepare a statement which he sent to the student and to many of his own friends. It asserts:

> Individuality is a myth. . . . All things to me are emanations and evolutions of cosmic forces and cosmic law. Buddha and Mary Baker Eddy affirmed an *over* or *one* universal soul, itself *being* and so con-taining all wisdom and all creative power. Modern science sees no other answer than this, but is not willing to affirm it. . . . As for the human soul—my scientific, as well as my philosophical studies, compel me to feel that there can be but one primary creative force or soul. . . . I am inspired by the conception of a primary source of all life or over-soul. . . . More, I am thrilled by life's endless grandeur and genius as it presents itself in time and space. Again I am profoundly grateful for any manifestation of itself that may be looked upon as *me*. I have no desire to flout such of its laws as are truly known—only to understand them. To know that I have been, and possibly may continue (in any form) as a part of it, is sufficient not only for my present well-being but my continuing peace of mind.

About 1943, Dreiser prepared an essay "My Creator," which showed that his skepticism now had been supplanted altogether by reverence and serenity: "I am moved not only to awe but to rever-ence for the Creator . . . concerning whom—his or its presence in all things from worm to star to thought—I meditate constantly even though it be, as I see it, that my import to this, my Creator, can be but as nothing, or less, if that were possible. Yes awe I have. And, at long last, profound reverence for so amazing and esthetic and wondrous a process, that may truly have been, and for all that I know, may yet continue to be forever and forever."

At the start of his career as novelist, Dreiser saw man at an "in-termediate stage . . . neither drawn into harmony with nature by his instincts nor yet wisely putting himself into harmony by his own free-will." For a long time he professed to believe most men

incapable of aligning themselves with Nature. Yet in those years, he
did conceive of change as a process essentially ameliorative. Thus
Newspaper Days states: "I have always rejoiced in the eagerness
of so-called living things for change, that strange something in nature that wants to be on the go." Dreiser's last novels each feature a
character who halts at the barrier of transiency and sees no way
to get past it. In *The Bulwark,* Etta Barnes confronts the barrier in
hesitant bewilderment. She senses a refuge in Nature but does not
wholly understand. In *The Stoic,* Cowperwood is unable to see what
lies on the far side of transiency. But Berenice has the purity of heart
to behold that elusive Grail. In a statement that must be Dreiser's
own final statement on a matter so long crucial to this thought, the
guru tells her:

> All motion in this universe is in the form of successively rising and
> falling. Systems after systems are coming out of the finer forms,
> evolving themselves, taking the grosser forms, again melting down,
> as it were, and going back again to the cause. So with all life. Each
> manifestation of life is coming up and then going back again. . . .
>   We are never born and we never die. Each atom is a living thing,
> leading its own independent life. These atoms combine into groups
> for an end, and the groups manifest a group intelligence, so long as
> it remains a group, these groups again combining in turn and form-
> ing bodies of a more complex nature, which serve as vehicles for
> higher forms of consciousness. When death comes to the physical
> body, the cells separate and scatter and that which we call decay
> sets in. The force which held the cells together is withdrawn, and
> they become free to go their own way and to form new combinations.
> Death is but an aspect of life, and the destruction of one material
> form is but a prelude to the building up of another.

Communism did not implant in Dreiser the desire to bring about
a better world. Communism appealed to him merely as a likely means
of getting results. A disposition toward social reform really was part
of Dreiser's commitment to the flux of Nature from the start. Robert
Ames warns Sister Carrie that if she lives to satisfy herself alone
she will lose the talents Nature has given her. Man seems meant to
uplift his fellowman, according to his abilities. In *Color of a Great
City* Dreiser says: "If you believe that hope is beautiful and that
mercy is a virtue, if you would have the world more lovely and its
inhabitants more kind, if you would have goodness triumph and sorrow laid aside, then you must be ready to make good to such ap-
plicants and supplications as fall to you the virtues thus pathetically
appealed to. You must act in the name of tenderness. If you cannot

or will not, by so much is the realization of human ideals, the possibility of living this life at all decently by any, made less." For years Dreiser hesitated to identify himself avowedly with social reform, beyond the protests he could make through his fiction. He was alienated by "that aggressive, pushing, self-seeking need which too often one finds motivating those who are professedly interested in reforms." The notion that meaningful social reforms might be carried forward under the auspices of organized religion seems to have first reached him through Quakerism. In 1934, he wrote: "I find very little difference between what the Friends are seeking to do here and what the communists are seeking to do in Russia. Both are laying aside the profit motive in order to help mankind to a better level and a happier life." To Dos Passos, in 1938, Dreiser described the kind of community he wanted in the United States as kindred to the Quaker concept of "spiritual relationship." The following year found him urging dissemination of "the two outstanding documents of the Quaker faith. . . . George Fox's and John Woolman's journals." Groundwork now was laid for sympathetic treatment of Quakerism, through a Woolman-like protagonist, in *The Bulwark*.

Dreiser took up the task of finishing *The Stoic* even as *The Bulwark* was undergoing final revisions. Cowperwood, an Episcopalian in *The Financier,* now peremptorily was provided, like his prototype, Yerkes, with a Quaker background. This motivates his final wish that part of his fortune should be used for a characteristic Quaker endeavor, the establishment of a hospital, free and without restrictions. When his estate is laid waste by despoilers before this plan can be executed, Berenice founds a children's hospital in Cowperwood's memory. Her social work is revealed to be God-directed, an evolution within the flux of Nature. Her heart touched by the starving children of India, she reflects: "this degradation must be met and overcome. And was not the All in All God speaking and directing her thus to assist, aid, change, until this earthly phase of Himself would be altered or transmuted into the exchange of evil for good?" By the end of his life, Elias says, Dreiser found "the principles of communism were . . . like the principles of Christ."

At the conclusion of *Sister Carrie,* Dreiser says of Carrie: "Sitting alone, she was now an illustration of the devious ways by which one who feels, rather than reasons, may be led in the pursuit of beauty. . . . Oh, blind strivings of the human heart! Onward, onward, it saith, and where beauty leads, there it follows. . . . Know, then, that for you is neither surfeit nor content. . . ." For many years

Dreiser was to see beauty thus—drawing man into the flux of Nature, but ever itself the unattainable goal. The preface to *Living Thoughts,* however, bares an altered perspective. Beauty at last becomes the mask of something beyond beauty: "Thoreau . . . was forever knocking at the door of the mystery. . . . was ever spellbound before the beauty of life. . . . nearly all that he has to say comes to you as a song, the song of a mystic force, embodying itself through beauty." Cowperwood had known the need for beauty. But as beauty had eluded Carrie, it eludes him also. He had sought it in women—Dreiser's reflections in "Protoplast" (1926) might have been Cowperwood's own:

> My error
> If at all
> Has been
> In seeking in mortal flesh . . .
> The Likeness
> Of something that is eternal. . . .

Again, Berenice completes Cowperwood's quest for him. She moves beyond beauty to that which beauty adumbrates. Even before Cowperwood's death Berenice had felt "a desire to create something utterly beautiful, so that her life would be complete and significant." The final revelation again is communicated to her through the guru. She observed: "So many people worshiped beauty in all its forms; in fact, they were slaves to beauty!" He explained:

> When you see a man being drawn to a beautiful face, do you think that it is a handful of arranged material molecules which really attracts the man? Not at all! Behind those material particles there must be and is the play of divine influence and divine love. The ignorant man does not know it, but yet, consciously or unconsciously, he is attracted by it, and it alone. . . . The Lord is the great magnet, and we are all like iron filings: all of us are being constantly attracted by Him, and all of us are struggling to reach Him, the face of Brahman reflected through all forms and designs. We think we worship beauty, but we are really worshiping the face of Brahman shining through.

Dreiser wants no mistake about this affirmation. Standing before Cowperwood's tomb, Berenice muses in almost the last words Dreiser wrote, "Cowperwood must know . . . that his worship and constant search for beauty in every form, and especially in the form of a woman, was nothing more than a search for the Divine design be-

hind all forms—the face of Brahman shining through." In reaching
this explanation for Cowperwood's pursuit of women Dreiser was
assured that his own hard-driving passions had not, after all, been
truly antagonistic to his need for spiritual fulfillment, but merely
a prompting from Nature responded to at too simplistic a level. His
conviction that Nature held the answer seemed vindicated.

To the question of man's status after death, Dreiser longest de-
ferred an answer. Religion's promise of eternal happiness for those
who held to the path of virtue in this life had seemed to him hostile
to progress and he would have none of it. "My Creator," written in
November 1943, expresses awe and reverence for the presence of
the Creator in all things—"a process that . . . may yet continue to
be forever and forever." Here Dreiser expresses a wish—indeed, prays
—to remain a part of this process. In his final works he brings the
matter under review and makes his choice. In *The Bulwark,* Etta
takes refuge in the realization that there is "something beyond human passion and its selfish desires and ambitions." She designates
it as "love and unity with all nature." In this she saw: "There was
nothing fitful or changing or disappointing—nothing that glowed
one minute and was gone the next. This love was rather as constant
as nature itself. . . . an intimate relation to the very heart of being." Even here, Dreiser does not insist this relation is eternal. In
The Stoic, however, he reaches a conclusion concerning the question of whether or not there is a destination for the spirit. Again
through the guru, the long withheld commitment is given: "In one
sense, bodies and forms are eternal. . . . We are never born and
we never die. Each atom is a living thing, leading its own independ-
ent life. . . . Death is but an aspect of life, and the destruction of
one material form is but a prelude to the building up of another."
In oneness with the Cosmic Intelligence, in a universe that swings
in unending flux, Dreiser found at last the haven he had sought,
through a lifetime of painstaking inquiry.

During the last six years of his life Dreiser labored under a two-
fold burden. The war filled him with concern for humanity: awareness of his own waning vigor stirred in him a driving compulsion to
meet unfulfilled commitments garnered in his passage through life.
These were the years to complete the books he had pledged himself
to write, to make a final ordering of his personal affairs, and above
all, to decide what life was all about. In 1941 *America Is Worth
Saving* was published. An attack on capitalism, it was a work both
hurried and inexact. Before the year was out, Dreiser was refusing
permission to organizations wanting to quote from it. Russia was

invaded in June of that year and his orientation toward the war was suddenly stood on its head. When the assault began, he took to his bed and remained there for days, sick at the thought of what was happening. Earlier that year Dreiser had prepared a final tribute to Sherwood Anderson, read at Anderson's funeral service, in which he spoke of "the well-outcoming of everything, guided as each thing plainly is by an enormous wisdom. . . ." There were times, surely, in the summer of 1941 when this courageous trust must have wavered.

The year 1942 was a tumultuous one. America was now in the war, allied with the Soviet Union, and Dreiser found less at home to complain about. When he heard that his books were selling well in Russia, war or no war, he fired off a note to Stalin asking for royalties. To his astonishment the Soviet government replied with a check for $34,600. Elatedly he told Helen: "I refuse to worry any more. This will carry me through to the end." Resolutely he worked on *Notes on Life,* already seven years underway. Meanwhile Hollywood bought *Sister Carrie.* When the fact was made public, Jug wrote him. For the $5000 he owed her, plus an additional $5000, she would give him a divorce. Dreiser saw that her back alimony was sent to her but ignored the divorce offer. Jug's death soon after, on October 1, 1942, in St. Louis, merely made official a freedom he long had taken for granted. Meanwhile, Dreiser had presented himself in Toronto on September 21 to speak on the need for a second front. At a press conference he stated candidly: "I would rather see the Germans in England than those damned aristocratic horse-riding snobs there now." When the story broke in the press, Ontario's Attorney General secured an order enjoining Dreiser from speaking further in public. Outraged, Dreiser at once entrained for Detroit. Banner headlines in John Blunt's *Weekly and Flash,* screamed after him expressing in patriotic indignation: *"Arch Traitor Flees Canada, One of the Most Dangerous Men on this Continent And If Cordell Hull is Alive to His Duty Dreiser will be Interned at Once or Shot."* That same autumn a coronary occlusion put Dreiser in bed for two months.

Even before his heart attack Dreiser must have experienced hints of his mortality, for a suggestion from Robert Elias that he should give his papers to the University of Pennsylvania had met with his cordial approval the previous spring. He dispatched to the university the first of several shipments which would see the bulk of his papers entrusted to Pennsylvania in the decade that followed. Dreiser now also collected, in labeled folders, data for nearly forty chapters of *Notes on Life*. These notes reached the university in 1955, following Helen Dreiser's death.

Although his weight and strength diminished steadily during 1944, Dreiser pushed on with *The Bulwark* and met other responsibilities as they arose. In June 1944, in New York, he received the Award of Merit Medal and $1000 from the American Academy of Arts and Letters. On his return from New York, Dreiser met Helen on June 9 at Stevenson, a hamlet in the state of Washington. As he got off the train he staggered and fell, but when he picked himself up it was not to complain but to hand to Helen the gold medal the Academy had given him. In 1898 Dreiser had gone to Washington, D. C., to marry Jug, after getting a letter from Jug's sister asking him to make good his promise. On his latest visit to New York he had received a letter from Helen's sister Myrtle asking him to marry Helen. Ever the fatalist who believed that certain events in our lives were destined to repeat themselves, Dreiser capitulated and wrote Helen to say he now would marry her. At Stevenson, on June 13, 1944, Dreiser and Helen were secretly married in a ceremony to which Myrtle and Myrtle's fiancé were sole witnesses.

Dreiser's marriage to Helen was but one of several decisive actions he took as his life drew to a close. In June 1944, in New York, he invited Marguerite Tjader Harris to come to Hollywood to give him editorial assistance with *The Bulwark*. She arrived in August, and through the fall worked with Dreiser daily from ten to four, at her cottage in Cadet Court, imposing some system on the materials he already had prepared. From November on, Dreiser dictated to Marguerite the further content of the novel, and on May 3, 1945, the book was completed. Within a month, Dreiser picked up with *The Stoic*. He explained to Helen: "My time on this earth may not be long and I want to finish *The Stoic*." At this time Dreiser also saw himself in the harvest season of his political and social involvements. He applied for membership in the Communist Party on July 20, 1945.

Dreiser's formal espousal of communism did not come easily. For several years he had been putting under rebuke aspects of communism which irritated him. In June 1938, he deplored the Soviet suppression of books hostile to communism, and denounced Soviet emphasis on a book's social content. Of American communists he said, in March 1943: "They have never interested me and I have never been interested by their gyrations and genuflections. I am—and have been—content to deal with the Russian Government direct. . . ." Far from being used by Russia to further its goals, Dreiser seems rather to have planned to use Russia to further *his* goals—naïve though this expectation may have been. He saw himself a chessmaster moving the pawns of the universe about to win his game. Soviet willingness to pay him enormous sums, in wartime, for the privilege of reading his books, was clear indication to him that he had something others wanted. To Dreiser, his conversion to communism was not an act of capitulation. In September 1945 he assured Elias that he intended to speak out (as an individual) just as he had always done, and if the Party did not like it, it could throw him out. Dreiser continued to form his own judgments. The extent to which *The Bulwark* and *The Stoic* concern themselves with man's kinship with Nature made them useless to the communist cause.

No man ever went about the business of writing a summary conclusion to each chapter of his life more methodically than Dreiser did in his last eighteen months on earth. His affairs of the heart ended in marriage to Helen; his quest for an agency through which to reform the world ended in his formal adoption of communism; his obligations to his publishers, his readership, and to himself as artist and philosopher, were met in his stubborn drive to complete his "literary schedule" with *The Bulwark* and *The Stoic*. The eighty-seven packets of *Notes on Life*, which he neatly wrapped and labeled, constitute a last polite plea to stand acknowledged as one who did his duty so far as strength would allow.

On September 16, 1945, Dreiser suffered a slight stroke which produced a brief but alarming impairment of his memory. The spell passed and he picked up again with his work, more determined than ever to complete *The Stoic*. On December 22, 1945, he returned the final proofs of *The Bulwark* to the publisher. Two days after Christmas, after working through the day with Helen on the penultimate chapter of *The Stoic*, he was stricken with a severe kidney attack shortly before midnight. At 6:50 the following evening (the forty-seventh anniversary of his marriage to Jug), as night thickened and a heavy fog swirled over the world beyond his door, a sudden heart attack brought Dreiser's life quietly to a close. Shortly before he died he asked Helen to kiss him. When she did so, he looked at her steadily and said, "You are beautiful!" It was less a farewell to earth than a salutation to eternity.

In August 1945, Dreiser had attended a friend's funeral at Forest Lawn, and confided to Helen that he had never seen a more beautiful resting place than the Whispering Pines section of that cemetary, an area noted for its typification of Nature. Helen arranged for his burial there. Though a simple headstone would mark his grave, the extravagant reputation of Forest Lawn inspired the legend that Dreiser went forth from this world clutching every adornment of materialism the grave could accommodate.

In the ambulance that carried Dreiser's remains to Forest Lawn, Marguerite Harris rode as a passenger seated beside the corpse. A few months before she had told Dreiser he was a natural mystic like Thoreau, but with much more *love*. He told her then: "Well, that's certainly encouraging. Maybe the Almighty will give me a chance." Now, during this solemn journey, Dreiser's hand clasped in her own in a last gesture of leave taking, she could not believe that that chance had not been given him. On the last Good Friday of his life Dreiser had taken communion at the Hollywood Congregational Church, whose pastor was his friend, the Reverend Allan Hunter. On the afternoon of the day Dreiser died, Hunter, who did not know of his illness, stopped by to pay the Dreisers an impromptu visit. With Dreiser's assent, he prayed over him. It was Hunter who conducted the funeral service, while friends, including Charlie Chaplin and Will Durant—a comedian and a philosopher—who were pallbearers, pondered with him Dreiser's compassion and spiritual awareness. Burial was delayed by a gravedigger's strike. Dreiser would have liked that. The funeral was in the new year—January 3, 1946—a time of beginnings. Dreiser would have liked that too.[1]

---

[1] At Forest Lawn, at the request of Dreiser's niece, Dr. Vera Scott, daughter of Edward Dreiser, the sculptor Edgardo Simone made a death mask of Dreiser, and a cast of his right hand. Before the lid of the coffin was closed Helen placed beside him the manuscript of "To a Poet," a sonnet she had written in tribute to him.

6

THE ARTIST

D REISER'S MASSIVENESS, more than any other factor, sponsored the common allegation that he lacked responsible critical standards. Dreiser himself blandly averred: "I need a large canvas." He explained further: "When a writer traces the course of a complete emotional cycle . . . he has his work laid out. . . . It is the amount of material which is involved in the feeling which determines the form of the work. . . . The idea or emotion completes itself, builds itself up." In consequence, the emotional cycle of each of his novels is enormous and its development massive.

With Dreiser, massiveness is functional. In an interview given Rose Feld, a *New York Times* reporter, in December 1923, Dreiser said: "If you want a great scene you cannot get it in miniature. The great realistic novels of the past, *The Idiot, Anna Karenina, The Brothers Karamazov*, could they have been written in the so-called present style of realism? Their authors needed breadth and length. They took the trouble to make their picture complete. The little canvases of today will never displace the larger ones of yesterday." [1]

Dreiser once told a correspondent that the structure of his books was always completely worked out in his mind before he began to write. The long delays which interrupted the writing of *Sister Carrie* were occasioned not by indolence, exhaustion, flagging interest, or a failure of fecundity, but by problems of architectonics which he refused to bluff his way past. He had to know that what came next was structurally right. In *A Traveler at Forty*, Dreiser wrote: "Of all known architectural forms the Gothic corresponds more nearly to the finest impulse in nature itself—that is, to produce the floreated form." Of the way his own books took form he wrote later: "I never make notes. I carry my plots around with me year after year before setting pen to paper. By the time I am ready to write I see the book as plainly as if it were a tree rising up before my eyes. Root, trunk, branches, twigs, so to speak, are all there; it is only the leaves

---

[1] The *New York Times,* December 23, 1923, III, pp. 6–7.

that require to be sketched in." That he should see his own works as carefully fashioned trees brought to leaf, suggests that, as a writer, he himself sought to hearken to nature's "finest impulse," liberally enclosing, in foliate abundance, a structure as sturdy as Gothic and as defiant of time.

Dreiser's critics are quicker to praise his ability to portray character than other areas of his achievement. The fact is Dreiser saw that the scope of the American scene was much broader than that which fiction under the Victorian consensus had accommodated. Accordingly he undertook to portray a class of people who never before had figured in American fiction. He gathered in, without prejudice, the unsanctified multitudes—factory girls, garage mechanics, lumberjacks, menials. Some of the criticism directed against Dreiser assuredly originated in resentment generated by his nonpejorative potrayal of these lower-class types. It may be that Dreiser did narrow the range of his art by restricting his choice of characters to people crude and repelling in their aesthetic unawareness. But, they were an actual segment of society, destined to become, in the twentieth century, that segment most written about because their lives reflected the inadequacies of the culture that had produced them.

Those who deplore Dreiser's concern for the lowly, offer in further proof of the essential triviality of his mind his documentation of events, facts, or customs of trite consequence. *Sister Carrie* chronicles the news that the term "masher" came into use about 1880, that America's first three department stores opened in Chicago about 1884, that Hurstwood used one of the first private telephone booths ever built, that Carrie could unlatch her front door with a push button in her kitchen. For Dreiser, no address is ever complete without its street number, no minor purchase concluded without an exact reckoning of cost. Although his grasp of transiency might have suggested to him the need for authenticating details relative to a given time and place, he did, in fact, describe an interest in history as one of his great failings and delights. This interest, moreover, was stimulated by the aloofness toward his work shown by his contemporaries, for it compelled him to write past his present public to posterity. It is this consciousness of addressing himself to posterity that gives to his historical accounts of the present a quiet authority which gains in appropriateness with the passage of time.

Dreiser's zealous compassion early addressed itself to humanity. At twenty, he "was filled with an intense sympathy for the woes of others, life in all its helpless degradation and poverty, the unsatisfied dreams of people, their sweaty labors, the things they were compelled to endure—nameless impositions, curses, brutalities—the things they would never have, their hungers, thirsts, half-formed dreams of pleasure, their gibbering insanities and beaten resignations at the end." It was a commonplace for him to press money on some forlorn vagrant, to supply a strange tyke with fare for a carrousel ride, or simply to stand on a city sidewalk weeping openly at the sad picture of passing humanity. He would confide: "The times unbidden tears have leaped to my eyes and my throat has become parched and painful over scenes of the streets, the hospitals, the jails! I have cried so often that I have felt myself to be a weakling; at other times I have been proud of them and of my great rages against fate and the blundering, inept cruelty of life." Dreiser champions not only maidens in distress, orphans, and fumbling oldsters, but child molesters, hobos, thieves, brutes, bad mothers, and even an eccentric ragpicker whose wild dogs tore a boy to pieces. He does not merely pity the unfortunate, he extenuates them. It is his amazing ability to see everyone's point of view that gives to his works a dimension absent from the works of his contemporaries. He wishes to put all the facts before his reader, to enable him to see how every action is undertaken with some apparent good in view. This intention lies behind the massiveness of his works and is its justification, for through it he liberates his reader from narrow prejudice, broadens his comprehension of human behavior, and brings him into compassionate communion with his fellow man. He deals always in the play of circumstances which those who confine themselves to rule-book morality never take into account.

In 1919, Dreiser told an interviewer: "I don't care a damn about the masses. It is the individual that concerns me." Dreiser's compassion is, in fact, qualified. He admires those who defy convention in response to compulsions of Nature more than timid transgressors who are committed still to society's fixed code. He has least sympathy of all for those who uphold conventions actively and seek to impose them on others. His real preference is for the liberated. The weak man is a creature of society, cowered by mandates; life goes with the man caught up in the flux of Nature. Yet Dreiser pities mankind in general, too; he regrets that even the strong must fall to earth, that the dreamer's dreams seldom are realized. In *A Traveler at Forty*, he says: *"Life seen through a temperament! that is the miracle of art."* He means the temperament of the character, not the artist, for his own personality never intervenes between his character and the reader. In fact, his characterizations are flecked constantly with insights into human nature

which can only have derived from shrewd observation of the usually
unobserved. Again and again, a character takes on individuality, a
situation its distinctive meaning, because Dreiser does not withhold
the precise detail that reality closely observed alone could supply.
Moreover, Dreiser is psychologically right in his portrayals. He is
able to see things authentically at the range that waitresses, lumberjacks, and ribbon clerks would view them from. He slips naturally
into their argot, and reproduces their naïve logic. Even as readers
are repelled by Hortense Briggs's crude bartering, they share her
wants and connive with her. Dreiser enters every scene from the
viewpoint of each character. He is submerged in their sensibilities,
his own presence scarcely felt. Carrie and Hurstwood, even in conflict with one another, both have his justification. Eugene and Suzanne are extenuated even when they pit themselves against the
dying Angela. Understanding all, Dreiser pardons all. "Giff" finds
Dreiser saying that the broken and weak can instruct as readily as
the profound and powerful. This view made him heir to perceptions
which self-complacency withheld from others. The modern reader
looks back to Dreiser now across an array of character types bolder
than any he cared to depict—rapists, junkies, fetishists, homo-
sexuals—and fails to credit his boldness. His own generation saw
him standing beyond an array of simpering, enthralled, bloodless
abstractions which made his creations seem the spawn of some great,
gray-dark wretchedness; its alarm was natural.

To say that Dreiser understands his characters is not to say that
they understand one another. On the contrary, Dreiser saw man's
inability to sustain his relationships with others as one of the most
profound facts of human existence. Each of his works offers a pleth-
ora of minor instances and at least one major instance of what can
be described as a "miscalculated gesture"—a gesture sometimes of
defiance, sometimes of compassion, sometimes of affection, but a
gesture predicated always on man's futile desire to be understood
by his neighbors. Dreiser's most dramatic miscalculated gestures
are those made by unrequited lovers. In *The 'Genius'*, Angela desperately seeks a renewal of Eugene's love for her by flinging aside
her peignoir to reacquaint him with her physical attractions. The
only response her gesture stirs in him is disgust. In *The Titan*, Aileen tries to quicken Cowperwood's languishing regard by taking a
lover. Her gesture arouses only a disdainful pity. When, in the same
work, she attempts suicide, hoping to shame Cowperwood into some
meaningful response toward her, the breach merely widens further;
pity is displaced now by contempt. In *An American Tragedy*, Ro-

berta Alden puts before Clyde a picture of her desperate need, in terms rich in pathos—heart-rending and anguishing. Her last appalling gesture of inept and fierce compassion which causes him to strike out blindly at her in revulsion, is as loathsome to him as it is precisely because it comes, at the worst of all possible times, as the latest in a series of such gestures. In each of the instances cited, a woman tries, without success, to rekindle in a man's heart a love that has flickered out. Understandably, this most vital of relationships would furnish Dreiser his best opportunities for illustrating the miscalculated gesture. But he uses it effectively elsewhere also, as in Carrie Meeber's break with Drouet, Aileen's estrangement from her father, and in Solon Barnes's disputes with Etta and Stewart. Wherever it appears, it points always to the same conclusion. So long as man's relationship to the cosmos eludes his understanding, he cannot hope to give lasting coherency to relationships with fellow mortals. Though Dreiser believed the answer was to be found in Nature, of all his characters, only Jennie and Lester and Solon and Etta are brought by it to a mutual understanding, and in each instance, death swiftly intervenes to omit from Dreiser's works any sustained example of such a relationship successfully maintained.

It is sometimes observed that Dreiser's failure to develop children as characters in his books suggests an area of deficiency in his understanding of human nature. It is true that Dreiser was childless, and that children are assigned no major parts in his works. The early life of Solon Barnes's five children is memorialized in a few anecdotes. Only Jennie Gerhardt's Vesta is developed as a character; yet her words are few and she is as antic as Hester Prynne's Pearl and, like Pearl, she is a personified abstraction, a reminder of her mother's fall from virtue. Possibly, the general exclusion of children from Dreiser's works is positive rather than negative in function. Dreiser enjoyed the company of children and found an easy comradeship with them. Yet, inasmuch as he saw all men as waifs or orphans, to portray children could only have diverted attention from his major contention that all men, in this world, are bewildered children, dolefully seeking their rightful abode. The child's view is well represented in Dreiser's works. Dreiser himself never lost a child's capacity for wonderment. His mind was ever open to life and to Nature just as a child's would be. To the best of his characters he extends this same endowment.

Although he was a professed naturalist, Dreiser's enormous compassion for mankind is at a far remove from the naturalistic ideal of clinical detachment, nor is his unorthodoxy as a naturalist limited to this one peculiarity. The true naturalist, by rejecting free will, filched from his characters that vital tension which derives from purposeful struggle. Dreiser's characters habitually refuse to show the acquiescence of the fated. Moreover, when they transgress the laws of society, he exculpates them on grounds implicitly moral. Carrie Meeber is driven to the role of kept woman by economic necessity. Jennie Gerhardt gives herself to her lovers out of a sense of responsibility for the well-being of her family—it is as important to Dreiser as it is to Jennie when her father, on his deathbed, acknowledges her as "a good woman." Eugene Witla, Clyde Griffiths, and Stewart Barnes are scarred not by fate but by the American Dream. Pessimism in Dreiser's works has habitually to contend with recrudescent hope. He could not find Nature, without provocation, hostile to man. Man's plight was social, not fated, and to struggle against it, with some hope of victory, was his prerogative and duty. All the tensions found in good writing done outside the naturalistic discipline are present in a Dreiser novel. A realist in his realizations, Dreiser was an idealist in his aspirations and the idealist in him would not let him violate the truth of Nature to stay within a limited theory of art. The only Dreiser characters without free will are conventionalists, and they have abdicated their will to society or synod. If Etta Barnes declares "I am crying for life," she cries not because Nature is indifferent to man's needs, but because mankind, though empowered to requite them, is indifferent to them, and persistently allows itself to be enticed by false goals.

The true artist does not structure his story on symbols, he functions through them. As a symbolist, Dreiser never has been given his due. Characteristic is the subtlety that inspirits the chair symbolism in *Sister Carrie* and *Jennie Gerhardt*, a subtlety hallmark to a persisting symbolism of vehicles, windows, stars, seasons, weather, water, light, electricity, clouds, attire, cities, flowers, colors, dancing, sports, crowds, birds, names, prisons, roads, hotels, and havens, real and ideal, that surges through the whole Dreiserian world. It is not tentative; nor is it a device selected and used with narrow deliberation. It is a function of that world which Dreiser is committed to explore. Out of the great raw substance from which America took its dreaming, he called forth implicit meaning.

Dreiser first understood that art went beyond ostensible appearances when, as a reporter, he found that artists did not illustrate his stories as he thought they should be illustrated. They failed to see all that he saw. He knew then that most men lacked the necessary dispositions for making a meaningful response to reality. This realization disposed him to make himself master of any subject he wrote about. When he began the trilogy of desire, he knew nothing about finance. Yet his passion for seeing things as they were brought him to so thorough a knowledge of the facts needed that bona fide financiers marveled at his perspicuity. His exactness was not the picayune detail work of the professional hack, but an entire impression of what he had had from Nature. Handling the guidelines extended up to him from past experience, he possessed so full a capacity for richly participating in the mere manner of ordinary life that sham or pretext were intolerable.

By responding intently to his environment, Dreiser did not suppose that he had done his whole duty as an artist. He saw the necessity of producing states of excitement through which situations or conditions could be experienced with heightened awareness. Once, after provoking a prostitute to anger, he explained: "It was brutal, but I wanted to get beneath the conventional lies these girls tell, if I could." To the last months of his life he liked the clash of personalities in conflict ringing about his ears. Where there was no strife, he stimulated it, to be stung into a response to life. Thus had he accounted for the existence of pain. Thus had he sought to give immediacy in his own life to that equation which he believed maintained all in a pulsing balance, never still, never finally determined.

Criticism of Dreiser's style is of two kinds. The first addresses itself to his diction which is deplored as worn, tasteless, florid, inexact, and clumsy. A second, more far-reaching charge, tasks him with being tediously prolix; he feels duty bound to include everything that has the remotest bearing on his subject, as though nothing would convince his readers that he has given them all the facts they need to arrive at just judgments. Dreiser once told Ford Madox Ford that since America was a country of businessmen, not *littérateurs,* he wrote as he did to bring himself closer to the people he wrote about. His process of creation by no means halted with a first draft. "There were three or four revisions of everything," says Mrs. Campbell, "plus one or two goings-over of the final proofs." The pages she received for editing "were always a maze of crisscross insertions and revisions." Swanberg says that Dreiser would "begin all over again, rather than cross out a sentence, or chop his writing line. The flow of his language was all important to him." And Swanberg even admits grudgingly: "Dreiser forgot his penury when his own writing was at stake. He made such sweeping correc-

tions in *The Financier* proofs that it cost him a staggering $726.90."
Dreiser, then, was faithful to the demands of his art. His scope and
purpose account for his infelicities.

Dreiser did realize that his methods of production and faulty
education left his manner, if not his matter, in need of mending.
His grammar was mere guesswork, his spelling censurable, his pro-
lixity so distressing to others that he realized he must yield where
yielding would cost him nothing in essentials. Usually he put more
than one reviser to work on his manuscripts, compared their suggestions and, as often as not, ignored them or got around them somehow. To be open to suggestion was, for Dreiser, part of the whole
process of learning from life. He revised just as a playwright might
revise once his script has been tried out on the ears of others. To his
editors he would suggest areas in which he saw certain kinds of
changes indicated, but once made, if not to his liking, they did not
stay. Of her revision work on *The Stoic,* Dreiser would instruct
Louise Campbell: "I would like a severe critical sandpapering in
order to shake me into closer work. . . ." Yet a short time later he
would tell her, concerning "Compromise," "Be sure not to overdo
the condensing. If a philosophic aside has any beauty it should in
my judgment be carried as poetic color." That he could present his
matter succinctly, directly, and matter-of-factly when his material
sanctioned it, is seen in his deft, quickly drawn account of Hurstwood's suicide in *Sister Carrie,* and in the drowning scene in *An
American Tragedy.* Closer work, to Dreiser, did not mean mere
abridgment. Subtleties other storytellers frugally eschewed, or were
without the wit to contrive, were not to Dreiser dispensable details.

Separate notice must be given to the character of the age in which
Dreiser emerged as a writer, since he took from it not only its diction but its preferred art form—the melodrama. Much of the quaint-
ness of his diction and situations becomes comprehensible if related
to the tradition of melodrama extant in his day, the melodrama not
only of a second-rate era in the theater but of Crane's *Maggie* and
Norris' *McTeague.* Just as he maniuplates diction to make mediocrity serve mythic and metaphoric ends, he manipulates situations
of melodrama to the same purpose. Working through the familiar,
Dreiser sophisticates it so that it serves all time, not some narrow
interval of time. Indeed, he made of melodrama an art form. His
stories retain but the thinnest veneer of the woodenness of the all
but unreadable melodramas that held the boards in his day. *Sister
Carrie* is only by incident a period piece; its contours assign its era
but the quality of the workmanship and its creator's intention, im-

part to the whole that worth which makes the great achievements of every era an heirloom for all times.

Dreiser's alleged lapses in style relate usually to his desire to put his characters in a language context appropriate to them. In "The Lost Phoebe," for example, he eschewed folk images and rhythms, which would have enhanced his rural dialogue, because he saw that they would have set up within the story a conflict of moods fatal to the spell it casts. "A Mayor and His People" not only captures the essence of individuals through diction, through its management it effects characterization. Where confusion arises is in Dreiser's practice of sometimes intensifying dialogue traits by allowing the omniscient narrator to share them, a technique which can be conceded validity as an achiever of harmony.

Nonetheless, in several areas Dreiser did fail as dialogist. His exchanges between men and women, whether lovers or friends, is halting and unconvincing. Nor does he handle crisis speeches well —his excited people lapse into unintentional melodrama. An exception is Clem Broderson's long delayed outburst in "Fine Furniture." When it does come it is convincing because it is conceived of as a rational statement of indignation and exasperation, suited to Clem's normal amiability rather than to his wife's whimsical folly.

Dreiser's art, even where it faltered, was not contrived haphazardly. His larger success as a writer rests, after all, not on a raw, undisciplined instinct for shaping fiction, as has been sometimes alleged, but on an understanding of his craft that was both reasoned and profound. An innovator whom the bludgeons of criticism could not turn from his purpose, he stands today in the front rank of those who have shaped the growth of the novel in the twentieth century.

7

SISTER CARRIE

WITH THE EXCEPTION of Henry James's last works no other American novel written at the turn of the century could approach the power of *Sister Carrie*. It was a powderhouse amid gazebos. The works of Norris, Frederic, Howells, and Garland all have been diminished by time, but *Sister Carrie,* owing to Dreiser's unusual ability to see his era in historical perspective, to extract from its flow of values those things which were not ephemeral, has the timelessness that attaches to all things which best evoke their times.

Carrie Meeber is seen first, eighteen years old, a simple country girl coming to the city to seek her fortune. Nature, not social thought, has formed her. Through the early, groping stages of her unsponsored excursion into the world she thinks that the visible show of the wealthy reflects inner contentment. *Sister Carrie* chronicles her discovery that human nature, to be spiritually sated, requires something more than the fruits of the American Dream. She never does find out what she is seeking, but at the novel's end she is redefining her goals and groping toward a fulfillment which is drawing her back toward Nature. She does appear to barter sex to put herself on the road to better opportunities. She entrusts herself first to Drouet, then to Hurstwood, not as an opportunist, however, but out of force of circumstance. Although she is impelled by a latent desire to participate in the flux of Nature, society misdirects her into a pursuit of the American Dream which hopefully she follows. By making her a creature not of calculation, but of instinct, Dreiser shows us that she is not a thoroughgoing materialist. Carrie moves slowly toward acceptance of Nature through a painstaking succession of goals. She is unequipped to quest for ultimates. Even at the end, her aspirations are felt rather than understood. Carrie, Dreiser says, was unwilling to wait until "the better thing would eventuate." This remark indicates a freedom of choice a strict mechanist never could sanction; it is enough to stress here the powerful desire within Carrie to push on toward something better. She never pretends that life with either Drouet or Hurstwood is the capstone of all her longings. Her goals, for her, are ineffable. She does not recognize them in any of the opportunities that present themselves to her. She accepts advantages as they accrue, but does not mistake their place in her life. When she first takes money from Drouet it is not, to her, a form of barter. Dreiser says: "No deep, sinister soul with ulterior motives could have given her fifteen cents under the guise of friendship." When she gives herself to Drouet it is an expression of gratitude. He has cleared obstacles from the path along which her spirit beckons her. Her friendship with Mrs. Hale, who is unaware of her true status, puts her under the pressure of accepted social thought. Even that pressure is counteracted by "the constant drag to something better"—the magnetic pull of the flux of Nature. Hers was "a passive and receptive rather than an active and aggressive nature." She does not create opportunities for herself; she merely is drawn into them as they present themselves. She wearies of her status, not because she is inconstant, but only because apart from Nature she feels restive and unrequited.

For a time, the novelty of her life with Hurstwood enables Carrie to stay complacent. Then she appraises the style of Mrs. Vance and senses the superficiality of Hurstwood's manner: "Her situation was cleared up for her. She felt that life was becoming stale. . . . The old helpful, urging melancholy was restored. The desirous Carrie was whispered to concerning her possibilities. There were no immediate results to this awakening, for Carrie had little power of initiative; but, nevertheless, she seemed ever capable of getting herself into the tide of change where she would be easily borne along."

The tidal metaphor points to the flux of Nature, rather than calculated ambition, as the force which impels Carrie. The search for fulfillment through the American Dream was proving inadequate while it was still far from attainment. First she thought she would be happy if she had nice clothes. After meeting Mrs. Vance she supposed "attitudes and smartness" were the warranty of happiness. Hurstwood's diminished income compels her to review her prospects. She had responded to Drouet's overtures because her whole nature protested the grinding woes of poverty. She will not accept these woes now. As Hurstwood begins to fail he looks less and less handsome to her. Dreiser now causes Hurstwood to tell Carrie that their marriage is not valid. The disclosure serves a multifarious need. Coming from Hurstwood it exonerates Carrie—she herself has not devised a pretext with which to end their alliance. Her astonishment reaffirms her status as a creature of simple trust; more-

over, it provides grounds for her to leave Hurstwood without the
sense of shirking an obligation. Now suddenly she finds herself
lacking status of any kind. In life, as well as in the play in which
she has procured a part, she is "nothing." She must understand this
fact if she is to alter her condition. Timidly, in the make-believe
world of the stage, she acts out her dream of aspiration, a dream she
lacks inner authority to express in practical terms. Her soulful daring, the utterance of her dream life, attracts appreciative notice and
her career is launched. It is no small point of Dreiser's artistry that
Carrie's chance comes in the role of harem slave, a Scheherazade
wooing, in her anonymity, the notice of her caliph.

Hurstwood soon is out of Carrie's thoughts entirely. By a supreme irony, a stage role as a disapproving religionist, a scowling
Quakeress, secures for her her immediate goals. Implications extend
in every direction. Society exacts conformity from those on whom
it would bestow its largesse. The world spurns the genuine to reward
the counterfeit. Virtue is a matter of appearances. There is irony in
the frank overtures made to Carrie by men of means who presumably would gather an added fillip in breaking down her fictitious
virtue. And there is irony in the new sense of values her success in
this role awakens in her. Dreiser is too good an artist to make Carrie responsible to the characterization itself. The very role, indeed,
he is careful to make clear, came about by purest serendipity. It is
success itself, resting on this part, which jogs her perspective: "She
was sufficiently wise to distinguish between her old condition and
her new one. She had not had fame or money before. Now they had
come. Wherefore? She smiled to think that men should suddenly
find her so much more attractive. In the least way it incited her to
coolness and indifference."

The renewed patronage of Drouet, and even of Mrs. Vance, now
constitute no enticement. Dreiser confides: "It does not take money
long to make plain its impotence, providing the desires are in the
realm of affection." By eschewing the obvious comforts that prosperity and fame can provide, Carrie shows that her eventual indifference to Drouet and Hurstwood never was rooted in calculation
and greed. It was, in fact, a by-product of her aspiring spirit, reaching out toward a goal that she is able to define only as "the-thing-
not-possessed." Ironically, her "lonely, self-withdrawing temper,"
which emblemized her status as cosmic waif, intrigues her public,
augmenting a reputation which, whatever its dimensions, can never
give her the satiety she is seeking. Dreiser recapitulates with a lucidity that points unmistakably to the failure of the American

Dream to requite her needs: "Chicago dawning, she saw the city offering more of loveliness than she had ever known, and instinctively, by force of her moods alone, clung to it. In fine raiment and elegant surroundings, men seemed to be contented. Hence, she drew near these things. Chicago, New York; Drouet, Hurstwood; the world of fashion and the world of stage—these were but incidents. Not them, but that which they represented, she longed for. Time proved the representation false."

Carrie's actual goal had been unity with Nature and her nearest approach to it was made through her craving for beauty. That she has looked for it in materialism is the fault of the society in which she lives. She adopted its goals because appearances and social pressures led her to believe happiness lay in their attainment:

> Here was Carrie, in the beginning, poor, unsophisticated, emotional; responding with desire to everything most lovely in life, yet finding herself turned as by a wall. Laws to say: "Be allured, if you will, by everything lovely, but draw not nigh unless by righteousness." Convention to say: "You shall not better your situation save by honest labor." If honest labor be unremunerative and difficult to endure; it be the long, long road, which never reaches beauty, but wearies the feet and the heart; if the drag [that is, the magnetic pull of the flux of Nature] to follow beauty be such that one abandons the admired way, taking rather the despised path leading to her dreams quickly, who shall cast the first stone? Not evil, but longing for that which is better, more often directs the steps of the erring.

Carrie's own thinking takes her this far: she had gone with Drouet, then with Hurstwood, in the expectation of being "lifted into that which is best." She sees now the false promise of the world's allurements. Dreiser discloses: "In her walks on Broadway, she no longer thought of the elegance of the creatures who passed her. Had they more of that peace and beauty which glimmered afar off, then they were to be envied."

Dreiser sees Carrie as "an illustration of the devious ways by which one who feels, rather than reasons, may be led in the pursuit of beauty." The final thrust which turns her from materialistic beauty to a higher beauty is, of course, administered by Robert Ames. It is his function to vindicate for her her own disquietude, to turn her from the American Dream, to assure her that she has, as yet, reached no true peak of accomplishment. He alone touches upon a possible explanation for her inner discontent. But he cannot offer a blueprint for happiness, much less the bluebird itself, for he is, himself, a seeker. In the closing passage of the book, Dreiser suggests that Carrie may never know personally the happiness she dreams of. He does not insist that happiness is out of reach for all men. He says merely that, led by instinct alone, Carrie may never attain it.

The rocking-chair symbol is the dominant flux allusion among several flux allusions generating from Carrie. She is encountered first, setting forth on a train journey; she is seen last, journeying compulsively in her rocker. The tidal motif, complementing the rocker motif, is a frequent feature of Dreiser's imagery throughout the work. Window and rocker, taken in association, are a persistent coupling relating to Carrie, and signify the spirit momentarily baffled but eager to go out into life and to be caught in its flux. The first night at her sister's flat, Carrie "drew the one small rocking-chair up to the open window, and sat looking out upon the night and streets in silent wonder." Many passages in *Dawn* reveal the youthful Dreiser taking a soulful stance before a window. One such passage carries the sum of the import of this activity as met with in the novels:

> From one of the windows of the store I could see the immense crowds of the city, bobbing along, and so rhythmically, under umbrellas, so that at last I was more conscious of the material rhythm than I was of the crowds or the units that composed them. There was rhythm, rhythm, rhythm—and somehow men and crowds and wagons and every moving thing fell into it, although they were unconscious of it . . . all life seemed to flow so softly and smoothly. . . to their homes, the barns, or to the city's heart and back again—systole—diastole. . . .

The unity implicit in such flux is, of course, the antithesis of waifhood. Seeking work Carrie is confused by the tug and turmoil of a world going about its business: "Men and women hurried by in long, shifting lines. She felt the flow of the tide of effort and interest—felt her own helplessness without quite realizing the wisp on the tide that she was." The great tidal turbulence of flux intrigues her. Once she gets a job her rocking chair becomes a catapult from which, via imagination, she is hurled into a life of brilliant pleasures: "She sat in her rocking chair these several evenings before going to bed and looked out upon the pleasantly lighted street, this money cleared for its prospective possessor the way to every joy and every bauble which the heart of woman may desire. 'I will have a fine time,' she thought." When the next crisis looms—Drouet's offer of protection—the window image and images of motion again are present: "Carrie looked out through the window into the busy street. There it was, the admirable great city, so fine when you are not poor. An elegant coach, with a prancing pair of bays, passed by, carrying in the upholstered depths a young lady." The coach here appeals to Carrie as representative of the flux she longs to ally herself with, as the coach's passenger apparently has done. Drouet seems to her her chance to ally herself with that flux. Once her commitment to him is made, adjustments follow. Looking at dusk from the window of the apartment which she shares with him, "Somehow the swaying of some dead branches of trees across the way brought back the picture with which she was familiar when she looked from their front window in December days at home." In the same season, the same experience later will be re-enacted by Jennie Gerhardt, by Ruby Kenny in *The 'Genius'*, and by Roberta Alden in *An American Tragedy*. Each occasion indicates that the heroine, in pursuing the American Dream, has allowed herself to be cut off from the flux of Nature. A few moments after she had looked from the window, Carrie, in an effort to revive her spirits, went walking with Drouet. It was then she saw a shabby factory girl, lately her co-worker, and "felt as if some great tide had rolled between them." The tidal image reflects her disposition to be caught up in the flux of Nature which, mistakenly, she now thinks she has come into.

Life with Drouet did not furnish the full involvement with the flux that Carrie sought. Alone, looking out her window, she ascribes her melancholy to surfeit rather than lack, an irony Dreiser could not resist, for it rebukes her conditioning. The direction he intends her to move in is clear: "Carrie sat at her window . . . looking out across the park as wistful and depressed as the nature which craves variety and life can be under such circumstances." When Hurstwood first meets her the whole spirit of motion with life, so strong in her, announces itself to him: "He looked into her pretty face and felt the subtle waves of young life radiating therefrom." Cosmic waif that she is, she struggles to discover what haven it is she seeks —riches, or the simple life of old: "At her window, she thought it over, rocking to and fro, and gazing out across the lamp-lit park. . . . too pensive to do aught but rock and sing. . . . She longed and longed and longed. It was now for the old cottage room in Columbia City, now the mansion upon the Shore Drive. . . . She was sad beyond measure, and yet uncertain, wishing, fancying." Caught in this pseudo-flux the rocker affords, Carrie comes to near knowledge of the emptiness of the material state to which she aspires. Her nature impels her in another direction. Given the limitations of her mind, she is destined not to understand. The tidal image reappears, as Carrie's infatuation with Hurstwood grows: "The little shop-girl was getting into deep water. She was letting her few supports float away from her." When Drouet praises her dramatic ability, a way to identify more fully with the flux of life suggests itself to her: "She sat down in her rocking chair by the window to think . . . she rocked to and fro . . . every illusion which she had concerning the stage—now came back as a returning tide after the ebb." The tidal image implies her instincts again have alerted her to her need to ally herself with the flux of Nature yet, as is to be expected, she harkens to it in the guise of the American Dream.

Dreiser had modest ambitions for Drouet, but these were met fully. Drouet is not money-centered. Nor does he have intellectual depth. He is a "butterfly" glissading in the flux of Nature. On his first walk with Carrie, after she becomes his mistress, he elatedly points out to her the swaying, strutting women they meet. By disposition he has allied himself with the rhythm of existence. The rocker becomes his refuge only briefly. A housemaid hints to him that Carrie is unfaithful: "He sat down in a rocking chair to think the better, drawing up one leg on his knee and frowning mightily."

The tale-bearing maid, who begrudges Carrie her responsiveness to life, habitually moves Carrie's rocker into a corner when she cleans the apartment—"Carrie as regularly moved it out." The day Carrie breaks with Drouet, once more she finds the rocker in the corner. At first she ignores it, while she deliberates, but by the time Drouet arrives home she is "sitting by the window . . . rocking and looking out." She has made her decision to indulge her questing spirit, even though uncertain of the direction in which it impels her. Drouet expresses concern for her future. She rocks complacently. Finally he departs.

Carrie's association with Drouet began aboard a train. Hurstwood courted her by taking her out for carriage rides. Her decision to cast her lot with him is made only after they have boarded a train and are being swept through the countryside. As soon as the fugitive couple arrive in Montreal, however, Carrie senses Hurstwood is not the answer to her longing to be caught up in the flux of existence. In her hotel room, "Carrie went over and looked out the window." A moment later, "She sat down in one of the rocking chairs. . . ." Yet the tidal image returns. Caught up "in the flood of his strong feeling" she lets herself be overwhelmed, accepting Hurstwood's pledge of protection. In New York, Dreiser introduces an unusual static-chair symbol to indicate that Carrie's instincts for alignment with Nature have yielded for the time being to a material goal. Attending a play in which the rich languish in luxury, she thinks: "Who would not grieve upon a gilded chair?" She is disturbed to realize "she had never achieved what she had expected." The evening with Ames brings matters to a crisis. Returning home "she sat in her chair and rocked . . . Through a fog of longing and conflicting desires she was beginning to see . . . She was rocking and beginning to see." This passage is a key one. Henceforth, Carrie acts on life instead of waiting for it to act upon her. The rocking-chair motif is abandoned to Hurstwood. Not until Carrie has reached her immediate goals of prosperity and renown will she pause to consider further what she needs to be happy.

When Carrie attains stardom she acquires a hotel suite. Its furnishings include "several huge easy rockers," an intimation that her quest for happiness is beginning anew. Presently, in consonance with a rocking-chair reference, the tidal image reappears. Ames tells her to aim higher: "The effect of this was like roiling helpless waters. Carrie troubled over it in her rocking chair for days." Her eagerness for flux reappears. Looking from her window she sees Hurstwood fall in the snow. She does not recognize him but concludes from the incident that when she goes out she must travel by coach. The world envies her, yet "In her rocking chair she sat, when not otherwise engaged—singing and dreaming." She is caught, perhaps forever, "in the ebb and flow of the ideal." *Sister Carrie* closes with this reflection: "Know, then, that for you is neither surfeit nor content. In your rocking chair, by your window dreaming shall you long, alone. In your rocking chair, by your window shall you dream such happiness as you may never feel." Motion as quest has not yet brought Carrie the answers she seeks; the motion continues.

Dreiser does not lose interest in Carrie when she enters the paradise of the American Dream. Her story has been written basically as a complaint against the goals of American life and their deleterious influence on the character of men and women who mistake them for the flux of Nature. Carrie has failed to find happiness in the attainment of these goals not because she has forfeited her virtue to attain them, but because the goals themselves were unworthy; the fault, then, is not hers but society's. She understands this much at the novel's end. Dreiser has made his point. Her future life properly lies outside the scope of this account. It is natural, therefore, that as Carrie dies to her old life, she should fade also from the pages of the book. She is one of the few survivors of the ordeal

American society imposes on the aspiring poor. Hurstwood is one of its victims. His history is therefore more consonant with the main concern of the book, the ruinous power of the American Dream, and the focus of attention naturally shifts from Carrie. Hers, henceforth, is the anguish of the gilded chair. By gradually withdrawing her from view, as he does, Dreiser emphasizes the isolation man experiences, as "orphan in space," when materialism estranges him from Nature.

In contradistinction to the scant coverage which he gives Carrie's material triumph, Dreiser offers a careful account of Hurstwood's decline. As Carrie withdraws into one kind of isolation, Hurstwood withdraws into another. Implicitly, in the contrast, Dreiser sets up a powerful commentary on Carrie's struggle, a necessary account if it is not to seem that he infers success is the lot of the majority. It is in his anxiety to create such a contrast that Dreiser exaggerates the social and financial prospects of a saloon manager. A Hurstwood plummeting from the pinnacle of success is more pathetic than some minor functionary forfeiting modest prospects. The picture is supplemented further by a final tableau of Hurstwood's money-centered daughter, caught up in a soul-wearying worldliness scarcely more desirable than her father's plight. One may see, also, that Dreiser builds up to the final phase of the book by presenting, throughout the first half, a Carrie who faces situations promptly and resolves them without prolonged deliberation. Her realization that her job offers her no chance to fulfill her dreams, her decision to go with Drouet, her break with Drouet, her reconciliation to her abduction, all are achieved without suspense. Only as she attains her material goals, and realizes that she remains unrequited, does her sense of dispatch falter.

Sister Carrie is the story of a poor miller's beautiful daughter who comes to the big city to pursue the American Dream. Given the environment she places herself in and the intensity of her longing, the pattern of her quest is evident from the start. She must stray or stifle. Dreiser pities Carrie because no other way to her goals is open to her. He admires her not because she elects to stray but for the force in her that will not allow her to stifle. In the same city in which Cowperwood is a great power, Carrie is the merest speck— a Meeber by name, an amoeba by circumstance. If she wishes to prosper she must be ruthless as Cowperwood was ruthless, according to her capabilities. Yet Dreiser's characters are not transgressors by preference. They would rather have a world in which they could behave other than they do. It is true that Carrie gives her heart to no one but, then, no one ever really wanted it. To Drouet, she was a part of the wardrobe of conspicuous affluence, to Hurstwood, a surrogate to negate middle-age disillusionment. She proves her spiritual worth by not confusing gratitude with love. Dreiser's characters are as moral as they dare to be in the world they live in. They inflict pain, never willfully, but only to get at some desired goal. Carrie is more fortunate than others in her pursuit of material goals and in her eventual awareness that happiness is to be found elsewhere—in the pursuit of beauty. Yet, Carrie's commitment to the goals of society has cut her off from direct contact with the flux of Nature. When Ames reappears, with his "call to the ideal," he must make his appeal not to Carrie's intuitions but to her intellect. Her "pain-touched mouth," her pensive face representative of "the world's longing," suggest she is inwardly unrequited. She knows already that materialism is not enough. His role is to explain to her why she has feelings that disquiet her, not to engender such feelings. He praises her successful Quaker portrayal as "a thing the world likes to see, because it's a natural expression of its longing." To know that she shares her unrest with all humanity ought to console Carrie. Possibly it will awaken in her also, as Ames wishes, a renewal of the journey of the spirit which she has forsaken on the mistaken and uneasy assumption that she has attained her destiny. Yet the last passage of the book owns to the probability that Carrie, in her search for full realization, is doomed to disappointment, because she has a capacity only to feel, not to think. Even when they attain their immediate aims Dreiser's protagonists never find happiness. They find merely that their concept of what constitutes happiness has been inadequate. Ames's function is not to suggest that Dreiser can envisage a joyous end to the journey of the spirit but to acknowledge that the flux of Nature wills that man move onward.

As Dreiser first sought to characterize Hurstwood, he stated that Hurstwood observed discretion in his personal affairs because his employers would have frowned upon scandal. Additional pressure is placed upon him by his wife, also, to conform to social thought; she is socially ambitious for herself and their children. Hers is a perfect dedication to materialism and she holds to it tenaciously. The way of life that she embodies, set in rigid social pattern, is so restrictive it invites, perhaps even compels, Hurstwood's rebellion. In this context, Hurstwood's first park assignation with Carrie abounds in symbolic activity: "In the shade of a green pagoda a bebuttoned officer of the law was resting, his arms folded, his club at rest in his belt. An old gardener was upon the lawn, with a pair of pruning shears, looking after some bushes. High overhead was the clear blue sky of the new summer, and in the thickness of the shiny green leaves of the trees hopped and twittered the busy sparrows." Here Hurstwood elects for Nature over social fixity. Seemingly the activities of the gardener release Hurstwood to analogous activities in his own life. Suddenly, with the law looking on, he declares his love for Carrie. Turning pointedly from the world of rigid goals to which his position and his wife hitherto have committed him, he makes his declaration here for the flux of Nature, symbolized, as often it is in Dreiser's work, by hopping, active birds. In this scene, both his theft and flight clearly are presaged. Hurstwood, conditioned strongly by the society in which he lives, possesses an ethical sense that must be deadened before he can take the money. It would be unnatural for him to put aside this ethical sense without some qualms. The theft, when it does occur, is not deliberate. In the original manuscript, Hurstwood actually put the money in his satchel and replaced the empty drawer before the safe, of its own accord, clicked shut. Dreiser saw something amiss with this scene as it stood then. To show that Hurstwood is not a bona fide thief, he introduces into the final version a mysterious voice which directs Hurstwood to rifle the safe—one will remember the mysterious efrit which later cajoled Clyde Griffiths as he hovered on the verge of a crime far worse than Hurstwood's. But just as Clyde was powerless to act, Hurstwood's nerve fails too. The farthest advance his courage vouchsafed to each was to allow to happen the thing which fear kept him from doing with full resolve.

Dreiser has no wish to diminish Hurstwood in the eyes of his readers, as he would be diminished if he was a genuine thief. This fact alone would give Dreiser enough reason to make Hurstwood's theft involuntary. But when it is remembered that Hurstwood gave back most of the money that he stole, a question arises as to what real purpose the theft served. Hurstwood tells himself that taking the money is a way to turn the tables on his wife, who is divorcing him. She is to have a $40,000 settlement; why should he not have $10,000? But this is mere sophistry. He steals the money for one reason —to establish an analogous mood that would fortify him to steal Carrie. The theft puts him in an untypical, lawless frame of mind, requisite here for a person who, after having been long conditioned to live within the confines of the social order, suddenly acts to defy it. It is a bridge-burning gesture. He has the name, now he will have the game. Taking Carrie cannot damage his reputation further.

The theft episode has further ramifications. It shows that Hurstwood lacks true Force. His rebellion, after all, is rooted not in his passions but in his dissatisfaction with his social goals. From this fact can be forecast his subsequent failure to push his fortunes. He is too shackled by the mores of the world he has tried to renounce to commit his crime with true impunity. Remorse should overtake a person with such a temperament, and it does. Even as the train carries him away from Chicago he is remorseful. And in Montreal, where he first breaks his journey, he is ashamed, on meeting a former associate, to realize that the theft has cut him off forever from social intercourse with friends and acquaintances. When, finally, he is impelled by a voice to destroy himself, the incident serves to recall that his decline began when he lost his social identity by perpetrating the mock theft which preludes the theft of Carrie. Had not Hurstwood stolen the money, pushed into the act finally by chance, he would not have had the courage to steal Carrie. Had he not stolen the money, therefore, he would not have perished in despair. When the voice comes again, urging him to self-destruction, he is only too ready to heed it, for it had begun his destruction from the time it was first heard, and summoned into existence the person he now is.

Well might Dreiser have hesitated over the theft scene. The theft is at the center of the novel. The events that follow the theft spring inevitably from it. The lack of deliberate planning that marks Hurstwood's abduction of Carrie illustrates the sudden dissolution of the old Hurstwood and points out unerringly the direction his future will take. Where hitherto order had governed his life, chaos now takes hold. By his violation of trust he has excluded himself from the world of conventional order to which he owed his sense of well-being. A man whose advances in life hitherto have been predicated on subservience to social thought, he is not equipped to live outside its context. His inability to move and function outside such a context is illustrated not only by his need to befuddle himself with drink before he can commit the theft and abduct Carrie; it is seen also in the ruse he uses to lure Carrie from Chicago. He addresses himself to her virtuous instincts, telling her that Drouet is hurt and needs her. Carrie herself, in her flight with Hurstwood, is somewhat extenuated because she has gone with him not as a mere wanton, but as an angel of mercy hurrying to solace the injured Drouet. But Hurstwood's lie achieves more than Carrie's extenuation, and it does more than safeguard Hurstwood against the possibility of a refusal from Carrie; it reflects his true state of mind.

Even as transgressor, his thoughts incline naturally to behavior patterns usual with the righteous; his moral nature is protesting and he tries to disguise his intentions not only from Carrie but from himself, to justify them. The usefulness of the fictions of justified theft and errand of mercy that have cloaked his deeds once being exhausted, Hurstwood becomes a remorseful moralist trapped in a dilemma regretted almost as soon as his train leaves the Michigan Central depot. His choice of a Baptist minister to perform the meaningless ceremony "marrying" him to Carrie is not the callous act it seems. More than seeking to offer reassurance through it to Carrie, he is trying to take up residence again within the enclave of respectability, both social and moral, lately renounced. And, of course, it rounds out the artificial interval of melodrama which Hurstwood has made the context of these events, appearing in his part like an actor interpreting a role for which he is without sympathy. Neither squeamishness nor prudence causes Dreiser to omit any mention of Hurstwood's pleasure in finally taking carnal possession of Carrie. Even as he procures her, his mind is so weighed with guilt he wonders if she has come to him at too high a price.

Hurstwood was not destroyed by a sense of inconsequence stirred by the impersonality of New York. He arrived there a man self-condemned; nothing in New York would have changed that. He had seen himself as a man of substance in Chicago and had liked the role. What he had not liked were the commitments to social thought and the money-centeredness of a family caught up in the pursuit of the American Dream. But his flight from discontentment found him unprepared to recognize the alternatives to the kind of life he knew. He arrived in New York shorn of the reputation and identity that went with his old life, yet unequipped to understand what the pattern of his new life should be. Everyone had to expect New York to tell him he was a nobody; everyone was free to prove New York wrong. But in his state of mind Hurstwood saw the sense of inconsequence with which the city envelops every man as affirmation of his personal unworthiness. And in his shame, in his almost insistent need for punishment, he is able only to bow his head and invite the blows of justice to rain upon him.

That remorse, rooted in a hankering for his old affluence, should be the wellspring of poisons that inveigh against Hurstwood's system, points clearly to his unreconstructed status as one committed to the recognized goals of American life. As one questing, without true awareness, the flux of Nature, he is miscast. His defiance had been only momentary and induced by mental stress brought on by the approaching breakup of his marriage. Yet, like Adam, his transgression has shut him out permanently from his former state. His sense of loss leaves him unable to face up to the exigencies of his new life. Nor can he look to Carrie for a clue as to what his new role should be. For she, too, seeks materiality and had found him attractive, not as a spurner of the American Dream, but as an embodiment of it and a means of access to it. As Hurstwood declines, waning enthusiasm and a yen for seclusion are accompanied by a growing conservatism about money, symptomatic of his shrinking sense of affluence and his shrinking expectations. And Carrie is disillusioned to realize that he can put on and off his manner of graciousness. Not only does his manner lapse, but his appearance. He neglects to shave or bathe, and strews his clothes about indifferently. The loss of sex urgency is reflected in his now listless eye. When Carrie denies him her bed he makes no complaint. His activities narrow to a desire to preserve himself, interspaced with incidents of fantasy. Newspapers become a window to the world from which he stands apart—reading about those caught up in life, and even in the American Dream, as he is not—he shares vicariously in their activities, so much to be preferred to his present lot. In a feeble attempt to reidentify with his past, as though the present has never been, he squanders thirty dollars—a traitor's price—on a day or two of self-indulgence. He falters in tact. He does not bother to go to the theater on opening night to see Carrie; her part is so small, it would be money wasted. How unlike his enthusiasm for Carrie's amateur theatricals in his days of prosperity! Even without money, Hurstwood might have kept Carrie had he kept his self-esteem. Devoid of it, the man who awed Carrie had ceased to exist. She tries to goad him into some response, but even insults stir no vestige of pride. He sinks to the role of menial, attending to domestic chores —cooking, shopping, bartering with clerks—while Carrie supports him. Now wholly pathetic, his condition is seen in its eventual impact on Carrie: "There was something sad in realizing that, after all, all that he wanted of her was something to eat."

The remainder of Hurstwood's story is one of fast unfolding immolation. He makes a final, desperate effort at rehabilitation offering himself as a strikebreaker in a streetcar strike, in an episode quite the finest in the book. Although Dreiser's sympathies must be with the strikers, he has the ingenuity to enlist our sympathies on Hurstwood's side. Hurstwood knows he is in the wrong so that, throughout the episode, his guilt feelings are being compounded. Although a lingering pride makes him reluctant even to ask for a

meal ticket when he first goes on the job, presently he is discovered
clutching about him the filthy blankets in the workers' bunkhouse
and washing at a horse trough.

Surely it is appropriate that Hurstwood, alias Wheeler, whose
downfall first took on visible form when a carriage ride he had taken
with Carrie had been reported to his wife, and had had finality conferred on it by his train flight with Carrie, should seek to begin his
rehabilitation, his realignment with life, as driver of a vehicle. In
Dreiser's scheme, Hurstwood, by taking to the rails, is trying to
join in the peristalsis of Nature. When he is driven from the train by
strikers, symbolically he loses more than a job, he loses a frantic
bid to get caught up in the flux of Nature. There is fierce irony intended also in the taunts hurled at the fleeing Hurstwood by the
strikers: "Steal a man's job, will you . . . you thief?" The mistake
he is trying to live down thus is brought searingly before his eyes.
The illusion of rehabilitation crumbles as he is reminded shame-
fully of who he is and what he has done. He runs from the streetcar,
he runs from life, and from his final attempt to surge in consonance
with its rhythms. Ironically, he had sought to regain his self-respect
doing that which had cost him his self-respect. The stones that rain
upon him, flung by angry strikers, seem a penance imposed for his
sins, a needful expiation. After the brief interlude of strikebreaking,
which had occurred in winter and marked the end of Hurstwood's
efforts to ally himself with the flux of Nature—just as earlier, in
springtime, his declaration of love to Carrie in the park had marked
its beginning—Hurstwood falls regularly into daydreams in which
he relives events out of his past. The world of the American Dream
again contains the whole of his aspirations. He talks to himself,
recapitulating past glories.

As Carrie begins her climb to success in the theater, transcending
her role as harem slave, Hurstwood approaches his final degradation
sinking to the slavelike role of being auctioned off on a street corner.
While passers-by pay, as for sport, the derelicts are gathered, the
fee for their night's lodging procured, and they are marched off to
their obscure haven. Hurstwood stands motionless on the street corner waiting to move only at the will of another—as completely removed from the flux of Nature as seems to be possible. Here is an
ironic coda to his material ambitions. This is the promised land he
has come into—a passer-by contributes and another vagrant goes
"to the blessed line of success." A final irony is reserved for a
view of Hurstwood falling in the snow outside Carrie's hotel, while
within, Carrie sighs comfortably over the fancied anguish of Balzac's

Goriot. This much-scoffed-at episode really is no violation of texture. Dreiser's chosen context is that of melodrama. Indeed, in these same final pages of *Sister Carrie* Dreiser rises to a triumph which ably proclaims his writing competence. The brilliant account of Hurstwood's suicide is quickly and sparingly told, yet a touch of melodrama persists. Carrie's appearance in *Under the Gaslight,* in Chicago, for the first time aroused in Hurstwood the determination to possess her. That first link in the chain now links to the last. In a squalid flophouse, Hurstwood snuffs out the gaslight and lies down to await the bliss of annihilation.

Hurstwood's story was meant to complement Carrie's story, to show how precarious is the ideal she pursues. Through Hurstwood, Dreiser strikes at those goals of American life which bade men live half-empty lives, or lured them to ruin. His emotional commitment to the American Dream made him unable to take up the harmony of Nature. When he fell it was from the pinnacle of the Dream. He was destroyed because he challenged the myth of the Dream without having the courage or understanding he needed to embrace Nature confidently. He died, not for love of Carrie, but for love of his old illusions.

In *Sister Carrie*, the rocking chair is both symbolic of the flux of Nature and a proxy for it. As has been seen, Dreiser makes the rocker serve as a clue to Carrie's degree of involvement in life. But during a significant interval extending over 150 pages midway through the book, the symbol transfers from Carrie to Hurstwood. For Hurstwood, the rocker is a flux situation in itself, a surrogate for both Nature and the American Dream, in neither of which he is able to participate. His loss of contact with a larger flux is first disclosed in one of the many marine images used throughout the book to give an additional symbolic dimension to Dreiser's theory of flux: "He was like a vessel, powerful and dangerous, but rolling and floundering without sail."

During her years with Hurstwood, until she acts to support herself, Carrie habitually sits in her rocker, deliberating, peering speculatively into the world that lies outside her windows. A prelude for her, it is an epilogue for Hurstwood. Weary of struggle, resentful of a world that has not used him well, the rocker becomes for him a womb surrogate. A new order rapidly takes hold. When Carrie tells him she is going to find work, Hurstwood, already deeply sunk into his uterine world, reacts with infantile passivity and gesture: "Hurstwood heard this, dead to the horror of it. He rocked a little to and fro, and chewed at his finger." Hurstwood's sole link with the world of flux now becomes his rocker. It is at this juncture that sexual congress with Carrie ends, a fact which serves to recall that the kinesthetic effect of rocking itself is sexual, and that Dreiser saw the sex act as symbolic of the flux of Nature and as a powerful manifestation of its degree of presence. When Hurstwood finds Carrie has left him permanently with the coming of spring, winter imagery hovers about him—"a sort of chill settling upon him. . . . Something colder and chillier confronted him." His severance from the flux of Nature now is complete: "He sat a long while without rocking, and added quite clearly, out loud: 'I tried, didn't I?' At midnight he was still rocking, staring at the floor." Hurstwood is not seen in the rocker again. It has done its job. He moves among men, thereafter, with automatic motions, in the breadline, in the march of many to the flophouse. His final involvement in flux is beyond his ken—the journey in "a slow black boat"—an ironic echo of the tidal motif—to the paupers' burial ground in New York harbor. In Dreiser's novels, the boat journey often is terminal: for Lester in *Jennie Gerhardt*, for Roberta in *An American Tragedy*, for Cowperwood in *The Stoic*, signifying that man, borne upon the endless flux of the earth's waters, does not, with death, cease his questing role in the universe.

Everyone agrees *Sister Carrie* is a landmark novel, but few can agree on why it is one. Some acclaim it as a book which, by daring to feature a heroine who gave up her virtue without shame or remorse, knocked down the barricades of censorship. Yet today Dreiser is cited, in some quarters, as a virtual guardian of morals. Others find its landmark value in its reflection of the human condition and in Dreiser's management of character. Yet criticism finds Dreiser, in his selection of detail, more nearly allied to Hardy than to Salinger and dismisses Carrie herself as cold and unappealing. The book is praised as a social document. Here, too, critics argue among themselves, wondering if, after all, in his attention to minute details reflecting time and place, Dreiser is less a prose artist than a journalist. In the last analysis, however, it must be seen that *Sister Carrie* is a landmark novel because in its compassionate avowal of the essential worth and dignity of the least of mortals, it disengages itself from the age that produced it to speak with undiminished relevancy to men of every era.

8

JENNIE GERHARDT

DREISER FIRST sketched out the plot of *Jennie Gerhardt* in 1901, under the title "The Transgressor." In 1908 he sent twenty completed chapters to Grant Richards. The book was finished in July 1910. In the first draft Lester marries Jennie. Since this denouement forfeited the poignancy the story seemed to require, Dreiser rewrote it, depriving Jennie not only of Lester but of her daughter Vesta, too. It was typical of Dreiser to be more severe with his characters in revision than in a first draft. By temperament he was disposed to want things to turn out well. From experience he knew life was not that obliging. In the spring of 1911, Harper's bought the book but cut its length from 723 pages to 425. It came out the following October. Favorable reviews convinced Dreiser that he had a mandate to continue. For the next several years at least, Jennie remained Dreiser's "pet heroine."

A fledgling reporter wrote *Sister Carrie*; *Jennie Gerhardt* was the work of a seasoned editor. The difference between the two books is the difference to be expected from two such varying backgrounds. As an editor, Dreiser knew the importance of coming to terms with accepted taste.

Those who protested Carrie's prosperity probably sympathized with Jennie for her misfortunes. Like Carrie Meeber, Jennie Gerhardt is a woman of feeling rather than of intellect. Yet where Carrie is self-seeking, Jennie is self-giving. Each has two lovers, yet acquires them under circumstances wholly unalike. Both Drouet and Hurstwood win Carrie with promises of a better life. Jennie gives herself to Senator Brander because he saved her brother from jail. She gives herself to Lester Kane to procure means to provide for her daughter and her parents. Both girls are victims of the society in which they live, but ambition betrays Carrie while Jennie is undone by her sense of duty. Thus while Carrie is a creature of the new age, Jennie (often depicted sighing to herself or "clenching her fingers in an agony of poetic feeling"), resembles the traditional heroines of romantic literature. At the time of her seduction, Jennie is seventeen, a mere bud of Nature, innocent, unawakened. Even when she gives birth to Vesta, she is still a creature of simple trust: "There was always that saving sense of eternal justice in life which would not permit her to be utterly crushed. To her way of thinking, people were not intentionally cruel. Vague thoughts of sympathy and divine goodness permeated her soul. Life at worst or best was beautiful—had always been so." Old Gerhardt's conventional understanding of right and wrong accounts for his severity toward Jennie. Yet his natural dispositions dispute his formal convictions. On his deathbed, he capitulates finally to Nature, just as later, Solon Barnes will. Then, echoing words that John Paul Dreiser once spoke to one of his own erring daughters, Gerhardt tells Jennie: "You've been good to me. You're a good woman."

Nowhere is Jennie's simple, nonevasive nature better revealed than in her confrontation with Lester concerning his inheritance. What it has taken a seasoned lawyer four pages to explain to her, she imparts to Lester in four sentences: "He said that if you married me you would only get ten thousand a year. That if you didn't and still lived with me you would get nothing at all. If you would leave me, or I would leave you, you would get all of a million and a half. Don't you think you had better leave me now?" The statement is not only a model of lucidity, it is a true image of the perfect innocency of Jennie's soul, contrasting sharply with the deviousness of the world with which she is in conflict. On several occasions a mystified Lester confesses he finds Jennie "beyond" him. And so she is— in a way he never suspects. Jennie has no American Dream goals. Her betrothal to Senator Brander brought her within a hair's breadth of the American Dream. That fact did not matter to her. Its loss mattered to her still less. She mourned not the prospect of material plenty snatched from her, but the man himself, father to her child. Cut off from society because she has borne a child out of wedlock, she is thrown back entirely upon Nature, and in hewing to Nature she sees things not visible to those beholden to convention. She lives by a code delivered by Nature. It lifts her above a world of convention that follows a dead letter and the goals of greed. For his part, Lester has defied society to live with Jennie, but his defiance never has been wholehearted. When he learns of Vesta, he at once suspects Jennie of double-dealing. She explains the deception and he finds her simple, reasonable account "beyond" him. He wonders how Vesta is to be explained to society and decides that she cannot be. He loves Jennie but does not understand her superiority to the world to which he is committed.

When Jennie made her first trial flight with Lester it was by train, to New York, recalling Carrie's flight with Hurstwood and, later, Etta Barnes's flight to Wisconsin. Although the train journey here indicates a disposition to flux, it is the flux of Lester's world, not of Jennie's world of Nature. Consider the scene that spreads itself before Jennie as the journey begins: "There were the forests, leafless and bare; the wide, brown fields, wet with the rains of winter. . . ." Such a scene is a fixed point in most Dreiser novels. Its significance is always the same. Here it tells us Jennie had left the sanctuary of Nature to try her fortunes in a world unfamiliar to her. Carrie and Roberta had done much the same. But, unlike them, Jennie has no expectation of being received into this new world on its terms; accordingly, she maintains her alliance with Nature. Later, after Lester has left her, she is found again, rusticated, living in a quiet country house. While others struggle in accordance with the formulas society has set down for attainment of happiness, Jennie possesses it all the while, through Nature. Not for her "the rush and hurry of a clamant world—a civilization, so-called—eager to possess itself of shows and chattels. . . ." Dreiser confides: "Only this daughter of the poor felt something—the beauty of the trees, the wonder of the rains, the color of existence . . . feeling their call of community in spirit, how could it be that she should hurry—that she should seek? Was it not all with her from the beginning?" None of Dreiser's characters is more perfectly attuned to the flux of Nature than is Jennie. Society does its worst against her but her integrity persists. To Lester, however, the world of Nature communicates nothing. When he decides, on the basis of his social needs, not to marry Jennie, and tells her so, he stands before a window: "There were some trees in the yard, where the darkness was settling." Nature is shutting itself away from him, yet he is unaware of it. It is a triumph for him, as well as for Jennie, therefore, when on his deathbed he acknowledges their spiritual marriage. His final efforts to prosper by the terms society sets down failed because his heart was not really with them. His contact with Jennie enables him, at last, to see their valuelessness. His final commitment is not to the pragmatic world of the American Dream which his brother Robert represents, but to Jennie's world—that of Nature. Yet, for a time, Jennie had thought Vesta the "prop" that "would sustain her in the face of a waning existence." In this hope for stability she departs, for once, from the rule of Nature, which is mobility, and is made to sacrifice Vesta. Then, in the classic gesture of the Dreiserian protagonist, she adopts two orphans. Had Jennie adopted one child, she might seem to have been reaching out to regain the stability Vesta had represented to her. Adopting two, she transcends her personal need to take up man's plight of uncertainty as he wanders the universe. Jennie is herself the most orphaned of creatures—an outcast, dispossessed of all those dear to her. Only the powerful rush of Nature in her sustains her; she reaches out to the orphans in affirmation of man's questing state in Nature. The orphan, to Dreiser, had a status uniquely acknowledging the plight of mankind. In professing orphanhood, one recognized a oneness with the human condition— with the universe. When Dreiser willed a portion of his own estate to support an orphanage, it was a hand extended to the going process of life. The passage with which *Jennie Gerhardt* ends underscores this belief in man's unfathomed condition: "Jennie loved, and loving, gave. Is there a superior wisdom? Are its signs and monuments in evidence? Of whom, then, have we life and all good things —and why?" Recognition of man's orphaned state was, for Dreiser, the first step toward an answer to this oldest of all questions.

Both *Sister Carrie* and *Jennie Gerhardt* attack the American Dream as a goal which diverts mobility, or flux, from its proper object, Nature. Carrie's contempt for the ethical content of the American Dream alienated Dreiser's readers. As one who craves material security, Carrie does not enlist our support for her behavior; our sympathy for her real longings accordingly is blunted. In creating Jennie, Dreiser does not repeat this mistake. She is victim beyond cavil. But outside the American Dream she finds the happiness Carrie vainly sought within it. Our hearts go out to her. If society had brought her plight to pass, then society must be wrong. But *Jennie Gerhardt* made its points without ruffling public complacency. *Sister Carrie* was an angry novel. It got its issues talked about as *Jennie Gerhardt* never could. Hence as a novel of protest it continues to be read while *Jennie Gerhardt* is little read and less discussed.

In her closeness to Nature, Jennie is superior to those who are guided by social thought. Yet their code excludes her. Ironically, the direction of her fortunes has been determined not by her kinship to Nature but by the society that condemns her. Her brother is arrested for stealing coal—needed to keep his family from freezing through the cold winter—and she goes to Brander. Her father is injured in an industrial accident and, without compensation, is thrown out of work—and, again in winter, Jennie goes to Lester. On each occasion she is a victim sacrificed to the injustice of the society she lives in. Her appeal, significantly, has been to men who see in

her a virtue superior to that of the world to which they are committed. Brander is a man reluctant to outrage his conscience further
—and his integrity costs him his senate seat. He has had enough of
the world's ways and in turning to Jennie symbolically he is turning
to Nature. At the hour of her seduction, she embodies "the perfec-
tion of Nature." In embracing her, Brander embraces all Nature.
Had he lived, Jennie would have been his wife. Lester is a man
committed by inheritance to the American Dream. He grasps only
dimly the alternative he finds in Jennie, so that when powerful pressures are brought to bear to make him break with Jennie, he yields
to them. But before he dies, Lester is vouchsafed the wisdom to understand the meaning of Jennie Gerhardt. Against her sweetness of
Nature he sees that the American Dream counts for little.

When Jennie traveled abroad with Lester, she acquired a perspective that released her from any sense of commitment to American social thought:

> Now from this point of view—of decayed Greece, of fallen Rome,
> of forgotten Egypt, she saw how pointless are our minor difficulties,
> our minor beliefs. . . . Her mother had worried so of what people—
> her neighbors—thought, but here were dead worlds of people, some
> bad, some good. . . . Admitting that she had been bad—locally it was
> important, perhaps, but in the sum of civilization . . . what did it
> all amount to? . . . Did anything matter except goodness—goodness
> of heart? What else was there that was real?

Although Jennie was "like the wood-dove . . . a voice of sweetness
in the summer time" (again, the inevitable bird image), society had
taught her to feel tainted. Foreign travels restore her self-assurance,
but Lester lacks her nearness to Nature and retains, in fact, commitments to the civilization which in theory he dismisses so easily.
Dreiser says: "We live in an age in which the impact of materialized forces is well-nigh irresistible; the spiritual nature is overwhelmed by the shock. . . . Lester Kane was the natural product
of a combination of elements—religious, commercial, social—modi-
fied by that pervading atmosphere of almost uncounted freedom of
thought and action." Lester, liberated, still is subject to the powerful drag of those elements that shaped him. The same man that
can pluck that "rare flower," Jennie Gerhardt, can judge her with
the austerity of a Puritan magistrate: "Jennie was before him as the
criminal at the bar. He, the righteous, the moral, the pure of heart,
was in the judgment seat. Now to sentence her—to make up his
mind what course of action he should pursue." When he decides he

cannot marry her, he concludes with aplomb: "It was a shame life could not be more decently organized." ("Life" is used here, as it is at the end of *The Bulwark*, as a synonym not for "Nature" but for society.) Thus Lester bows to the will of society. A marriage to Jennie would not be approved, therefore it cannot take place. Lester's father, a man of thoroughgoing orthodoxy catechizes Lester: "How do you suppose I can seriously contemplate entrusting any share of my fortune to a man who has so little regard for what the world considers right and proper?" Though Kane, senior, has prospered in business, the key to his success has been hard work and integrity. He stands dead center in the old righteous tradition which kept the American Dream as an ideal. But just as Lester, in his personal life, has veered away from his father's moral principles, his brother Robert has veered from his father's business ethics, to become money-centered. When Lester capitulates to family pressure and gives up Jennie to return to business, he seems to rationalize the move by determining to succeed by his father's standards rather than by his brother's.

Lester is assisted to his decision by Mrs. Letty Gerald. Mrs. Gerald is ingeniously contrived. She must be sufficiently beguiling to detach Lester from Jennie. Yet she must not be resourceful in the conniving sense so as to make it seem that Jennie has lost out to the wiles of a rival rather than to the American Dream. Moreover, her presence is needed to extenuate Lester. He cannot forsake Jennie merely to take possession of his fortune—even so sizable a fortune. He is not that undeserving of Jennie's love. But no great burden of blame must fall on Mrs. Gerald, otherwise the point Dreiser wishes to make about Lester's renunciation of Jennie will be lost. Perhaps this is why Dreiser at once links Mrs. Gerald to the flux of Nature, by causing her, in her first approach to Lester, to ask him to dance with her. The compulsion for material success really draws Lester from Jennie. Society compels men to look upon themselves as failures unless they prosper in business. Once Lester comes to see he has no destiny in business after all, however, Letty is without a function in his life. And she, worthy of the respect she awakens in the reader, has the good sense to realize it. In tribute to her basic worth, during Lester's final illness Dreiser does not cause her to hover in competition with Jennie at his bedside. She is absent on a cruise—itself, of course, a symbol of impending events.

The manner of Lester's life when he is first introduced, reveals him to be even then in a state of rebellion. He is "chemically drawn" to Jennie because he senses in her a capacity to requite needs which actually are spiritual before they are physical: "She was his natural affinity, though he did not know it—the one woman who answered somehow the biggest need in his nature." Lester is unable to appreciate the change Jennie has wrought in him, until too late. This tardiness is the fault of his conditioning. But the force of Nature is not dead in him. When he returns to business, Dreiser says of him: "He lacked the ruthless, narrow-minded insistence on his individual superiority which is a necessary element in almost every great business success." His association with Jennie has confirmed his original dissatisfaction with the American Dream. Yet nothing less than the confrontation of death itself opens his eyes to a realization of what his life ought to have been and what Jennie has been in it.

As a moral force acting on Jennie, old Gerhardt counterbalances the elder Kane as a force of social thought acting on Lester. Lester never succeeds in softening his father's attitude. Old Gerhardt, however, becomes reconciled to Jennie through her persisting kindness and his own love for her child. Of Vesta and old Gerhardt, Dreiser says: "By some strange leading of fate this stigma on his family's honor, this blotch on conventional morality, had twined its helpless baby fingers about the tendons of his heart." Having to choose between orthodoxy and life as it confronts him, Gerhardt sees that orthodoxy must bend. When, with his final breath, he acknowledges Jennie's goodness, his capitulation is complete. Jennie, in hewing to the course of Nature, has routed society, as it touches her, on two fronts. As moralist, her father comes to realize that Jennie's conduct transcends the strict code he has held to—as would-be materialist Lester has come to realize, through his association with Jennie, that she represents a superior force which puts to rout society's faith in material riches. Dreiser sees old Gerhardt as the victim of restrictive conditioning. Presumably if he had harkened to the harmonies of Nature rather than to arbitrary standards of a society geared to exploitation of the masses, his old age would not have seemed so ludicrous or his fortunes so cruelly twisted.

Death makes frequent appearances in *Jennie Gerhardt*. Brander, Mrs. Gerhardt, old Gerhardt, Vesta, Lester, one after another pass to the grave. Yet each death is dictated by the circumstances as they progress to the event. Throughout the book Dreiser increasingly isolates Jennie to focus attention on her representative waifhood. Moreover, by leaving her to survive while others perish, Dreiser stresses his belief that her acceptance of the flux of Nature, rather than of the fixed position society decrees, is the only role which allows for man's perpetuation. Civilizations and their values, ar-

bitrarily arrived at, come and go. Jennie's values will endure because
they are of the law that upholds life. One of Jennie's two orphans is
named Rose Perpetua. This "everlasting rose" is symbolic of Nature
—Dreiser's placing her under Jennie's care provides a symbol of
hope, a belief not only that Nature is undying but that the values
represented by Jennie can be communicated to others.

Several symbols found in *Sister Carrie* reappear in *Jennie Gerhardt*—the chair, window, tide, vehicle (carriage, train, and boat)
are the most striking. As the device which he makes amplest use of
in *Jennie Gerhardt*, the chair allusions merit first attention. Unlike
Carrie, Jennie does not sit and deliberate; she is caught up already
in the flux of Nature. Lester is a deliberator. It is related in a passage recalling Satan's temptation of Christ: "Lester sat down in an
easy chair by the window . . . and gazed ruminatively out over the
flourishing city. Yonder was spread out before him life with its con-
comitant phases of energy, hope, prosperity, and pleasure, and
here he was suddenly struck by a wind of misfortune and blown
aside for the time being—his prospects and purposes dissipated
. . . by this sudden tide of opposition." An alien flux, significantly
described here in a tidal image, opposes him.

Unlike Lester, Senator Brander plays a most elaborate game of
chairs. On their first visit to his room, Brander makes both Mrs.
Gerhardt and Jennie take chairs while he talks with them. When
Jennie comes again he makes her leave her laundry bundle in one
chair and seat herself in another. When she leaves he sits in his chair
and gives himself over to pleasant speculations about her. On a later
visit, reclining in his chair, he calls Jennie to his side and kisses her.
Next she is made to sit on the arm of his chair. In a subsequent scene
she stands by his chair stroking his hair. Next he broods in his easy
chair when Mrs. Gerhardt tells him of the gossip circulating about
himself and Jennie. When the chair is mentioned again, Brander
makes Jennie sit in it. Her seduction follows. So concludes Brander's armchair campaign.

Brander's easy chair had been for him haven as well as ambus-
cade. Brooding over the loss of his senate seat to political schemers
he grows increasingly disenchanted with American opportunism.
Jennie becomes to him a way to replenish himself in Nature. Her
oneness with Nature is emphasized when it is realized that she is a
Persephone whose mother, like Ceres, has placed her in the environment of her seduction, leaving her in an Enna where, gathering, she
herself is gathered.

As in *Sister Carrie*, in *Jennie Gerhardt* the carriage symbolizes flux. From the start Brander courts Jennie by taking her for drives on which, significantly, she touches his heart by addressing his notice to the beauties of Nature. From the start, Lester (whose family trade is carriage making), compels her to ride with him. When her mother is ill, Jennie (as Dreiser himself had done for Sarah in her last illness) takes her on daily drives, trying to set running strong again the ebbing flux of Nature. But the season is late autumn and the falling leaves give Mrs. Gerhardt a sense of fading with Nature. Later, when a newspaper publishes a romantic story concerning Lester and Jennie, the article is illustrated with a drawing showing Jennie out driving with Lester at her side. The carriage, even as the train, serves Dreiser as a would-be proxy for the flux of Nature. In it one is whirling with the motion of existence.

Allied to the vehicle, and linked also with the tidal and orphanhood images, is the premonitory dream Jennie has shortly before Lester's death:

> It had seemed to her that she was out on a dark, mystic body of water over which was hanging something like a fog . . . then out of the surrounding darkness a boat appeared . . . in it were her mother, and Vesta, and some one whom she could not make out . . . then suddenly Jennie realized that the third occupant of the boat was Lester. He looked at her gloomily—an expression she had never seen on his face before—and then her mother remarked, "Well, we must go now." The boat began to move, a great sense of loss came over her, and she cried. "Oh, don't leave me, mamma!" But her mother only looked at her out of deep, sad, still eyes, and the boat was gone.

Lester dies, indeed, soon after he returns home from a cruise.

Dreiser's boat and water symbolism instructs the reader that some mysterious destiny awaits man within the flux of Nature. Here also does the reader sense Jennie's "orphaned ache," which impels her, even in this dream which foretells Lester's death, to cry out not for Lester, but for her mother.

The last chapters of *The Financier, An American Tragedy,* and *The Bulwark* move to the prison cell. *Jennie Gerhardt,* alone among Dreiser's novels, both ends and begins with "prison" scenes. The arrest and confinement of her brother Bass sends Jennie to Brander's room and precipitates her own tragedy. At the end of the story, Jennie goes to the railroad station from whence Lester's body is to be shipped home. There, standing behind an "iron grating," which separates the passengers from the tracks, she furtively watches the coffin being placed on board the train. Jennie's prison here, though unofficial, is yet wholly a prison, and society has shut her in it quite as it has shut Bass, Cowperwood, Clyde, and Stewart in theirs. It is more evocative, in fact, for it separates Jennie not from ambition and pleasure, but from the manifestation of love. The iron grillwork interposed finally between Jennie and Lester merely gives visible form to a condition that has persisted throughout their relationship, with Jennie the victim of an uncompromising society.

Dreiser uses Vesta also to reproach society for its condemnation of Jennie. Through Vesta, old Gerhardt's reconciliation with Jennie is effected. And when she comes, scarcely wanted, into Lester's life, she fixes him with a frank eye (a curious counterthrust of the mesmerism he used to woo her mother) and melts away his opposition. The events which bring Lester to an awareness of Vesta's existence begin with his discovery of a toy lamb she had left in the apartment while playing there in his absence. This symbol both of innocence and sacrifice points to the role Dreiser has assigned this child. On the night Lester tells Jennie he will not marry her, because of Vesta, Jennie lights the candles on the dinner table before she begins to cook dinner. Criticism cites this incident as a Dreiserian faux pas. The action may be ritualistic, however, for the dish in preparation is a small roast lamb. Jennie, too, is a lamb—sacrificed to social thought. The crisis over Vesta which began with a lamb, ends now with one. Vesta, as the lamb of innocence, embodies Jennie's faith in the goodness of Nature—and Nature itself.

Old Gerhardt finds Vesta's dancing lessons "devil's fol-de-rol," but, in the usual scheme of motion activities in Dreiser's works, dancing signifies Vesta's affinity with the flux of Nature. Vesta, unlike Hester Prynne's natural daughter, is not solely a symbol of the disharmony sin brings into the world, she represents primarily tranquillity and order. Through her the narrow goals of the American Dream are not upheld but repudiated. In her, Jennie's faith in "eternal justice in life" finds confirming bond.

9

THE TRILOGY OF DESIRE

THE FINANCIER

DREISER ONCE PLANNED to call his entire trilogy *The Financier*, but later found separate titles for the second volume (*The Titan*) and the third (*The Stoic*). The trilogy was first projected in December 1911. Dreiser's first step toward writing the opening volume was to go to Philadelphia and pore over newspaper files on Charles Tyson Yerkes, prototype of his financier, Frank Algernon Cowperwood. Late in February 1912 Dreiser wrote Mencken that he had not yet "written a line" of the new book, but by mid-September Mencken had in his possession the completed manuscript. Financial need had made Dreiser press on with it, at a sacrifice of style and content. Fifteen years later, with the help of Louise Campbell, he brought out a second edition, extensively revised and improved. In revision, *The Financier* is surpassed only by *Sister Carrie* and *An American Tragedy* among Dreiser's novels.

Dreiser never meant to embody in Cowperwood his own ideal. True enough, both sought to approach through the feminine form some "imperishable bliss." But to suppose that Dreiser shared Cowperwood's materialistic aggressions shows understanding neither of Dreiser nor of his intentions as a writer. In *A Traveler at Forty*, Dreiser, without condoning the aims and methods of the Borgias, acknowledges their sense of purpose, their enthusiasm, and their decisiveness. These are the qualities Dreiser confers on Cowperwood and these are things he likes about him. From the moment when Cowperwood, as a boy, saw the outcome of a battle between a lobster and a squid in a display tank, he decided that man made his way in life by turning aside, through an unabashed use of Force, every obstacle that appeared in his path. Sentimentality and success, then, were incompatible. To Dreiser, the values stressed by organized religion and society were a form of sentimentality used by the self-seeking to exploit the masses. He did not respect the man who, beholden to moral or social commitments, was reluctant to realize himself. He cared still less for the man who hid behind moral views while he furtively betrayed them or would have betrayed them, if he dared. Once Cowperwood opts for the American Dream he rejects every religious principle that might impede his progress. Without approving Cowperwood's goals, Dreiser recognized him for a vital, consistent man who had thrown off all inhibitions to follow his ambitions boldly. Dreiser admits that Cowperwood lacks a first-rate speculative mind—but, even at that, finds him superior to narrow men of righteousness whose complacency leaves them unresponsive to every subtlety of existence. The moral mind, Dreiser reflected, saw everything as wrong or right, recognizing no middle ground. Throughout *The Financier* emphasis is laid on Cowperwood's subtlety. His superiority to conventional men is shown graphically at the time of his trial when the righteous, incapable of taking into account extenuating nuances, sit in judgment over him. The trial evokes less a sense of Cowperwood's wrongdoing than heightened awareness of the extent to which an inherited set of values, accepted without reasoned deliberation, can darken the intellect. The society that condemns Cowperwood, however much he may be deserving of punishment, forms its judgments capriciously and only rarely with real justice. The conniving that goes on to jail Cowperwood —not because of his misuse of public funds (the offense for which he is tried and condemned), but because of his seduction of Aileen Butler, daughter of a powerful political boss—illustrates the dissembling that so-called moral men can stoop to when their interests are menaced.

American literature, prior to Dreiser, had depicted justice as a simple matter of passing on human actions as right or wrong. By dwelling on the caprice that makes the jurymen believe one thing rather than another, Dreiser suggests that much more is involved. The florist on the jury is for Cowperwood—in a sentimental way; the architect thinks Cowperwood too talented to be sent to prison; the glue manufacturer thinks he is guilty of breaking the law but feels that, under the circumstances, he had acted prudently; the Irish contractor wants to see him punished as a transgressor of God's law; the Jewish clothier sees a certain inevitability in what has happened and thinks Cowperwood should be freed. The whole process seems slovenly, archaic, and rote. The judge who sits on the case is "absolutely unconscious of that subtle chemistry of things that transcends all written law and makes for the spirit and, beyond that, the inutility of all law, as all wise judges know." Dennis Shannon, the district attorney, is a man of force, subtle and resourceful.

He is not "opposed to Cowperwood's having made money as he did
. . . if he had been in Cowperwood's position he would have done
exactly the same thing." He differs from Cowperwood in just one
way. Cowperwood acted as he did in order to advance himself; he
never pretended otherwise. Shannon is the servant of the state.
While acting to advance himself he must seem to serve the interests
of others. The system that condemns Cowperwood, then, is itself
corrupt and, in a sense, far worse than Cowperwood, for it sins
against itself. The final irony comes when Cowperwood's appeal is
acted on by the State Supreme Court. Its justices allow political obligations to plot their course for them.

In *The Financier*, religion is spoken of as the haven of those deficient in Force. When Stener begs Mollenhauer to keep him out of
jail, Mollenhauer ruminates: "Stener was lacking in force and brains
—not morals. This lack was his principal crime. There were people
who believed in some esoteric standard of right—some ideal of conduct absolutely and very far removed from practical life; but he had
never seen them practice it save to their own financial (not moral—
he would not say that) destruction. They were never significant,
practical men who clung to these fatuous ideals. They were always
poor, nondescript, negligible dreamers." One by one, as fortune fails
them, those deficient in Force seek the "nebulous solace" of religion
—Cowperwood's first wife, Aileen's bereaved mother, and, finally,
Cowperwood's own father.

Dreiser uses the term "a definite force personality" to refer to
Aileen Butler. Cowperwood first is attracted by the sight of her as she
"bounded in from the street." She further excites him, dancing with
him. She first yields herself to him by the bank of a tumbling stream.
She is strongly allied to Nature. The scene in which Cowperwood
lets Aileen mother him serves both to emphasize his role as cosmic
waif, suffering the "orphaned ache" of havenless mankind, and to
point to his later relationship with Berenice when it will become
apparent that his material triumphs have left a part of his nature
unrequited:

> She could only put her arms around him and stroke his head, mur-
> muring: "My poor boy—my darling . . ." She held his head while
> Cowperwood . . . winced and trembled, too. Her love was so full—
> so genuine. It was so soothing at the same time that it was unmanning
> . . . making of him a child again. And for the first time in his life
> . . . he lost his self-control. The depth of Aileen's feelings, the coo-
> ing sound of her voice, the velvety tenderness of her hands, that
> beauty that had drawn him all the time . . . completely unmanned

him. . . . He was crying, and he could not stop. . . . "Oh, my sweet,
my sweet, my darling boy! . . . Cry here on my shoulder, cry here
with me. My baby—my honey pet."

Dreiser drew with unusual care his account of Cowperwood's imprisonment. Allegorical allusions intervene to deepen the drama.
Like Christ, Cowperwood is condemned with two thieves, is stripped
and blindfolded; his persecutors "cast lots" on his possessions.
Some of these acts are multifaceted. His reaction to the blindfold
is notably different, however: "This simple thing of a blue-and-white
striped bag over his head almost cost him his sense of self-posses-
sion." It intercepts his eye magnetism, the outward manifestation
of his Force. Psychology says it could produce also a sense of castration, implying a loss of the very source of Force.

Throughout *The Financier*, by apposite allusions to Nature,
Dreiser emphasizes that Cowperwood's proper kinship is with Nature, rather than society. The news of Cowperwood's nemesis, the
Chicago fire, comes "with that tinge of the dying year in the foli-
age. . . ." As his trial ends, night falls and artificial light suddenly
illumines the courtroom. Outside snow begins to fall. When he first
leaves home for jail, after his trial, it is said of his family: "Surely
a brilliant sun had set on their local scene. . . ." When he is sen-
tenced: "The day had now become cloudy, lowery, and it looked as
if there might be snow." When Cowperwood ends his marriage,
darkness descends over the prison, and there is a promise of rain before nightfall. These allusions anticipate a pattern of solar and
light symbolism that attaches to him through *The Titan* and *The
Stoic*.

The Financier also utilizes animal imagery, a commonplace of
naturalistic writing, handled here with Dreiser's usual individual-
ism. At the outset, Cowperwood identifies with the lobster as preda-
tor; at the end he is identified by Dreiser with the Black Grouper.
The whys of the lobster-squid relationship never disturb Cowperwood. He concludes it is better to eat than be eaten. The Black
Grouper analogy does advance the matter further, however. An
"overruling power" ordains this creature's duplicity, though society
can find no place for such duplicity in its scheme of rectitude. Therefore, society's confidence in the correctness of its standards is unwarranted. As Dreiser sees it, the Black Grouper is representative "of
the constructive genius of nature, which is not beatific." Once
again, then Cowperwood's disposition to follow Nature is vindicated.
Addressing the jury, Shannon describes Cowperwood as "a vicious,

greedy, unmerciful financial wolf," as a man "as shrewd as a fox," as one possessed of "wolfish nerve," as one "who came smiling and in sheep's clothing." If animal instincts, in truth, had not impelled Cowperwood before his condemnation, they do thereafter. Then: "Like a wolf prowling under glittering, bitter stars in the night, he was looking down into the humble folds of simple men and seeing what their ignorance and their unsophistication would cost them." He is, henceforth, an animal contending against animals. In prison, in what was obviously a surrogate activity, daily he baited traps for rats. The account of warden Desmas (namesake of the "good thief" crucified with Christ), like Cowperwood, a man of force, ascribes to him "savage-looking teeth, which showed the least bit in a slightly wolfish way when he smiled." Confronting Cowperwood, "He was like one tiger looking at another." He speaks and his "even teeth showed in a friendly, yet wolfish, way." Indications are that Desmas and Cowperwood are two of a kind.

Dreiser's alternating accounts of Cowperwood's love-making and money-making parallel Yerkes's personal history. This alternate-presentation method, sometimes cited as a structural blunder, is functional in that it reproduces a brisk businesslike pattern in Cowperwood's affairs that is in keeping with his image. The fashion in which Dreiser shunts business and women (Cowperwood's other business) on and off, reproduces the effect of the world coming and going from a mecca of business and, at the same time, creates around Cowperwood an aura of uncanny methodicalness. Dreiser takes care to insist that Cowperwood is a man of Force. Force enables him to carry off his business dealings with such verve. And since Force, as Dreiser understood it, is an outward manifestation of a vital sexual nature, it is requisite that a record of Cowperwood's sexual vitality be given. Moreover, its presence extenuates Cowperwood by showing that he pursues "spiritual" aims—through the goal of beauty—put before him by Nature.

But the way Cowperwood uses women to requite his need for beauty, qualifies his relationship with them. He acts to procure a mistress much as he would set about acquiring a traction company. He disapproves of emotional people and accordingly his own emotional life is managed professionally. As something which conveys to him assurance that his contact with the flux of Nature has not been broken by his material interests, the pursuit of beauty, whether as woman or art treasures, is for Cowperwood a calculated undertaking, tainted by business methods, which carry over into everything he does.

In prison, Cowperwood is given the chance to reflect on his material goals. He looked up at the stars and, as cosmic waif, "thought of the earth floating like a little ball in immeasurable reaches of ether." Here, for a rare moment, he saw his own life as trivial in comparison. But the mood is brief. Confidently, he turned back to thinking of himself as a man of destiny—yet not before he has shown a speculative side to his mind coextensive with his material concerns. When later, in *The Titan*, he makes a gift of a telescope to the University of Chicago (as did his prototype, Yerkes), he does so to mislead his foes about the state of his finances. Furthermore, at the time the gift is made, Mars dominates the skies, a reminder that Cowperwood himself is a god of battles. Yet his pragmatism is not entire. The gift appeals to him also as a chance to press man's inquiries into the mysteries of the universe and the riddle of man's origins.

As *The Financier* ends, Cowperwood recoups his fortunes and leaves Philadelphia to begin a new life in Chicago. An afterword offers a description of the Black Grouper, a subtle marine animal endowed with remarkable powers of deception. Since the "overruling power" that governs the universe decrees the existence of such a creature, Dreiser concludes that some men are meant to govern, others to serve. Yet it is said finally, in the spirit of the closing paragraphs of *Sister Carrie*, that in the attainment of his material goals Cowperwood will find happiness still eludes him. A lack persists. Dreiser, like a fairy godmother (or weird sister), appears, to predict a brilliant future for Cowperwood. Like Macbeth, however, he is to be "Master, and no master, prince of a world of dreams, whose reality was disillusion!" Nothing better disproves the assumption of later critics that the author of *The Stoic* was an old and frightened man who had lost the courage of earlier convictions. *The Stoic* points to a man working out his plan for the trilogy just as he had formulated it more than thirty years earlier.

THE TITAN

In December 1912, fortified with letters of introduction to people who had known Yerkes, Dreiser went to Chicago to research *The Titan*. The work went ahead relentlessly. By 1914, Harper's had the book in press and had begun to advertise it. Then, suddenly, publication was halted. The probability is that Emilie Griggsby, Berenice Fleming's prototype, had used her influence to keep the book from appearing. Dreiser himself finds Harper's reneging because "the realism is too hard and uncompromising and their policy cannot stand it." Within three weeks he had found another publisher for the book, the John Lane Company, which brought it out later that same year.

Despite his ruthlessness, the protagonist of *The Financier*, as a victim of the American Dream, is a worthy object of compassion. He has married to advance himself, he has speculated to advance himself; neither venture has prospered. Those who judge him betray their unfitness when they resort to duplicity and political pressure to win a conviction. In *The Titan*, however, Cowperwood is ruthless, selfish, and invulnerable. Our inclinations no longer connive for his well-being. Even those repelled by the duplicity of righteous men who oppose Cowperwood find it hard now to prefer him in their stead. Actually, Dreiser does not expect readers of *The Titan* to like Cowperwood. Indeed, he wants to suggest that Cowperwood's imprisonment has destroyed whatever humanity he possessed earlier. The best he can do is to maintain a readiness to acknowledge the supremacy of Nature, by pursuing Beauty, always from the same distance, through successive romances. Thus is his gift of Force kept active. But the resultant impression is of cold self-sufficiency, of a man who neither wants nor deserves the sympathy of others. Without redeeming passages of reflection, or philosophical stock-taking, the book moves forward in brisk, episodic fashion, as Cowperwood whirls through a bewildering array of business ventures and amorous interludes.

It is in the nature of the subject matter that Cowperwood, in *The Titan*, should be shown moving juggernaut-fashion, through many affairs of business and romance. While he could not alter the pattern without falsifying his material, Dreiser was aware of the need to bring in an alternate emphasis built up along nonrepetitive lines. If everything should happen as his protagonist decrees, essential elements of tension would be lacking. Dreiser does not want his reader to forget, even in the midst of Cowperwood's business successes, that powerful forces militate against man's happiness. Consequently he develops the tragedy of Aileen which, in many ways, is counterpart to the decline of Hurstwood. At times Aileen's story surpasses that of Hurstwood in poignancy. She gave up more. She loved more. Her sex was the frailer. Her expectations had been greater. She falls from the pinnacle of youth, not from the treacherous crags of middle age. Even when she is unfaithful to him, Cowperwood realizes she is only trying to hurt his pride as he has hurt hers, and her gesture merely becomes a further humiliation for her. Assessing Aileen, Berenice concludes that she "had not kept pace with" Cowperwood. She "had not run swiftly before, like a winged victory." The irony of this appraisal is immediately evident. Cowperwood had based Aileen's original appeal for him on her likeness to a "fine, spirited animal," a veritable personification of the flux of Nature. Her savage attack on Rita Sohlberg shows the reader the extent to which Aileen's animal nature has altered. The noble animal has become a hellcat possessed now of "a courage and rage born of a purely animal despair." The Sohlberg incident shows Cowperwood the altered state of Aileen's temperament and, with that, the major phase of her life abruptly ends. She is no longer necessary to Cowperwood since she no longer embodies Nature to him. As a businessman, Cowperwood's instinct is to cut his losses to a minimum by breaking clear of a faltering investment. He spares no place to sentiment. When finally Aileen breaks with him, Dreiser has done his work so well that our sympathies are as much with him as they were with Carrie when she left Hurstwood. It seems unreasonable to ask either Carrie or Cowperwood to sever their affinities with Nature in order to persevere in relationships that can only drag them to ruin.

In *The Financier*, Dreiser uses weather references to parallel the fortunes of his hero. Radiant sunlight accompanies his prosperity; darkness and storms presage his misfortunes. In *The Titan* and again in *The Stoic*, Dreiser builds an imagery of light around Cowperwood—a man around whom other men orbit, "as planets around the sun." Cowperwood builds his great home in New York using a decor which favors "a morning-sun effect." One room is designated by him his "sunrise room." Immediately after its existence is disclosed, Berenice, who has radiant red-gold hair (even as Aileen has), appears, in two separate scenes, bathed in morning sunlight. In one she admits her desire to marry a man such as Cowperwood; in the other, she dismisses Cowperwood's principal rival. Presently when Cowperwood visits her, the landscape is bathed in "a crystalline light," and his car emits "a lacquered light." It stands outside her door, "radiant in the snow," an exalted flux symbol introduced at the high moment of his courtship. He was, it is stated, "impelled by some blazing internal force which harried him on and on." His status as sun-king soon receives further enhancement. He is credited with "a creative, constructive sense of beauty that, like sunlit spray, glowing with all the irradiative glories of the morning, danced and fled, spun driftwise over a heavy sea of circumstance." Mrs. Carter, Berenice's mother, acknowledges him "a Heaven-sent son of light." Then, in the scene which leads to Aileen's attempted suicide, he is "a rainbow dancing over an abyss." These images are hard to accept unless their metaphoric function is conceded. The events that follow help establish an awareness of that function. Aiming at the very heart of Cowperwood's being, Aileen shuts herself in his sunrise room and there tries to kill herself. Resolutely, Cowperwood breaks into the room to find her, "the sunrise glow over everything," bleeding from a self-inflicted wound. Undaunted, he takes charge. As the scene ends, there is a "light of control, even of victory, in his eyes."

The break with Aileen disturbs Cowperwood more than the knowledge that he has turned the whole social element in Chicago against him. What it stirs up, however, is not animosity but inner perplexity: "He harbored . . . a kind of sorrow over the inevitable consequences of his own ungovernable disposition, the will to freedom within himself. Change! Change! the inevitable passing of things!" The pull toward Nature is there, yet it is as though instinct, not reason, induced him to yield to or cooperate with it. He moves from woman to woman seeking some mysterious fulfillment. And paralleling his frequent changes of mistress are his changes of locale, houses, clothes, and artistic enthusiasms, all, in a way, a part of his quest for beauty. He moves in an ascending spiral, constantly reaching out into the beyond, striving to fill his lacks as they appear. Often his mistresses are young women, even the daughters of friends—Butler's daughter, Haguenin's daughter, Cochrane's daughter, Mrs. Carter's daughter—the child-wife of Hand, or his own "grand-niece." Youth represented for him a closeness to Nature, an instinct for life not yet contaminated by the rigid impositions of society or the wariness which disappointment fosters. In approaching it, he could partake of its freshness and renew his own spontaneity, find haven from the encroachments of age and the mystery of approaching dissolution. (Hence the "mothering affection" he awakens in Berenice—her recognition of his need, of his orphanhood before the mystery of existence.) If there is a certain sameness to Cowperwood's successive amours, Dreiser so ordained it. Cowperwood repeatedly tries to return to the starting point in his quest for the meaning of beauty. Berenice succeeds in holding him only because she draws him after her in her quest for beauty. Through her he surmises that there is a beauty in both women and art that is beyond physical beauty.

As the woman who would succeed with Cowperwood where others failed, Berenice had to be exceptional in every attribute. But Drei-

ser had to conjecture her merits because she had no real life counterpart. Before she appears, she is idealized beyond all range of realization. The reader is asked to believe she is a goddess. When she appears she is the living embodiment of "the Winged Victory." Images
of flux intermingle with those of Nature to suggest how thoroughly
she seeks union with Nature. Berenice's affinities are not with Carrie
Meeber but Jennie Gerhardt. Nature, not the world, entices her. Yet,
unlike Jennie, her pursuit of Nature is not instinctual but by design.
Dreiser suggests this in her first face-to-face encounter with Cowperwood: "Her arms were full of sweet-peas and roses which she
had ruthlessly gathered." At Pocono, "all eyes for any movement of
hers," Cowperwood is enthralled watching her pursue and capture a
sparrow. Then, at Southampton, she runs on the beach, pursuing
minnows, and her dancing, splendid motions betray Cowperwood into
an open expression of his admiration. Never had the flux of Nature
been so visibly before him. In depicting Berenice, Dreiser attempts
more than could be managed, but his theme demanded her presence.
It was not for lack of daring that he failed. She was a dream; as a
dream she eluded him.

While Cowperwood, through Berenice, pursues the ideal of Nature at one level, at another he must contend with clumsy paragons
of mediocrity. Typical is Chaffee Thayer Sluss, "a rag-bag, moral-
istic ass." A pagan at heart, he lacks Cowperwood's courage to follow his instincts: "On Sunday when he went to church with his wife,
he felt that religion was essential and purifying. In his own business he found himself frequently confronted by various little flaws
of logic relating to undue profits, misrepresentations and the like
. . . God was God, morality was superior, the church was important.
It was wrong to yield to one's impulses, as he found it so fascinating
to do. One should be better than his neighbor, or pretend to be."
Recognizing Sluss's vulnerability Cowperwood lures him into an
adulterous liaison, then threatens his exposure. Sluss is compelled to
come to terms. For Cowperwood there is poetic irony in carrying off
this maneuver. He routs the righteous by thrusting back in their
teeth their own moral hypocrisy.

Cowperwood is ruthless, but he never pretended not to be. His
adversaries posture as men of integrity, yet "are willing to sacrifice
every principle of justice and fair play to see him eliminated." There
seems but two kinds of men. Those who defy convention openly,
and those who defy it surreptitiously. Although Dreiser prefers the
amoralist to the moral weakling, his truest regard is for the man of
self-sacrificing integrity, the rarest type of all. When Governor

Swanson proves to be a man who cannot be bought, Cowperwood comes to his financial assistance, free of obligation. He respects him as a man who has rejected society's goals in order to pursue higher values.

Musing on why obstacles continually impede his progress, Cowperwood concludes: "The humdrum conventional world could not brook his daring, his insouciance, his constant desire to call a spade a spade. His genial sufficiency was a taunt and a mockery to many." Here at once is the secret of Cowperwood's superiority, the secret of his alienating some and drawing others. He is what he seems to be. Those cowered by convention resent his being as he his; those stifled by convention are grateful to him for the precedent he sets. Florence Cochrane exemplifies this last type: "In a tentative way she was in revolt against an apple-pie order of existence which was being forced upon her." Cowperwood did not seek social acceptance out of any mistaken notion of its worth. He sought it as another chance to dominate. His failure to get it spurred him on to greater partiality to the flux of Nature. As in adversity he puts on a jaunty presence, bespeaking an unimpaired inner Force, so too, he defies the censure of society by cultivating around himself an enviable opulence, and a communicable beauty. His first business house incorporates into its construction features of imperial Rome and of Venice in the resplendent days of the Doges. The growing interest he shows in gathering about him priceless objets d'art, is not only a reassurance that he is materially and aesthetically superior to the society that rejects him—it is a bond by which he lashes himself to Nature. At the close of *The Titan*, only in his passion for beauty does hope exist that Cowperwood will some day let go his hold on materiality, seeking, if not knowledge, then a kind of comfort found neither in wealth, nor fame, nor power, but in the mothering embrace of beauty.

THE STOIC

The third part of the trilogy of desire appeared posthumously in 1947. Dreiser had begun work on it in the early 1920s, but set it aside to write *An American Tragedy*. In 1926 his thoughts returned to it and he went to England to gather more material about Yerkes. The actual writing of the book, which he had now entitled *The Stoic,* began in October 1928. Louise Campbell received fifteen chapters to edit in April 1932. By the end of July, Dreiser had com-

pleted chapter fifty-four, but a month later he abandoned the manuscript once again. Thirteen years passed before he went back to it.
On May 26, 1945, he wrote James T. Farrell to say that *The Stoic*
was three quarters done and that he was now resolved to finish it.
His efforts prospered so well that he was able, on December 3, to
send the manuscript on to Farrell for his opinion. A week before
his death, however, Dreiser wrote his publisher, Donald P. Elder:
"I do not consider the manuscript finished. I intended to write
another chapter and a half about Berenice—a psychological study
of her at the end of the book." Pleading exhaustion, he went on to
say that this had to wait, at least for "a short period." He had, however, completed an epilogue which, in fact, amounted to a dis-
tillation of his personal philosophy in its culminating phase. All
the metaphysical problems that had troubled him throughout his
lifetime are seen here in resolution. A four-page summary of the
material that was to have gone into the final chapter on Berenice
Fleming was prepared by Helen Dreiser and appended to the book.
It is based on the notes and remarks Dreiser had made indicating
how he meant to develop it.

The Stoic is the story of Cowperwood's gradual extrication from
the morass of the American Dream. Dreiser thus makes expert use
of Yerkes's physical absence from America during much of the closing phase of his career. For Cowperwood, the absence fosters detachment; and it impels him more rapidly in the direction in which
Berenice beckons him. Through the questing, metaphysical spirit
of Berenice, he is drawn steadily into deeper involvement with the
aesthetic and the spiritual. As a man of Force, Cowperwood had
made the goals of American life his own in an effort to fulfill the
needs of his spirit. So long as obstacles stood between him and attainment of these goals he could feel unfulfilled and challenged. In
the attainment of many successes, however, and in the experience
of certain failures, he came to see that fulfillment did not lie in material things. This realization impelled him at last to seek self-realization in that part of his nature which responded to beauty. On
his final journey homeward from London to New York, on board
ship—and again this symbol of flux is allied to death—Cowperwood, as cosmic waif, at last confronts the change which supersedes
all other changes: "Once on the boat, Cowperwood felt alone, spiritually alone, at last admitting that neither he nor any man knew anything about life or its Creator. He now felt that for some reason he
was facing a change which involved all this great and beautiful
mystery as it related itself to him." Such thoughts would have ill

become the Cowperwood who dazzled Chicago and New York. But *The Stoic* was to be Dreiser's most meaningful commentary on the failure of the American Dream to satisfy the needs of the human spirit. When Carrie Meeber scaled the heights of her modest ambitions, Dreiser was there to insist that success had not brought her happiness. When Clyde Griffiths let his dreams entangle him in mortal complications, Dreiser was there to state that his goals, from the start, had been illusory. And Dreiser assures us that Lester Kane, Eugene Witla, and Solon Barnes all turn at last from the American Dream with none of their expectations realized. Cowperwood differs from Dreiser's other protagonists only in that he pursued, on a vaster scale, the same goals they pursued and had the drive and acumen to push them nearly to their logical conclusions.

As a concession to Cowperwood's determined quest for beauty, however, Dreiser does let him draw closer to a vision of the Grail he seeks than any of his protagonists with the exception of Solon Barnes. Toward the end of *The Titan,* Dreiser says specifically: "At last he saw clearly, as within a chalice-like nimbus, that the ultimate end of fame, power, vigor was beauty, and that beauty was a compound of the taste, the emotion, the innate culture, passion, and dreams of a woman like Berenice Fleming. That was it: that *was* IT. And beyond was nothing save crumbling age, darkness, silence."

Although the profaneness of Cowperwood's materiality bars him from the true Grail vision, in his appreciation of Berenice, in conferring upon her the status of quasi-mother, he shows his disposition to follow where she leads. Although once Berenice had thought of giving herself to Cowperwood in order to escape the burdens of poverty, when she did give herself to him, it was unselfishly—an act of compassion. Thus—Berenice, as surrogate, not like Carrie Meeber but like Jennie Gerhardt—truly untainted by materialism, her spiritual nature intact, can extend Cowperwood's quest for him after his death, to the spiritual realizations he himself craved but was personally unworthy to approach. In a most direct sense, therefore, the adventures of Berenice, after Cowperwood's death, form an integral part of *The Stoic.*

The light imagery attaching to Cowperwood in *The Titan* persists in *The Stoic.* As Cowperwood arrives in England he is greeted by "the sun dimly piercing an English fog." Before he disembarks a telegram comes from Berenice: "The sun shines on the England you step upon. The sea has been grey without you. *Oro del oro.*" For a time it seems that Cowperwood must share his sun-kingship with

Lord Stane. Dreiser explains: "Stane being proportionately excluded from the practical realm in which Cowperwood shone, was more effectively radiant in that atmosphere which Berenice most enjoyed, that of an aesthetically controlled luxury." The interposition of Stane (whose name means "rock") is only temporary: "He lacked the blazing force of Cowperwood. There was not about him that nimbus of great affairs and powers." Although the device of linking leadership with the solar eminence finds ample precedence in both history and literature, Dreiser possibly held a view of it that was unique. He believed that the seat of sexual power and of Force was located in the solar plexus—the place, therefore, whence originated man's impulse to ally himself with the flux of Nature. As early as *The 'Genius'*, he had attributed to Eugene Witla a belief in mysterious powers emanating from the solar plexus. In *The Stoic*, when Berenice places herself under yoga discipline, the plexuses are emphasized as the pathway to "superconsciousness." Cowperwood, even without the advantage of a guru's instruction, derives power from this source: "He was one who could not only sense danger but fairly register the vigorous thoughts of others in regard to himself. . . . Long before he reached England, he had been fully convinced that his affair with Lorna was known to Berenice. He could feel it in the region of his solar plexus." The light imagery around Cowperwood may be meant, then, to externalize that inner mastery of solar plexus from which strength of personality and Force in affairs generates. If Nature had in the impulses of the solar plexus an ally, then here would exist an explanation for the extraordinary way Cowperwood's sexual energy serves as a bond between himself and Nature, a bond stronger than the competing ties of materialism.

In "The Victor" (1927), published just before he began writing *The Stoic*, Dreiser sketches a businessman, J. H. Osterman, in many ways a work-up of Cowperwood in his final phase. By methods kindred to Cowperwood's, Osterman amasses a fortune of nearly forty million dollars. As death approaches, Osterman, like Cowperwood, surveys his achievements and ponders the vacuity of material success. For Osterman, as for Cowperwood, the building of houses or art galleries constituted a renewal of the search for happiness that eluded him in mere material accomplishments. His will stipulates that his fortune be used to establish a chain of orphan asylums across America. Before he can sign it, however, he is stricken fatally. On his sickbed the will is propped up before him—on a Ouija board—but he expires before he can put his name to it. The presence of the Ouija board implies that it is the will of destiny that Osterman should die unfulfilled. Possibly, at the time he began *The Stoic,* Dreiser envisaged a similar end for Cowperwood. Vestiges of just such a denouement survive in the final version of the book but, by the grace of Berenice, their negative emphasis is muted. Though estranged, as Osterman was, from his wife as the hour of death approaches, Cowperwood is compensated with the presence of Berenice—a bond with Nature unknown to Osterman. Yet the sorrowful incompleteness of Cowperwood's life cannot go unrecorded. His body must be smuggled into his own home at one o'clock in the morning, where it lies unattended, in stately isolation, strikingly signifying Cowperwood's orphanhood—until Aileen discovers it and is reconciled. After the death of her daughter, Vesta, Jennie Gerhardt had adopted two orphans; after the death of Angela, Eugene Wilta committed himself to the task of raising the infant whose birth had signaled Angela's death; after the death of Clyde Griffiths, his mother was consoled by the task of rearing her daughter's fatherless son; after Cowperwood's death, Berenice Fleming devotes herself to the care of "neglected waifs." It was not inappropriate, therefore, that Dreiser's own last testament makes provision for orphans. It comes as final affirmation of his concern for the welfare of the waifs of the world, among whom he never had ceased to number himself.

In his plans to benefit the world out of the fortune he has accumulated, Cowperwood is no more successful than Osterman had been. His estate is fallen upon by the greedy. His art collection is dispersed at auction. Judge Severing (a name evocative of the Eumenides) presides over the liquidation of his business holdings. Money designated for a charity hospital vanishes before the hospital can be built. Dreiser does not look to Aileen for a philosophical response to the loss of her husband and the sudden scattering of his vast holdings. Her death, a few years later, is that of a lonely, bewildered woman, one of Dreiser's most pitiable waifs. Something more can be expected from Berenice, however. Surely, Cowperwood's death must draw from her some exceptional response to justify his conviction that she held the key to questions which he himself was unable to answer. The trilogy has equally a dramatic and a philosophical need of Berenice. Her presence is needed to break the pattern set in the first volume and built up through much of the second. Speculatively she is the oracle through which Cowperwood's unarticulated desires will find utterance. To give these utterances a profundity commensurate with the expectations he raises, Dreiser could not make them less than his own final reflections on the philosophical mysteries which he had pondered throughout his life.

Briefly, in *The Titan,* Aileen shares Cowperwood's solar kingship when he opens his new home to Chicago society. On that occasion Aileen appears in a gown of "golden-yellow silk" complementing her glinting "reddish gold hair" that was set off by a diamond sunburst. But her social triumph is abortive and the solar effect is not repeated. Throughout this final volume of the trilogy, however, solar imagery gradually transfers from Cowperwood to Berenice, showing that it is through Berenice that Cowperwood's quest will be carried on. Cowperwood speaks first of her "sunburst of hair." Then, presently, Berenice surprises Cowperwood with his likeness sculptured in snow: "Suddenly confronted with this figure at dusk, a wintry wind whispering among the trees and the last rays of a blood-red sun spearing through, Cowperwood was startled." The stress on a dying sun, on a winter night, gathers further meaning when it is said of Berenice, "All of a sudden she dashed the figure apart with Cowperwood's cane. 'See, I made you, and now I'm unmaking you!'"

The night Cowperwood is stricken at Lord Stane's, Berenice enters on Cowperwood's arm, dominating the scene "in a trailing white gown of Greek design and simplicity, held at the waist with a golden cord, her red hair crowning this costume as might a wreath of gold." When Cowperwood is dying, Berenice enters his room clad as a nurse—in Cowperwood's words, " 'Immaculately white!' " He hails her: " 'A goddess. . . . The golden red of your hair!' " He continues: " 'That smile. . . . It is like sunshine.' " When Berenice, following Cowperwood's death, goes to India in quest of the guru who will lead her "into a realm of light or spiritual peace," she finds him in a black forest, where the trees grow so closely together they shut out the sun. Here she learns that the search for beauty in every form is "nothing more than a search for the Divine design behind all forms—the face of Brahman shining through." To this realization she voluntarily abdicates her own solar radiance.

As Berenice's temporary assumption of Cowperwood's solar rulership indicates, her own journey to spiritual understanding is not without troublesome incident. But the name of her English retreat, "Pryor's Cove," is promise of the direction she will take eventually. With Cowperwood dead, as cosmic waif she feels a need "to seek sanctuary somewhere." She desires to "equip herself with the mental and spiritual data that would brush completely out of her consideration the whole Western materialistic viewpoint which made money and luxury its only god." She recalls remarks made by Lord Severence [sic] (a name, like Judge Severing's, indicative of the need of radical pruning) concerning the Bhagavad-Gita and a remarkable guru, and she journeys to India. Even though Berenice's conversations with the guru do reduce the major problems of philosophy to a series of simple declarations, the questions asked are the same questions Dreiser had pondered for fifty years, and the answers are offered sincerely as the best he has been able to give. It may have been injudicious of him to present this matter in a form uncomfortably close to the catechisms of his parochial boyhood, but he probably adopted this technique for the same reason it was adopted by church schools, as a means of communicating succinctly and lucidly a sum of vital information constituting the essence of his belief. This philosophical coda, far from being an afterthought, must have been envisaged by Dreiser as an integral part of his trilogy from the time the plan for writing it first took shape in his mind. He would have found it impossible to end his most extended work with a mere shrug at the emptiness of Cowperwood's world. Every novel Dreiser wrote left his protagonist groping for something more at the end. Moreover, it is usual for Dreiser to apportion out the stages of quest to two characters in the same book—a Hurstwood and a Carrie, a Lester and a Jennie, an Angela and a Eugene, a Clyde and a McMillan, a Solon and an Etta—leaving one to pick up where the other left off. Berenice alters the whole pattern of her life to care for "neglected waifs." The only difference between her and Jennie Gerhardt is that what Jennie is moved to do intuitively, Berenice undertakes through reason.

Chapter seventy-eight of *The Stoic* is indispensable to an understanding of Dreiser. Here he gives, conscientiously, the answers, as he was able to formulate them, to the question which appears in everything he wrote: "What is life?" " 'Love God in All,' and you will escape the bondage of the senses," the guru tells Berenice. "Brahman is 'the supreme Reality.' Knowledge cannot go beyond that. 'This is the most sacred of all the truths I have taught you. He who has realized it becomes truly wise. The purpose of his life is fulfilled.' " It was left only for Berenice to apply what she had learned—for the cosmic waif to reach out to other orphans of the universe in order to share with them the haven that now enclosed her.

10

THE 'GENIUS'

I<small>N</small> 1903 Dreiser wrote thirty-two chapters of a book, obviously autobiographical, about a St. Louis newspaperman—but in 1907 he fed them to the fire. Dreiser recognized the fact that he was too close to his material to deal with it with proper detachment. He did not escape this pitfall even later. The second version of *The 'Genius'* was not begun until 1910. Its artist-protagonist, Eugene Witla, has touches that suggest Everett Shinn, one of the painters of the "Ash-Can" school, but chiefly resembles Dreiser himself. Dreiser had *The 'Genius'* "on ice, all nicely typewritten," by October 1911. But when he decided to go ahead with its publication in 1914 new copies had to be prepared because both original typed copies had been lost in separate misfortunes. The retyping brought at least one major change. In the 1910–1911 version, Eugene marries Suzanne Dale; in the 1914 version he does not. Further revised by Floyd Dell and Frederic Chapman, who cut 100,000 words, the book was published by the Lane Company in October 1915. The first year it sold fitfully. Then in July 1916 the Comstock Society struck, and *The 'Genius'* became a *cause célèbre*.

In fictional form, *The 'Genius'* recapitulates in detail Dreiser's years with Jug. He writes as a bruised mortal, seeking in disclosure a healing therapy. In *The 'Genius'*, Dreiser concentrated all his aspirations, disappointments, and self-doubts as a man, and all his schemes, conjectures, and contrivings as a writer. Their presence there, though often not well compensated for, is highly instructive to anyone interested in Dreiser's maturation as an artist.

Eugene Witla's marriage vows, and his affirmation of them, preface *The 'Genius'*. The tale that follows records the long list of his infidelities and culminates in the death of Angela, hastened by Eugene's mistreatment. But *The 'Genius'* is not a condemnation of Eugene's behavior; it is rather an attempt to explain its inevitability in a society designed to serve material ends. Years later, Dreiser would begin another novel with a statement of marriage vows. Whereas *The 'Genius'* suggests that the onslaught of materialism is irresistible, *The Bulwark* says an enlightened adherence to Nature can safeguard integrity. Thirty years had worked a profound change in Dreiser's thinking.

As a youth Eugene Witla "liked to lie in the hammock at home, spring, summer or fall, and look at the blue sky showing through the trees. A soaring buzzard poised in speculative flight held his attention fixedly. . . . The beauty of a bird in flight, a rose in bloom, a tree swaying in the wind—these held him." Here again is seen the young Dreiser, sharing in the rhythms of existence—hammock, bird, and tree—eager to be caught up in the flux of Nature. Yet Eugene is a creature of feeling rather than intellect, and the hurt he will have from life can be anticipated. His dilemma is presented in the contrast offered by his parents. His mother, a dreamer, gave him the middle name "Tennyson" because of her fondness for the *Idylls*. His father, a strong believer in initiative, is by conviction if not by opportunity, a go-getter. Dreiser's sympathies patently are with Eugene's mother. In the early scenes of the book, Eugene's eyes often are on the stars. His first girl friend, aptly enough, is named Stella, sustaining this emphasis. But while Eugene's earliest feeling has been "an intense sense of beauty," there coexists within him a desire for material well-being, a longing for fine clothes, vehicles, and attractive women—a duality America fosters. He goes to Chicago as much to make money as to become an artist. When he visits the Chicago business district a tidal image, representative of the flux, promptly appears: "The section was running with a tide of people which represented the youth, the illusions, the untrained aspirations, of millions of souls." There, his interest in fine clothes takes on a practicality which partially extenuates him: "social prestige went with them. . . . You could really starve if you didn't look sharp. . . ." Soon, to open the way to employment, he buys a suit. Dreiser is not extolling clothes as a status symbol; he is rebuking a society which judges success in terms of wearing apparel.

Even as Eugene's yen for material advancement awakens, vague stirrings toward beauty contend with it: "He loved women, the beauty of the curves of their bodies. He loved beauty of feature and after a while was to love beauty of mind . . . but his ideal was as yet not clear to him." The conflict between Nature and material aspirations was mounting. Despite his efforts to take on the appearances of the world in which he is competing, he continues to look more like an idealist than a man of affairs. Trying to satisfy the antithetical demands made on him by both Nature and society, he gives his heart to two girls—Ruby Kenny, a spontaneous, free creature, and Angela Blue, a conservative product of American social thought. Ruby poses for nude art studies at night school; Angela, a pillar of orthodoxy, dresses always in virginal white.

Fortune soon summons Eugene to New York; dutifully, before setting out, he binds himself to Angela with a promise of marriage. Ruby is left looking out on the dead world of Nature from behind a closed window.

A letter Dreiser received from Lois Zahn, when he left Chicago to work in St. Louis, describes just such a scene. It affected him deeply, and is commemorated in many of his novels. In New York, Eugene is "overawed by the material face of things," although he continues to pursue beauty—through his art and through an infatuation with Christina Channing. On a visit to the white and radiant Angela, in Blackwood, Wisconsin, he nearly seduces her, separating her from the world of convention, to make her part of his quest for beauty—drawing her into the flux of Nature. Although moved toward Nature, she clings desperately to her status. Eugene, as a result, finds himself unsure of what goal to pursue. A cosmic waif "He wandered about dazed, hurt, moody, like a lost child. . . . To think that beauty should blossom for a little while and disappear for ever seemed sad. . . . It hurt him to think of this, but it made him all the more eager to live, to be loved while he was here. If he could only have a lovely girl's arms to shut him in safely always!" He tries then, through marriage, to reconcile his dual goals. Angela is to be his passport to orthodoxy, his access to beauty— mother to the cosmic waif. After marriage, as a creature committed to social thought, Angela wants to attain the goals of American life and wants to pursue them in keeping with the Algerine formula. Eugene is surprised at the fixity of her code. The strain of conforming to her expectations soon begins to impair his powers as an artist. He tries to satisfy his yen for Nature in the pleasures of the marriage bed, only to find himself further weakened. Angela suggests he needs relaxation and rest. Vaguely he senses that what he really needs is peace of mind. But he does not know where to look for it.

Seeking health, Eugene returns to his parents' home in Alexandria. He contrasts his own state with that of his sister's husband, an active churchgoer and a shrewd businessman, dedicated to those things which "make a conventionally successful life."— the very embodiment of the small town American success ideal. Eugene tries to take up his old, easy abode in the hammock, symbolic of flux, but peace of mind eludes him. Dimly suspecting it is the conflict between Nature and materialism that has unsettled him, he becomes infatuated with the eighteen-year-old daughter of a neighbor. She could be his new link with Nature; even more, she represents for him "the holy grail of beauty." Angela is slow to suspect. When she does, they leave Alexandria for Blackwood. There, Eugene again is shown seated in hammock and swing. His spirits dip steadily lower. He has only to regard Angela's "four solid Western brothers-in-law. . . . banker, lawyer, grain merchant, and real estate dealer. . . ." Their tidy material achievements seem a further reproach to his own will-o'-the-wisp ambitions.

In an effort to rehabilitate himself, Eugene takes work as a day laborer for a Long Island railroad. He finds a quiet boardinghouse where, in the evening, he can sit "in one of the rocking chairs and look at the water." But soon he takes up again the pursuit of Nature as adumbrated in the beauty of his landlady's daughter, Carlotta Wilson. Significantly, this affair begins with Carlotta's invitation to Eugene to ride with her in her auto—his first ride in such a vehicle. The vehicle here again is a symbol of flux, but the flux symbols Eugene is now becoming identified with, train and automobile, anticipate the move he is soon to make, toward the world of materialism. For the moment, wholly absorbed in the pursuit of beauty, to the immediate exclusion of the American Dream, Eugene's sense of well-being returns. When he recovers his health, as a first step toward rebuilding his life, he inventories his outlook. Dreiser speaks now specifically, at last, of his "dual point of view." The natural object of the flux of Nature is personal fulfillment in Nature. For this, society has substituted material goals. Eugene craves personal fulfillment but is not sure whether it lies in Nature or in materialism. Like Cowperwood, he has reached for it through the beauty of women. But he knows society frowns on promiscuity and accordingly is remorseful: "This love of beauty which haunted him seemed much more important than anything else in the world, and his pursuit of that seemed to fly in the face of everything else which was established and important. But if society cannot approve his efforts to attain personal fulfillment through the beauty of women, he cannot approve the avarice which society sanctions in those who pursue material ends. Since the men who hold society's respect have such avarice, he upbraids himself for being unable to be like them: "Had he not better be seeking wealth, distinction. . . . Shame upon his weak-kneed disposition, not to be able to recover from this illusion of beauty." Carlotta pushes him further: "Only fools were held by religion. . . . The honest man might be very fine but he wasn't very successful." Striving to satisfy material longings even as he was striving to respond to Nature, Eugene had superimposed the pursuit of the American Dream upon his pursuit of personal fulfillment; this confusion of goals induced his breakdown. Carlotta, like himself, prefers personal fulfillment to material ends and in this harmonious relationship his health is restored. Unfortunately, Eugene understands neither what brought about his illness nor to what he owes his recovery.

While Eugene's affair with Carlotta shows him that the way of Nature is the proper direction to take, this affair ironically ends by turning him away from his career in art to one in commerce. Angela finds a note Carlotta has sent to Eugene. An emotional storm follows. Eugene is persuaded: "One had to be strong, eager, determined and abstemious if wealth was to come, and then it had to be held by the same qualities." He recalled the successful artists he knew: "They put the emphasis upon the hard facts of life and not upon the romance connected with their work." He goes to work for a masterful businessman, Daniel C. Summerfield. Summerfield has created in his firm, a goading, Darwinian atmosphere of ruthless struggle. Eugene adapts even his dress to his new station. He looks "more like a young merchant than an artist." Soon, moving on to a better position, he is "bold and determined-looking. . . He had learned to fight." Eugene's new venture in business is with Hiram Colfax, a man of merciless determination and utter practicality.

Although Eugene looks like a businessman and maintains a standard of living commensurate with his new affluence—his annual income soon tops $25,000—within himself he has not changed. In the midst of his prosperity, realizing "a long cherished dream" he makes a great crucifix the dominant motif of his sumptuous new apartment. Groping again toward personal fulfillment and beauty, at thirty-eight he falls in love with Suzanne Dale, a girl of eighteen. Typical Dreiserian flux images announce the affair. As he dances with Suzanne, he is overwhelmed by "the poetry of motion." In a scene in which first they sit together in rockers, then transfer to a double seated swing, Eugene finds the courage to declare his passion. They play tennis together and Eugene experiences "a strange vibration." Mention is made of "the weary longing that was in him for something new and delightful in the way of a sympathetic friendship with beauty." He has proven his ability to succeed in business, but has not found happiness in its attainment: "The lure of beauty had never for one moment during all these years of upward mounting effort been stilled." His restiveness does not escape Angela's vigilance; she allows herself to become pregnant, thinking that fatherhood might give him the stability he lacks. Joyfully, she reveals her condition to him. To Eugene, her disclosure seems a nightmare. His dilemma is the classic American tragedy. He cannot marry the girl of his dreams because his first love is pregnant. Eugene reacts just as Clyde Griffiths will. He wishes Angela dead.

One morning, following a spirited showdown with Angela, Eugene, seeking Nature, goes for a drive in the country with Suzanne. As they ride, they talk:

> Suzanne told Eugene of a book she had read in French, *The Blue Bird*. The allegory touched Eugene to the quick—its quest for happiness, and he named Suzanne then and there "The Blue Bird." She made him stop the car and go back to get her an exquisite lavender-hued blossom growing wild on a tall stalk which she saw in a field as they sped by. Eugene objected genially, because it was beyond a wire fence and set among thorns, but she said, "Yes, now, you must. You've been spoiled. You're a bad boy. . . . I am going to reform you."

In this passage Dreiser concentrates allegory. Maeterlinck's blue bird is Eugene's goal of personal fulfillment. He thinks he has found it in Suzanne. From the start of their relationship, Eugene has seen Suzanne as a "perfect flower." But she is a flower set among thorns. Although Suzanne senses the cosmic waif in Eugene and has her mothering instinct awakened by her "bad boy," neither as blue bird nor flower is Eugene destined to attain her.

At the connivance of her mother, Suzanne is abducted to Canada by train. Suzanne's train journey, unlike Carrie's, is not shared with the man who loves her. Their failure to share this flux experience seems to imply that their relationship has been breached—one recalls similar lonely train journeys made by Clyde and Roberta, by Solon and Etta, and by Cowperwood, which pointed to imminent estrangement. It is not the abduction, however, but Eugene's conflicting goals that finally betray him. Even as he reaches out for his ideal, he still thinks it possible to retain the practical advantages of material success. Now in a bargaining position, Mrs. Dale offers to arrange a brilliant marriage for Eugene and Suzanne if they will remain apart while Eugene divorces Angela. The realization that Eugene is willing to barter with her love for practical advantage, ends the romance for Suzanne. Although Eugene sees Mrs. Dale as architect of the breakup of his romance, in reality it has stood forfeit to his pursuit of materiality.

Eugene's romance gave his business rivals an advantage they exploited fully; he emerges from his ordeal deprived not only of

Suzanne but of his foothold in the world of materialism as well. His mind now gropes for a new point of view. He ruminates on omens rooted in superstitions, and on Christian Science. These specula- tions become a bridge by which he crosses from materialism back to his pursuit of beauty. In a scene which presages the disclosures of the guru to Berenice, in *The Stoic,* Eugene's eclectic readings and reflections point to the existence of a ruling power, immanent and "not malicious." By such deliberations Eugene is tempered at last for life and work. Reinforcing these spiritual inquiries is the example set him by Angela, whose life rapidly ebbs as the birth of her child nears. Eugene recognizes her now as "a representative of some great creative force which gave her power at once to suffer greatly and to endure greatly." Once again she is arrayed in white, although now it is the clinical white of hospital procedure. It is winter. While Angela undergoes a fatal Caesarean section, Eugene, from a window of the hospital, watches trains, automobiles, and people, moving through the snow. He seems cut off from the flux of life. With Angela's death comes catharsis. Eugene names the newborn child Angela, at- testing that he places no blame on her mother for his wretchedness. He turns again to his art and achieves the distinction that so long has eluded him. Everything that has happened communicates to him no clear understanding of life, but, under the stars once more, he makes a quiet affirmation of life as he finds it. At the last, his thoughts are broken in on by the sudden appearance of little Angela, clad in Harlequin costume, as spokesman for the human comedy— Dreiser, after all, was a disciple of Balzac. Dreiser's unasked ques- tion here, where the book ends, seems to be—Is man's clownish role in the universe to be taken seriously after all?

11

AN AMERICAN TRAGEDY

A BOUT 1894 Dreiser became interested in a type of crime which the American Dream seemed designed to generate. A young man, struggling to rise out of poverty, murders a working girl whose prior claim on him blocks his marriage to a rich girl. Over the years he explored the facts in fifteen typical cases, wrote six chapters on the Linnell-Richeson case (Massachusetts, 1911), then switched finally to the Chester Gillette-Grace Brown case (New York, 1906). Initially, Dreiser called this book "Mirage"; he was at work on it as early as December 1920. In the summer of 1922, he had twenty chapters written and had persuaded Liveright to accept it in lieu of *The Bulwark*. By May 1924, chapters for revision were flowing to Mrs. Campbell. Over the next months the manuscript was reduced to about 385,000 words, a third its original size. On November 25, 1925, after at least six revisions, the book was finished. It appeared for sale in mid-December in two volumes.

Grace Brown was murdered at Big Moose Lake, upper New York State, on July 11, 1906. Chester Gillette died in the electric chair on March 31, 1908, after making a full confession of the crime the day before. Some time after *An American Tragedy* was published, hostile critics charged that Dreiser had incorporated into his book many excerpts from the original trial transcript. The charge at most affects only a few pages in the concluding section of the book. *An American Tragedy* is pre-eminently a re-creation of American experience, into which Dreiser pours the anguish and frustrations of his own life. *An American Tragedy* is the definitive repudiation of the American Dream. It states that such tragedies not only can occur in the United States but, in such a social order, must occur regularly.

When Clyde dreams at last of being trapped by vipers and horned monsters in a narrow divide, Dreiser is offering, in a climactic statement, a conclusion inevitable from the onset—for Clyde, the American Dream has become the American nightmare. It is, of course, a further feature of Dreiserian irony that Dreiser has cast his attack on the American Dream in the Algerine format, suddenly abandoning it at the moment of expected triumph in order to dramatize with greater effectiveness the insubstantiality of the Dream, and its cruel deceptiveness. When the elder Griffiths offers to help Clyde because he is impressed by Clyde's clean-cut, purposeful demeanor, it seems a reassuring Algerine situation, where virtue has harvested its reward. Yet it is clear that both Samuel and his son, Gilbert, are veritable Dickensian creations. They saw it as essential to drill "lower individuals," in fundamentals, to hold them "to a clear realization of how difficult it was to come by money." They told themselves: "It informed and strengthened the minds and spirits of those who were destined to rise. And those who were not should be kept right where they were." This was fine old American doctrine. The Griffithses, indeed, had been natives of Bertwick, Vermont, and were, therefore, from New England, heartland of the Protestant ethic. The Yankee virtues of self-reliance, self-denial, hard work, and hard cash had become a nation's heritage. So far, so good. Clyde is being schooled in a revered tradition. Perhaps Clyde misunderstood when he thought that being rich "meant that you did what you pleased." Under the protection of the Griffithses of Lycurgus, he supposes he is soon to drive ahead and prosper. And then there is Roberta—leaving the farm to seek her fortune in the city. She is staying with people of good repute and is dutiful to her parents. Of course she will be accommodated by the Algerine formula, too. Dreiser creates a certain complacency, suddenly shattered as it is realized that the old merits, to be made to work, require a subtle ruthlessness. They elevate the few but grind the many to perdition.

If the orthodox thought *An American Tragedy* subversive, they were not mistaken. The book challenges the basis upon which their prosperity was reared; moreover, it insists that the attainment of the American Dream is possible for some only because it is impossible for many. When Clyde falls, he falls from the shining pinnacle of the American Dream, and in his fall he sunders the heart of the American moral tradition. Dreiser shows genius and daring in giving Clyde a virtuous early environment rather than a sordid one. He thus affirms that the custom-decreed American way of life is Clyde's undoing, not some bizarre exception to it. Hereby he underscores the failure of conventional American morality, as promulgated by church and state—the handmaiden of an impossible idealism.

The book opens in "the commercial heart of an American city. . . ." The personages first encountered, however, are not the

Original Drawing by Ruth Hudson

A MAN OF FORCE

barons of finance but a drab family of street preachers. The wife alone shows something of the hardihood that "makes for self-preservation, if not success in life." To passers-by, the group seems a pitiable example of the folly of rejecting the opportunities American life affords. But the street preachers are being judged not only by onlookers. Their own son, the youthful Clyde, is restive—he wants his parents to be like other people, and he wants to have his share of material comforts. Even though he thinks constantly about how he may better himself, Clyde has much of his father's impractical make-up. Clyde's dilemma is, for the moment, even more acutely felt by his older sister, Esta, who had given herself to a seducer who promised her clothes and the glamour of travel, and then abandoned her when she became pregnant.

Clyde's first step toward realizing his ambitions is to take a job in a drugstore patronized by actors and theatergoers. To him it seems, at first, "the true mirage of the lost and thirsting and seeking victim of the desert." But soon he realizes that he again wants more than he has. He takes a job as bellhop at the Green-Davidson, the principal hotel in Kansas City, and thinks—"What a realization of paradise!" With him the reader thrills to the splendor of his new situation. Soon, though, an earthy notion of paradise seizes him. It was "like looking through the gates of paradise" to catch sight of young couples rendezvousing at the hotel. His education is "advanced" further when he finds that people who have discarded the code which his parents uphold seem none the worse for it. This realization leads to some mild duplicity of his own. To spend money on clothes, he deceives his mother about his earnings. The deviousness he resorts to in order to carry off this deception sponsors in him a moral evasiveness which opens the way to the major involvements that later beset him. The sensuous side of his nature precipitates this rebellion, and soon involves him in the pursuit of Hortense Briggs, a creature of surpassing commonplaceness. Her fascination for Clyde rests in the promise of sexual adventure. Hortense's willingness to sell her favors in exchange for a fur jacket re-enforces his conviction in the power which clothes have to open the way to good fortune. The pursuit of Hortense involves him in an outrageous dilemma. His mother appeals to him for money to help his seduced sister. He rejects her plea because he is saving up his money to seduce Hortense. This episode foreshadows his failure, later, to stand by Roberta.

Part One of *An American Tragedy* ends with an auto trip into the country taken by Clyde and Hortense and several of their friends, in a "borrowed" vehicle. Here is a familiar situation in Dreiser's works—a vehicle ride taken by someone eager to be caught up in the flux of Nature. From the outset, Clyde's motor trip is marred by the fickleness of Hortense. At a roadhouse, enticed by "his rhythmic skill," she elects to dance with Sparser, the driver of the car, instead of with Clyde. While Hortense and the others are "dipping and lurching and spinning," Clyde must content himself doing an inadequate one-step with a pudgy, spiritless girl. Afterwards, at an impromptu ice-sliding party, on a neighboring river, Hortense again chooses Sparser as her partner. From all these flux activities she excludes Clyde. The extent to which he can be imposed upon, however, is seen in her successful last minute bid to reinstate herself in his affections. After all, her fur jacket is at stake! On the homeward trip he feels confident that Hortense will yield herself to him when he meets his pledge. But then an accident occurs; the car strikes and kills a young girl. The instinct Clyde shows now, to run away, prefigures his later choice, when his involvement with Roberta reaches a crisis, not to shoulder his responsibilities manfully. Dreiser suggests Clyde is responding at brute level. He makes his exit from the scene crawling through a field on all fours.

At the Union League Club in Chicago, where Clyde found work after fleeing Kansas City, he meets his uncle, Samuel Griffiths, a manufacturer from Lycurgus, New York. While working at the club, Clyde sought to emulate the manners of the people he met there. Now, although he is oriented toward the fruits of success rather than toward the process through which success is obtained, his uncle is impressed enough to offer him a job in his factory. The pattern of Clyde's expectations is set when, on his arrival in Lycurgus, he makes an on foot inspection of the upper-class residential area of the town, savoring its splendor and leaping ahead in his anticipations to the time when he will be part of such a world. What he does not know, however, is that his cousin Gilbert, Samuel's son, resents his presence in Lycurgus and fears his own social standing will be impaired if it becomes known that Clyde is an erstwhile bellhop. Gilbert is irritated still more to realize that Clyde and he are look-alikes, a detail which Dreiser puts to remarkable use. Throughout Part One of *An American Tragedy* Dreiser has given Clyde, torn between his moral upbringing and his material desires, a dual personality. Juxtaposed with Gilbert, a veritable Doppelgänger who possesses the very things he wants, Clyde finds the struggle that hitherto has taken place within himself now is externalized. Incidentally, in most versions of the myth, as Dreiser surely knew, meeting one's Doppelgänger presaged a reversal of fortunes.

As a poor relation, Clyde is separated promptly by Gilbert from the affluent life he expects to share in. Considering his expanding hopes, he is put to a task unmistakably symbolic—working in the shrinking room, the lowliest job in the Griffiths' factory. His is to be a machinelike existence seemingly without relief or hope. This situation will wear on him terribly once he realizes how far he stands from the fulfillment of his dreams. And the climate in which these realizations will come to him is quickly established. He is forced, by reason of his small salary, to seek cheap lodgings and to associate with people who possess none of the arts by which a man might advance himself. The ultraconservative moral climate of Lycurgus imposes another difficulty. Irrevocable social ostracism would be the swift and certain fate of anyone disputing Lycurgus's solid middle-class notions of what is "most essential to the order and well being of the world." After the Kansas City episode his conduct had been exemplary, yet—"It was such an Eveless paradise, that." Obviously Clyde is chafing under his self-imposed prohibitions. Coming to Lycurgus, he had dreamed of legitimate outlets for his passions. The call, instead, for still greater restraint is provocative. Despite his humble job and meager pay, others obviously are impressed that he is a Griffiths! Then an invitation to dine at the Griffiths' home brings a chance introduction to a local society belle, Sondra Finchley, and a decision on the part of Samuel Griffiths to advance Clyde. Clyde's expectations of social recognition leap forward again. But an envious Gilbert places him in a situation which makes his tragedy inevitable. He insists that the family socialize with Clyde no further. At the same time, he tells Clyde that the Griffiths name imposes upon him a responsibility to comport himself impeccably. His future, it appears, will depend upon his ability to stay aloof from the women whose work he will oversee. Clyde is to have no social contact with his betters, and none with his inferiors. Ingeniously, Dreiser superimposes upon the American Dream the condition of happiness theme, as ancient as Eden, and here curiously fitted to complement Clyde's vision of an earthly paradise; even as he comes in view of the paradise for which he yearns, the condition is laid down by which he will be induced to forfeit it. A youth of shrewder wit than Clyde may have been able to abide by such a mandate, in certain expectation that it could not remain in force forever, but Clyde began furtively to defy it as soon as he found himself in love with Roberta Alden, a Griffiths' employee under his supervision.

Like Clyde, Roberta has been stifled by her early environment and is resolved to move upward. What could be more natural than that Clyde and Roberta should think that they have found in each other the difference they have been craving? Although Roberta works in his department, Clyde at first resists the temptation to cultivate her. Virtuously, he takes up swimming and boating in order to be more accomplished should the Griffiths begin to include him in their set—ironically, these flux activities are the very skills he brings into play finally to rid himself of Roberta, to the permanent destruction of all his hopes. He goes now to Crum Lake, one of the less fashionable lakes, to practice his new skills. In his mind's eye, he sees himself "riding or playing tennis, or in the evening dancing or racing from place to place in some high-powered car, Sondra by his side." Soon he sees that his lonesome canoeing is only a surrogate for meaningful participation in the flux of existence. He decides Gilbert's mandate that he refrain from association with such a girl as Roberta is unjust. He would not marry such a girl but she would be a nice companion "to idle and dream with." Suddenly, as he is thus ruminating, in a canoe on Crum Lake, he is astonished to pick out the figure of Roberta herself standing on the lake shore. Coincidences of this kind are not unusual in Clyde's life. By coincidence he had seen his mother going to minister to his sister Esta in her trouble; by coincidence he had met his uncle in Chicago; by coincidence he will meet Sondra again. An element of foreshadowing colors most of these episodes. Esta's trouble and his mother's secretiveness, for example, anticipate Roberta's trouble and his own secretiveness. This first July encounter with Roberta—canoeing, hunting water lilies with her—anticipates their last boat trip together the following July, and the vision of Roberta's body entangled among water lilies.

Water, like vehicles, is for Dreiser representative of flux. Lake and boat here are a magnetic force of Nature drawing Clyde and Roberta toward one another. On this first outing, in symbolism luxuriantly sexual, Clyde flings lilies "with their long, wet stems at her feet as she lay reclining in the seat. . . ." Despite their material ambitions the romance begins under the auspices of Nature rather than the American Dream; it ends disastrously not because Nature fails them, but because they fail Nature.

The evening following the Crum Lake idyll Clyde is lonely. He wonders what Sondra is doing—"Where dancing? Where speeding?"

The flux of existence moves on but he is not participating in it. He ends inevitably, telling Roberta: "I'm not going to let any old rule come between me and you, if I can help it." Yet what Nature proposes, the American Dream opposes. Clyde has been "carried away by a bravado which was three-fourths her conception of him as a member of the Lycurgus upper crust and possessor of means and position. . . ." This notion gives him the illusion of having attained the status to which he has aspired. To Roberta, Clyde is the dazzling prospect of the American Dream coming within grasp. He had never supposed he would have to settle for so little; she never dared hope for so much. Yet their desperation impels them recklessly—he, to rashness of action; she, to rashness of expectation. Their first date is made possible when Roberta tells a falsehood to avoid going to a church service—a gesture that foreshadows her break with the accepted mores of her world. They next contrive a weekend away from Lycurgus—the train journey, so often found in Dreiser's works, is a prelude to seduction. Their stolen weekend is highlighted by dancing at Starlight Pleasure Park, Roberta's first experience of this exotic pastime: "They moved rhythmically and instinctively together. . . . the wondering rhythm of his body coinciding with hers." Both at last feel themselves caught up in the flux of Nature.

The dancing interlude leads fatefully to Roberta's alienation from the restrictive moral environment that has encompassed her since she came to Lycurgus. Guests at her boarding house have seen her dancing with Clyde. She rationalizes a need to move, subconsciously choosing a place where Clyde can visit her without exposure. If she is going to hold him, she tells herself, she must not seem narrow. She has no knowledge of Clyde's own struggle. If she denies herself to him, it will seem to him that his expectations of advancing up the ladder of success, via his new connections, are a pipe dream. Threatening to seek consolation elsewhere, he compels her to receive him in her room. Recognizing how great is the moral barrier that is now overcome, Dreiser shrewdly fixes the actual seduction in the moment of verbal consent rather than in the sex act itself. Her resistance crumbles; she agrees to receive him. A surging tidal image suggests full alliance at last with the flux of Nature.

Unbeknown to either of them, Clyde and Roberta have come as far along the path to the attainment of the American Dream as they ever will—"in the silence of the middle night, to slip into this unlighted room which was proving so much more of a Paradise than either might ever know again. . . . " Dreiser's theme is not fleshly delirium anymore than it is sin. Nature has brought Clyde and

Roberta together, but their relationship is overshadowed by the American Dream. She sees in him a way to the attainment of material and social distinction; she is his assurance that the pleasures of life are within his grasp.

Predictably, Clyde's fondness for Roberta dwindles once he has taken physical possession of her. He decides he is not truly allied to the flux of existence after all. He pictures "Gilbert Griffiths racing in his big car, Bella, Bertine and Sondra dancing, canoeing in the moonlight, playing tennis, riding at some of the smart resorts. . . ." As for Roberta: "Who was she? A factory girl! . . . Was this to be the end of all his dreams in connection with his perspective [*sic*] superior life here?" Coincidence intervenes again. Sondra, seated in an impressive limousine, mistakes him for Gilbert. Sondra has been "the one girl of this upper level who had most materialized and magnified for him the meaning of that upper level itself." Enthralled by this casual encounter Clyde cancels a date with Roberta, to leave himself free to dream undisturbed dreams about Sondra and upper-level life. Dreiser builds to his crisis. The duality of Clyde's nature is utilized here subtly when Sondra, on a whim, decides to make him a proxy for Gilbert, to get back at Gilbert. The unsuspecting Clyde receives an invitation from her to a dinner dance—a characteristically Dreiserian flux occasion.

At the dinner dance, one girl tells him bluntly: "People like money even more than they do looks." Artfully, Clyde hints that other prospects are open to him besides those his uncle can proffer. Sondra and her friends are reassured. Then she finds out Clyde shares her interest in sports. She invites him to ride with her and to play tennis. She talks of aquaplaning and of her swift motor boat. He envisages her in "riding or tennis or dancing or automobile costume." They dance together "dipping and swaying here and there—harmoniously abandoning themselves to the rhythm of the music—like two small chips being tossed about on a rough but friendly sea." At last Clyde is caught in a current that can sweep him onward to the attainment of the American Dream.

Sondra had told Clyde she liked him when he was not being sentimental. But sentimentality is his bane. Pitying Roberta, he keeps up a pretext of courtship although she has become little more than a physical outlet for the passion building up within him for the inviolable Sondra. Then, while visiting her parents at Christmas, Roberta chances on a newspaper item recounting Clyde's Christmas rambles with Lycurgus society. She senses danger: "She got up and walked to the window and looked out on that same orchard where as a girl so many times she had been thrilled by the beauty of life. The scene was miserably bleak and bare." Thus, deftly, in a scene which is a fixed point in many of his novels, Dreiser discloses her estrangement from the flux of Nature.

Meanwhile, Clyde's social success is forcing his uncle to re-evaluate their relationship. He invites Clyde to Christmas dinner, and Clyde, relishing his new status, fails to keep a date with Roberta. A late visit to her is fraught with recriminations. Roberta compares her humble lot to Sondra's affluence. Pitying her, Clyde enters into a reconciliation which leads inevitably to Roberta's pregnancy.

Even as Clyde's love for Roberta diminishes, his passion for Sondra mounts. At the same time, Sondra is being drawn to him because she senses in him an animal spontaneity unknown in her world. Thus, ironically, in loving him she draws away from the American Dream toward Nature, while he, loving her, draws away from Nature toward the American Dream. Clyde at length resolves to break with Roberta, cost what it may. But just at this juncture, she becomes aware of her pregnancy. Clyde searches for remedies to induce abortion, the crisis intensifying steadily as dread for the security of his social position grows. He sees himself so close to becoming a second Gilbert, that he feels a need even to keep out of sight when Roberta visits a doctor lest he be mistaken for Gilbert! Even as he schemes to arrange an abortion for the luckless Roberta, he focuses selfishly on "the glorious denouement that lay directly before him"—this obstacle alone intervening.

Roberta's visit to the country doctor is disquieting. He puts her off with "solemn moralizing." The import of the doctor's refusal to perform an abortion now is stated concisely: "Illegitimacy and disgrace for Roberta. Exposure and destruction for Clyde." An intimation that money could have procured the desired end with the doctor consulted emphasizes their plight is less one of the morally wayward than of those lacking money and station. Their entanglements are the inevitable consequence of questing the acknowledged goals of American life, yet they are to be destroyed for pursuing these goals in the one way inexperience advised. Their desperation now reduces them to instinctual struggle: she is "a cornered animal"; he is "a harried animal, deftly pursued by hunter and hound." Roberta's pregnancy urges her toward decisive action. Clyde's rapidly improving situation with Sondra urges him toward decisive action. Yet the decisions they are impelled toward negate one another. For Roberta to succeed, Clyde must fail; she must fail if he is to succeed.

For Clyde, the crisis soon intensifies. On a motor trip with Sondra and her friends he stops at a farmhouse to ask directions. It chances to be the Alden farm—in its dilapidation the embodiment of all that he is fleeing from. The specter of his own future confronts him. He runs back to the car and the safe refuge it offers. Sondra instinctively turns to mothering him, dropping into baby talk, the classic mothering scene enacted in each of Dreiser's novels. In her, this cosmic waif has found a haven from a world that both terrifies and dismays him. This retreat back into the safety of Sondra's world, fixes Clyde in his resolve to stand his ground and find a way out of his dilemma. Fittingly, he chooses this moment of crisis to look back on his violation of the condition of happiness Gilbert had imposed on him: "Oh, why couldn't he have waited and then this other world would have opened up to him just the same? If only he could have waited!"

Upon his return to Lycurgus, Clyde receives, in successive mails, two letters which blueprint his dilemma. Sondra, at Pine Point Landing, wants him to come up to "ride and drive and swim and dance," with her. Her letter is written in baby talk. The second letter is from Roberta, who has gone home to her family. She says her friends want her to dance, but she is not well enough. She presses Clyde to join her. A contrast obviously is intended between the participation in the flux of life which Sondra offers Clyde and the shunted curtailment which awaits him if he joins Roberta. Immediately thereafter, as the plan for killing Roberta insinuates itself into Clyde's mind, he finds himself intrigued with the realization that she cannot swim. Her inadequacy in the area of flux is to serve as instrument of her destruction.

Even as he deliberates his next move, Clyde joins Sondra for the weekend—"It was as though he were in Paradise." He has attained the promised land of the American Dream, yet is menaced with the threat of expulsion. And now his last desperate gambit—elopement with Sondra—fails. Sondra's hard core common sense routs romance. She will not risk estrangement from her parents. Desperation seizes Clyde. A motor trip with Sondra and her friends, to Big Bittern and neighboring lakes, introduces him to a locale where a drowning death might occur under isolated circumstances. He had read a newspaper account of an alleged double drowning in just such a locale. A Gothic aura hangs over the Big Bittern environment, a world, it seemed, out of harmony with Nature—"Decadent . . . weird . . . bogs and tarns," "funereal or viperous vines," "green slime," "rotting logs," snakes and "poisonous grasses," the weir-weir bird, uttering "it's ouphe and barghest cry, flying from

somewhere near into some darker recess within the woods." While
Dreiser often uses birds as symbols of the flux of Nature, this bird
is ill-omened; in flight it interposes itself between Clyde and Nature, shutting him out of a world he has turned away from to follow
the American Dream.

Returning to Lycurgus, separated now from both Roberta and
Sondra, Clyde's mind enters into a morality play dialogue with itself. His interlocutor, however, is a genie appropriate to his Arabian
Nights fantasies of fabulous fulfillment. Clyde's personality, ever
torn between his moral upbringing with its emphasis on privation,
and his worldly aspirations with their emphasis on material pleasure,
has at last split in schizoid disorder, with the rebellious voice of his
"dark personality" striving to put to rout the conservatism of his
light personality. This device separates with a bright line the alternatives Clyde must choose between. It also advances the story to
the point of crisis. In two phrases, everything is established. The
genie says: "Pah—how cowardly—how lacking in courage to win
the thing that above all things you desire—beauty—wealth—position—the solution of your every material and spiritual desire. And
with poverty, commonplace, hard and poor work as the alternative
to all this." The emphasis on "material and spiritual desire" shows
how the American Dream and Nature have lost separateness in
Clyde's mind. The voice of the genie is the utterance of Clyde's own
suppressed consciousness, stating with cold calculation what he has
never had courage to say before. Even now, a part of his mind with-
holds recognition. He allows his second personality to take command
—he is ready to do what he believes must be done, acting it out as
fantasy. In his expectations, Clyde long has occupied a land of
make-believe. Now, as that fantasy is menaced, he produces another
fantasy to protect it.

Clyde's July fourth weekend with Sondra is passed over without
comment in order to plunge the reader directly into the final scene
with Roberta. The train journey to Utica is flashed before us. Clyde's
thoughts, random, anxious, agitated, reflecting the indecision and
determination that coexist in his mind, here are interspaced with
parenthetical asides mostly drawn from his distracted observation
of the external world from the train window. He sees birds flying,
streams flowing, automobiles keeping pace with the train—all symbols of flux. But Clyde, because of the fixed commitment he now has
to the American Dream, stands apart from Nature. He is onlooker
only, as Roberta had become on her visit home at Christmas. The
completeness of his separation from Nature is marked further by

his separation from Roberta herself, who is aboard the same train but, to avoid detection, riding in another coach. A stop at Grass Lake follows—and a "pestilential search for water-lilies," signifying, in its mood, Clyde's estrangement from Nature. Finally the boat puts out on Big Bittern and, again, a search for water-lilies ensues. The boat enters a tree-fringed tarn, Moon Cove. The wandering orphan, buffeted by the world, suddenly finds miraculous peace. A strange comforter intervenes. Clyde now felt:

> . . . the grip of some seemingly strong, and yet friendly sympathetic, hands laid firmly on his shoulders. The comfort of them! The warmth! The strength! For now they seemed to have a steadying effect on him and he liked them—their reassurance—their support. If only they would not be removed. If only they would remain always—the hands of this friend! For where had he ever known this comforting and almost tender sensation before in all his life? Not anywhere—and somehow this calmed him and he seemed to slip away from the reality of all things.

Thus, briefly, the wandering, unrequited Clyde—whose very name is of a troubled river that struggles to the sea over inhospitable terrain—whose search is, after all, summed up in the one word "security," comes to this brief moment when he has a fantasy of peace possessed. Then the Jobian comforter vanishes. Clyde hears the enigmatic cry of the weir-weir bird, sees it soaring from one dead branch to another—announcing, if he but knew it, his permanent estrangement from the flux of Nature. The perverse drama unfolds. Clyde's courage fails him. His face contorts in anguish and frustration, and Roberta (anticipating West's Miss Lonelyhearts) stumbles toward him in an unbearable gesture of sympathy, stunned by his look of undecipherable distress. Her unwanted solace revulses Clyde; his hand thrusts out to stay her. The forgotten camera cuts her face. He springs up, abject and solicitous. The pitching boat capsizes. The genie reappears to whisper exonerating words. Hesitation—and Roberta sinks to lie entangled among water lilies, received back at last by Nature. Then the weir-weir bird's cry is heard anew. Part Two ends, as Part One had, with Clyde in flight from a girl's death.

With the opening of Part Three, a brisk, subtle, opportunistic society takes hold of events. As soon as news of the drowning reaches the coroner's office it triggers a political response. Both party newspapers must be told of the event immediately so that neither can gain an edge with the electorate at the expense of the other. Nor is this precaution an idle one, for the district attorney, Orville W.

Mason, seizes upon Clyde's plight as a means to further his own ambitions. As Clyde sought to destroy Roberta to realize his material ambitions, Mason now seeks to destroy Clyde to gain the same goal. Yet even Mason is manipulated by factors he has not willed. His childhood had been blighted by poverty and hard work. At fourteen, an accident to his nose had left him with a "psychic sex scar" which made him girl-shy and easily scandalized by the promiscuity of others. He had reached his present position by putting himself at the disposal of ambitious men. He had married money. He differs from Clyde merely in that he has advanced himself with more shrewdness. In fact, he is the greater transgressor. Quite possibly, Clyde has broken no law at all. Mason has prostituted the law even while he has professed to serve it.

When Mason first considers the case, the realization that Clyde has made Roberta cohabit with him before marriage strangely agitates him: "And was that not part and parcel of a rich and sophisticated youth's attitude toward a poor girl? By reason of his own early buffetings at the mood of chance and established prosperity the idea appealed to him intensely. The wretched rich! The indifferent rich!" Yet when he learns Clyde's actual status he is reluctant to carry through his intitial conjectures to their logical conclusions.

After his flight from the Big Bittern, Clyde joined Sondra and her friends at Pine Point, the bliss of having his dilemma resolved overshadowed by fear of imminent detection. Even Sondra's baby talk fails to soothe him. He goes through the motions of enjoying himself, half in a dream, shuddering when he joins his friends on a lake outing and one jocosely complains when the boat is rocked, "Oh, say, what do you want to do? Drown us all?" At length, he slips into the woods "as might a hunted animal," in experimental flight. But Nature is unreceptive to him now. Hovering at the edge of the woodlands, he is taken into custody. When he arrives at the jail at three in the morning, a crowd, alerted to the report that he had murdered "a young and charming working-girl" in order to free himself to marry a rich girl, is there to jeer him. "At the sight of the outer steel jail door swinging open to receive him, he actually gave vent to a sigh of relief because of the protection it afforded." Clyde had found a haven—an ironic commentary on the vistas the American Dream had opened to him.

Society presides over Clyde's destruction with solemn insistence. His jailers are exultant at housing the nephew of a rich manufacturer. Mason's assistant threads a few strands of Roberta's hair into Clyde's camera, to heighten the probability that Clyde's blow had been deliberate, thus eradicating any hope that a truthful account of what took place would be credited by the jurors. The local press features human interest stories on Roberta, building up sentiment in her support. Meanwhile society, which with its lures, pressures, and taboos, had sponsored this crime, now moves to protect itself from possible reprisal. The Finchleys take steps to keep their name from public view. The Griffithses veto a strenuous defense for Clyde because they do not relish the publicity it would elicit. Meanwhile, Democratic leaders, realizing the case can advance the political ambitions of Mason, a Republican, scheme to narrow his advantage. They suggest Clyde should be defended by Alvin Belknap, a man of considerable resourcefulness in the field of criminal law. Belknap himself is amenable only because he thinks he, too, may gain some political advantage from the case.

By recognizing and appealing to Clyde's need to be mothered, even, in a phrase reminiscent of the genie, "placing his hands on Clyde's shoulders"—Belknap draws from him a veracious account of what had occurred. Nevertheless, knowing the temper of backwoods jurors, he resolves to build the case on half truths. His first instruction to Clyde enjoins moral hypocrisy: "They hold services here in the jail on Sundays, and I want you to attend 'em regularly—that is, if they ask you to. For this is a religious community and I want you to make as good an impression as you can." He decides also that Clyde will be defended as "a moral coward," with emphasis on his remorsefulness, to appeal to the "religious and moral" nature of the jurors. The one sentimental counterthrust Clyde might use, the testimony of his parents, is forfeited when the Lycurgus Griffithses insist the social gap separating the two families must not be exploited by the press. When an account of Clyde's parents did reach the press, it "shocked Lycurgus and Twelfth Lake society. . . ." To some, Clyde's upbringing itself seemed not the least of his offenses against society. Even Sondra deliberates: "Was he not a murderer? And in addition, that miserable western family of his, pictured as street preachers, and he, too—or as a singing and praying boy from a mission!" *An American Tragedy* is much more than an attempt to reproduce fictionally an authentic criminal trial. Dreiser is conducting an inquiry into moods and opinions underlying American life.

The trial begins like a harvest festival. Crowds outside the courthouse are in holiday mood. Copies of Roberta's letters are hawked alongside hot dogs and peanuts. The irony is huge when one realizes that Roberta's "giant fear of exposure" had pushed Clyde to the

point of formulating his desperate plan to rid himself of her. Those
who would avenge her care nothing for her dignity as a person.

The jurors selected are, "with but one exception, all religious, if
not moral, and all convinced of Clyde's guilt before ever they sat
down. . . ." The prosecuting attorney addresses himself to sacro-
sanct emotions and convictions: "The secret and intended and im-
moral and illegal and socially unwarranted and condemned use of
her body outside the regenerative and ennobling pale of matrimony!"
—so much for Clyde's moral turpitude. "She loved him with that
love . . . that transcends in its strength and its weakness all fear
of shame or punishment from even the immortal throne above. "—so
much for Roberta's part in the same wrongdoing. "Good enough to
betray but not good enough to marry"—so much for Clyde's patri-
cian disdain of the poor.

Then Mason reads Roberta's letters aloud to the jurors, inducing
Roberta's mother to faint in the courtroom—"the audience almost
. . . as moved and incensed against Clyde by that development as
though, then and there, he had committed some additional crime."
And Clyde, through it all, wishing he might run away to the woods—
to a sheltering Nature no longer disposed to receive him. Sondra
is not mentioned by name during the trial. Clyde muses: "That was
what a family with money could do for you." Clyde's defenders meet
the situation boldly. The jury is cautioned not to come to any "mistaken judgment based on any local or religious or moral theory of
conduct or bias. . . ." Clyde was furtive because of "mental and
moral fear of the great social mistake as well as sin that he had committed in pursuing and eventually allowing himself to fall into this
unhallowed relationship. . . ." Mason's pursuit of Clyde is animal,
instinctual. He is "a restless harrier anxious to be off at the heels of
its prey. . . ." The very boat that Clyde had hired is produced in
the courtroom and Clyde made to step into it to re-enact events as
he had described them. This episode inevitably is unfair to Clyde
since the boat is not subject to the same caprice it had shown at
Moon Cove. But the effect on the jury of this piece of showmanship
is overwhelming. The boat again serves Dreiser as a death omen.
Nor does Mason stop here. Every technique of playing on the emotions of the jury is invoked. Each time Clyde registered at a hotel
with Roberta, it was under a different name, causing her to appear
"the unhallowed consort of presumably three different men in three
different days." Clyde's annotated travel folders from Lycurgus
House are introduced, to show he plotted his escape route before setting out on his fateful journey.

The summation appeal of the defense touches on the influence of the American Dream: "Mental and moral cowardice . . . inflamed or at least operated on by various lacks in Clyde's early life, plus new opportunities such as previously had never appeared to be within his grasp, had affected his *perhaps too pliable and sensual and impractical and dreamy mind*." But Mason spends a full day bringing the jurors to "the verge of tears." Individually polled, they vote like so many puppets: "They were like a blackish-brown group of wooden toys with creamish-brown or old ivory faces and hands." Puppetlike, they find Clyde guilty, their verdict directed by their social conditioning. In this crisis, Clyde instinctively sends a telegram to his mother, "But now . . . now . . . oh, he needed her now— so much." The cosmic waif who had wandered the world seeking the solacing comforts of the American Dream turns now to the only security he had ever known—his mother's arms. She who conducts a mission offering haven to the waifs of the world will learn too late that maternity begins at home. While the world of materialism closes in—jailers relating to reporters Clyde's moods and behavior; the press giving his mother travel fare *in exchange for an exclusive* —Clyde welcomes the seclusion and safety his cell proffers.

Mrs. Griffiths forthwith takes the offensive for her son. She points out that Roberta was three years Clyde's senior. She remarks: "And might it not be said in Clyde's favor—as in the very beginning of life in the Garden of Eden—'the woman tempted me?' " She notes that the district attorney had built his case on Roberta's letters. What Clyde is looking for when he is reunited with his mother is "sanctuary, sympathy, help, perhaps—and that without criticism— in her heart." In her arms he seems to find it. Meanwhile, shutting their eyes to the effect their own faint-hearted treatment of Clyde has had in sponsoring the disaster, the Griffithses of Lycurgus retreat into their money. Just as the American Dream had made Clyde willing to sacrifice Roberta, his wealthy relatives sacrifice him in order to salvage their own social well-being.

The concluding phases of Clyde's ordeal compel him to grope for new values. His black wavy hair and carefully chosen wardrobe give way to prison clip and prison drab. His companions in the death house regard him as "a little like mamma's boy. . . ." Initially he observes that most of his companions have turned "to some form of shielding or comforting faith. . . ." He himself drifts into familiar patterns of fantasy. A fellow prisoner, a lawyer, who like Clyde had seen murder as a short cut to the attainment of the American Dream, on the eve of his own execution sends Clyde two books, *Robinson*

Crusoe, gospel of the self-reliant man, and *The Arabian Nights,* refuge of the dreamer. Dreiser says now of Clyde: "His was a mind that . . . was naturally more drawn to romance than to reality. . . . He preferred the light, romantic novel that pictured some such world as he would have liked to share, to anything that even approximated the hard reality of the world without, let alone this." Into this world Mrs. Griffiths introduces the Reverend Duncan McMillan, a young evangelist. Caught up by the minister's personal attractiveness and honest ardor, Clyde begins his quest for spiritual peace: "Tortured by the need of some mental if not material support in the face of his great danger, Clyde was now doing what every other human in related circumstances invariably does—seeking . . . the presence or existence at least of some superhuman or supernatural personality or power that could and would aid him in some way. . . ." Still he wavers. Then he receives an unsigned letter from Sondra, tender, but final: "His last hope—the last trace of his dream vanished. . . . So this was the end of all that wonderful dream. . . . A vain—impossible dream." At last, for Clyde, a quietus to the American Dream which, in astonishing testimony to its tenacity, had not relinquished its hold on him to this point. Religion survives as his one possible solace. Sober deliberation, then a clean breast is made to McMillan concerning the exact circumstances of Roberta's death. McMillan, a religious prig, fails to realize that legally Clyde is not guilty of the crime for which he has been condemned. Clyde falls back into his familiar duality. McMillan's certitude disposes Clyde to think himself guilty, yet—how can McMillan and others really know? After all, McMillan had not been tortured as he had by Roberta with her determination that he marry her and thus ruin his whole life. He had not burned with that unquenchable passion for the Sondra of his beautiful dream, as Clyde had. They had not been harassed, tortured, mocked by the ill fate of his early life and training, when his whole heart and soul cried out for better things.

His mother cannot see things as they are. Clyde himself concludes: "She would never understand his craving for ease and luxury, for beauty, for love. . . . She would look on all of it as sin—evil, selfishness." She wanted him "terribly sorry and wholly repentant." But, somehow—"although great was his desire now to take refuge in God, but better yet, if it were only possible, in her own understanding and sympathetic heart,"—to end his status as waif—he could not find full conviction that he was the sinner society said he was.

Meanwhile the righteous McMillan stands before the governor empowered to save Clyde. He elects to remain silent, convinced Clyde had committed murder in intention if not in fact. Eventually he elicits from Clyde an edifying statement on the merits of Christian life, and embraces him believing the victory won. Yet Clyde's doubts persist. Even in his final parting with his mother, he does not truly possess peace of mind. In that last maternal embrace in which she "gathering him in her arms and holding him long and firmly to her," says, "My son—my baby," Clyde does not come to rest in that perfect peace that so long has escaped him. Seated in the electric chair, it is to McMillan that Clyde turns seeking the courage of belief that he has not been able to achieve. In the final crisis, McMillan's strength is not communicated to Clyde—Clyde's doubts are communicated to McMillan. At the moment of the execution McMillan has to be assisted from the room, sick and trembling, torn with disquieting thoughts. Had he, after all, sacrificed Clyde to his own convictions? Through McMillan, Dreiser emphasizes that society smugly upholds organizing values which Nature disputes. Yet McMillan alone, in his deep, sensitive sincerity, has been given the chance to realize that factors existed which neither society nor he himself had had the honesty to confront. As he had done with old Gerhardt, as he would do with Solon Barnes, Dreiser, in his portrayal of McMillan, breaks in on the complacency of the strict religionist to make him aware that there are values beyond those he has been willing to recognize. Meanwhile, Mrs. Griffiths kneels in prayer at home, trying to visualize her son having attained to perfect peace at last "in the arms of his Maker." She is spared the mental disquietude that promises to haunt McMillan through the rest of his life.

The phrasings of the epilogue to *An American Tragedy*, often identical to the phrasings of the prologue, suggest that the same things happen over and over again in such a world as man finds himself. Mrs. Griffiths has at her side her grandson, Russell, Esta's natural son. The events commemorated in Clyde's life are destined, it seems, to be repeated over and over again, not necessarily in the person of little Russell, but in each generation so long as the American Dream persists. Dreiser's title for Clyde's story stresses that the most typical thing that can happen to an American is the destruction of himself in the pursuit of riches. Mrs. Griffiths does not understand how Clyde's fate came to pass. Nor does society understand. So men must go on repeating the same mistakes, lamenting the sorrows of a harsh destiny.

The year after *An American Tragedy* appeared, Dreiser published a short story, "Typhoon." Ida Zobel, protagonist of this story, is repressed by her parents. While young people her age go joy riding, her outings are chaperoned. She accepts an invitation from a young man, Edward Hauptwanger, to drive to a beach in his father's car. Her seduction follows. When she realizes she is pregnant, she confronts Hauptwanger and insists he marry her. When he denies his paternity and seeks contemptuously to shove her aside, she shoots him, crying irrelevantly, "You will marry me." While her father characteristically worries, "that now the world would know all," she goes on trial for murder and, on a tide of public sympathy, is acquitted. Then she returns to the scene of her seduction and drowns herself.

"Typhoon" is a coda to *An American Tragedy*. Through it, Dreiser suggests that if Roberta had slain Clyde, society would have exonerated her. He wishes to show further that neither Ida nor Roberta desired only the approbation of society. Society could act on Roberta's and Ida's behalf but could not understand their needs. Both died seeking a love they might have found if arbitrary goals and decrees of society had not blocked access to Nature, thrusting them thereby into inhospitable liaisons.

12

THE BULWARK

D REISER FIRST conceived the idea of writing *The Bulwark* in 1910. The actual writing was begun in 1914, and a draft was completed. By 1916 a third of the book was in substantial form. Then things lagged until 1920 when Dreiser, working on it anew, wrote Liveright: "It will be a fine bit of literary property when it is finished." But soon he abandoned the manuscript again, to make way for *An American Tragedy,* and not until he wrote William Lengel in October 1941, offering to finish it for Putnam's Sons in six months, did he resume work on it in earnest. In July 1942 he wrote Louise Campbell that the newest version had reached chapter twenty—"the structure . . . well in hand." Work once more stopped as Dreiser came up against "a psychologic barrage [*sic*] of some kind." Finally, in August 1944, Marguerite Tjader Harris went to California to help him with it and Dreiser put himself on a daily work schedule. Working together, they assembled from four earlier drafts—especially the third one—and a fifty-page introduction written in 1943, the first and second parts of the final version of *The Bulwark.* The third part Dreiser partly wrote himself and partly dictated to Mrs. Harris. On May 6, 1945, the completed manuscript was dispatched to Louise Campbell, who suggested many excisions. Mrs. Harris protested. James T. Farrell was consulted and agreed there should be fewer cuts. Dreiser then left it to Donald P. Elder, of Doubleday and Company, to do as he saw fit, and the major changes which Mrs. Campbell advocated were held to. Looking over the galleys a week before his death, Dreiser approved the final version.

The Bulwark and *The Stoic* are novels of spiritual rapprochement. Dreiser was aware when he was writing them that his strength was ebbing, and he was anxious to offer his summary statement on life. Even before he wrote *Sister Carrie* he had spurned materialism and, at least since 1902, when he wrote "A Doer of the Word," he had paid homage to the sincere believer. In Charlie Potter, old Gerhardt, Mrs. Johns, Mrs. Griffiths, and Duncan McMillan, he had tried to understand the enigma of faith that brought serenity to some minds.

Not until he wrote the last part of *The Bulwark* did he find a way
to account for it. With consistency he continues to find that answer outside organized religion, in Nature. *The Stoic* merely gives
philosophical exegesis to conclusions already set down in *The Bulwark*.

Helen Dreiser says: "Teddie used the Bible extensively in writing
The Bulwark . . . Bible quotations had always interested him, and
I would say that not ten days passed in which he did not quote from
The Sermon on the Mount or some of the other sayings of Christ."
Helen saw Solon, with superficial perception, as Dreiser's attempt to
"psychologize the limited religionist." Mrs. Harris says Dreiser first
intended for Solon to die a disillusioned man, and restored his hero's
faith only as his own awakened. Eugene Witla had sought comfort in
religion and then concluded it was merely a haven to retreat to in
times of adversity. Clyde Griffiths' execution shook McMillan's
faith. Clyde, at the last, could not rid himself of spiritual misgivings.
Solon alone among Dreiser's protagonists is fortified by faith when
death comes. How reliably *The Bulwark* reflects Dreiser's own quest
for values may be gathered from a perusal of successive drafts of
the book preserved at the University of Pennsylvania. These, Elias
points out, offer a clear record of Dreiser's "progress from objec-
tive determinist through active social reformer to reverent, mystical
believer in an ordered universe." During his visit to New York in
June 1944, Dreiser had said to Mrs. Harris: "I believe in God now
—a Creative Force. . . . not just a blind force, but a great Artist,
who made all these things with such love and care. . . ." On this
same visit he told his niece, Dr. Vera Dreiser, "I not only believe in
God, but I can go in any scientific laboratory and prove His existence." "It's funny," Dreiser told Elias, about this same time, "how
a fellow can go along for years and not get it [awareness of the existence of God] . . . when it's there all the time." The reconciliation
was not with organized religion, however. It concerns, as Mrs. Harris says, "a faith that goes beyond sect to universal principles of love
and the brotherhood of man. . . ." The affirmation of faith that
appears in *The Bulwark* is prefaced by everything Dreiser wrote.
Possibly he is direct here because he thought the theme of his book
required him to present, in a way commensurate with Quaker illumination, not the dark ordeal of his spiritual journey, but only its
radiant conclusion. The influence of John Woolman, strongly per-
meating his text, suggests the graciousness of the mood that touched
him as he wrote.

The enviable calm of a bygone age dominates *The Bulwark* at the outset. The protagonist, Solon Barnes, is a fervent Quaker. Dreiser always strove for functional idiom in his stories, and here he matches the quiet, firm assurance that hallows the prose of Fox, Woolman, and Rufus Jones. To have placed Quaker idiom in an alien prose pattern would have been unthinkable to Dreiser. The only departures in the book are calculated departures—in Solon's and Etta's encounter at Wisconsin (where Etta defiantly caps Solon's "thou" with her own "you"), in the exuberant utterances of Volida La Porte and young Stewart, chiefly—and their disharmonious effect compels the reader to see that not only the style of the narrative but the fabric of the Quaker world itself is being rent.

Theme, structure, and style interlock in *The Bulwark*. Fundamentally, the book portrays the conflict between faith and materialism; it ends in an affirmation of the superiority of Nature, approached through Christian love. It is a measure of Dreiser's architectonic genius that he has structured the book on the public life of Christ, beginning with a wedding and ending with death and resurrection. Like Christ, Solon Barnes bears witness to the Word of Faith, is turned upon by those whom he would help, and undergoes a passion, a harrowing, and a crucifixion between two thieves—his own children. Before his actual death he dies "unto" himself to be reborn in Christ. In his extremity, a Magdalene (his daughter, Etta) attends him. Mrs. Harris deplores the excision from the text of the phrase, "beauty of spirit must hang upon a cross," which she believes central to Dreiser's basic intention in writing the book. Although the use of these analogies can be defended as a literary expedient, it supports subtly, not merely the characterization of Solon Barnes, but the beliefs to which he owes tenacious commitment. Possibly Dreiser has erred in allowing too much of this relationship to await statement in the parallel drawn between Solon and Woolman in the last pages of the book. It may be here that those who task him with superficiality implant their standards. If so, they owe it to him to re-examine their ground.

The Bulwark follows the model of *The 'Genius', An American Tragedy*, and the trilogy of desire in dividing into three parts. The four works have parallel actions. Part One brings a commitment to materialism. This commitment leads to the crisis climaxing Part Two. Part Three brings a reckoning and, finally, spiritual adjustment. The brief introduction to *The Bulwark*, in its recitation of the marriage promises exchanged by Solon and Benecia, echoes the ironic epigraph of *The 'Genius'*. While the scene is one of apparent bliss, the emphasis is on subtle forces, already well advanced, which are undermining

Quakerism. Quaker integrity has been worn away by the materiality of the modern day. Solon and Benecia cling to a belief few still take seriously. People cannot be spared much longer from the consequences of their inconsistencies.

Part One of *The Bulwark* tells of Solon's life prior to his marriage. He was born in Maine, in humble circumstances. Shy, grave, alert but not clever, he was trained easily to piety by devout Quaker parents. Rufus, his father, relocates the family in New Jersey, in order to manage the estate of his wife's widowed sister. Thus the children are thrust into conditions of materiality hardly consistent with Quakerism. Rufus justifies his activities by thinking of them as a kind of stewardship. He restores Thornbrough, a decayed manor house, as a homestead for his family, and tells himself that the atmosphere created is not one of sinful leisure but of contemplative quietude. When he clothes his family better than before, the change is rationalized: if he wishes to have the confidence of the men he does business with, he must maintain himself in a way reassuring to them. Unconsciously seeking a saving link with Nature, he also restores Thornbrough's gardens which had run to ruin. Here one suspects that Dreiser, in dealing in Edenic imagery, goes beyond the strict dimensions of his plot to suggest every man's archetypal yearning to repossess the condition of prelapsarian bliss.

Solon's sense of evil was first awakened when he killed a catbird with a sling (an incident out of Woolman's *Journal*). Rocked and petted in his mother's arms, surrogate refuge of the spiritually orphaned, he tells her what had occurred. Not only had he killed the bird, he has doomed her squabs. Why "so much ill could come about accidentally when plainly no cruelty or evil was intended" Hannah cannot explain. For Solon, the thoughts of evil and orphanhood are traumatic. The perplexity discovered here will follow him through life. Other accounts of Solon's early life stress his pacificity, his horror of promiscuity, and his supposition that all sinners are irrevocably damned. Dreiser explains that Solon was unaware of the effect social and environmental pressures have in shaping a man's behavior.

Even in accepting a higher standard of living than he had been accustomed to, Solon still believes practice will readily follow precept. When he is brought to contend with the restive temperaments of his own children, this naïveté will do him a grave disservice; their natural dispositions are to be far removed from the tranquil moods which have been his heritage, and the world they will live in will possess little of the stability he was able to take for granted through his own youthful years.

If Rufus Barnes is haunted by the description of wealth in Quakerism's Book of Discipline as "fettering and disqualifying," Benecia's father, Justus Wallin, is not similarly perturbed. He is banker and Quaker, in that order. Servants serve his meals on silver plates, upon massive carved mahogany tables. When he rises at meeting it is to reiterate the one insight the Inner Light has vouchsafed him, a "formula concerning material wealth as a stewardship under the direction of the Lord." He makes his formula so plausible that both Rufus and Solon enter his employ. Only Hannah feels wealth is inimical to the Quaker ideal, but she cannot say too much because their sudden affluence came about through the intervention of her own sister, the owner of Thornbrough and other properties Rufus manages. Solon and his father raise no objection when Wallin urges them to buy a fine carriage and bay (surrogates for the flux of Nature), but presently Hannah dreams of Solon astride a proud black mare that throws him, injuring him severely. This beautiful, seemingly calm, yet treacherous mare represents "the sudden shift in their material and social status." Nowhere is Dreiser's use of the vehicle as flux symbol as open as it is in this instance. Hannah's premonitions, in fact, are not premature. Her sister's oldest daughter, Rhoda, already is wearied of Quakerism, and eager to escape its restraints. When Rhoda reminds her friends that Thornbrough belongs not to Rufus but to her mother, Solon humbly corroborates her, eager to disavow material taint. But in avoiding one snare Solon steps into another. His frankness here so impresses Benecia she confesses her love for him. Ironically, despite his good intentions, their marriage will draw him into a fateful commitment to materialism.

Solon is an upright Clyde Griffiths, an Alger hero who follows the rules of the game. It was the dream of his youth to have "a good position, a handsome home, a beautiful young wife, powerful friends and relatives, health and strength." Unlike Clyde, Solon saw his dream come true. But, as in the experience of Carrie, Cowperwood, and Witla, its attainment did not bring his happiness. All of Part One in *The Bulwark* is uneventful if events are to be measured in blows of fortune. Every step Solon and his father take is reconciled carefully to Quaker scruples; nothing seems ever to miscarry. Solon wonders if "fate or luck or the Inner Light" has put him in the company of the Wallins, but chiefly he supposes it is Quaker discipline that disposes everything to happen in his favor. Solon (and this fact supplies relevance to his name) found life "a series of law-governed details." Wallin's bank, the Traders and Builders, had been founded in 1811 to profit from money-manufacturing franchises the govern-

ment had made available to the favored few. As Dreiser describes the
bank's present officers and directors, their kinship with the founders
is self-evident. Skidmore, the president, is indifferent to the character of his customers; Sableworth, the first vice-president, wor-
ships successful men. Cashier Averard has one ambition: to become
a millionaire, and he is not particular about the means he must use
to succeed. Into this fetid environment Wallin sends Solon. Yet he
means him no injury. He merely wants for his daughter a husband
who will protect her inheritance.

Solon thinks all successful men are honest and that every wrong-
doer is brought to justice. Yet within a short time after coming to the
bank, he mistakes an innocent man for a thief and hires a clerk who
becomes an embezzler. None of Dreiser's characters disavows the role
of cosmic waif more vehemently than Solon, yet his very lack of so-
phistication points to an unconscious need for him to find haven in
Nature. Dreiser relates, at the close of Part One, that on Solon's wedding night "His ardor was tempered by a yearning, voiceless desire
to be mothered by this girl whom he loved so fervently. . . ." As
Part Two opens, Solon is experiencing qualms of conscience concerning the fortune the Wallins have bestowed on him and his bride.
Benecia, as naïve as her bridegroom, placates him with her father's
doctrine of stewardship. At the close of the conversation in which she
accomplishes this feat, Solon is looking out the window in a mood of
serenity. Hopping birds and a hammock (familiar symbols of the flux
of Nature) lay under his view, but he is cut off from them. He has
plighted his troth with materialism. Yet this same chapter ends with
the death of Hannah, whose uncompromising integrity has made
her Solon's strongest link with Nature. The loss of his mother plunges
him into a depression that tries his faith. The birth of his daughter,
is a rallying point—but a qualified one; the child, Isobel, is plain
and in frail health.

The diction, as well as the events encountered in Part Two of *The
Bulwark,* imply that Solon's idyll is over. A brisk, cacophonous tone
succeeds the tranquil flow of words in Part One. Moreover, the pace
of events itself accelerates as chaos overwhelms the quiet world Solon is conditioned to cope with. Up to now he had judged men and
events by fixed standards. Soon, as the father of five, he must make
his principles work not only for Benecia and himself, but for a generation confronted—in part due to his own compromise with materialism—with temptations he himself had never known. For a time,
extending the happy idyll of his youth into his adult years, he has
kept his way clear of strife by petty equivocations. In banking he

side-stepped a confrontation with materialism by confining himself to modest dealings and being content with small profits. Wondering how to distinguish ambition from greed, he consulted the Book of Discipline. In fact, he wanted "not to bolster his faith but to strengthen his convictions in this matter of prosecuting a vigorous business career." The sight of Skidmore and Sableworth coming and going in expensive limousines (material proxies, of course, for the flux of Nature) excited him and he would have emulated them had it not been for an unnerving experience that occurred at this time. A youthful Quaker embezzled bank funds to indulge worldly appetites. The ordeal both mystifies and alarms Solon.

During this period, other things occur to bring Solon to a confrontation with reality, specifically, the death of his father and the restive antics of his children. He had set exacting standards for his children. Bicycling, roller skating, sleigh riding, bobsledding, playing games (all flux activities), as well as fairy tales and candy making, were under interdict. When Rufus died, Solon moved his own family to Thornbrough, telling himself he had done this to shield them, in the environs of Nature, from worldly influences. But subtle forces work against his expectations. The ill-favored Isobel feels thwarted; Dorothea, popular and vain, yearns for a fuller life; Orville is money-centered. The two youngest children, Etta and Stewart, are drawn to the flux of Nature. Etta is a dreamer. Wafted away by fairy stories clandestinely told her by a neighbor, "slowly rocking in her little rocking chair," she would dream of "paradise." Stewart is a sensualist. He jumped and screamed when he saw a parade go by and wanted to march with the marchers. "Color, motion, beauty, the more vivid forms of life" attracted him and, on visits to Philadelphia "the crowded streets, the moving people, the cars, the shop windows seemed terribly exciting." The flux of life beckons. Solon's only instinct "to love him past the dangers which might lie ahead," is "to take him in his arms and rock him." Given Stewart's tempestuous spirit, this surrogate flux activity could not contain him for long. Solon cannot understand why life is filled with mischance. As once he had wondered about the bird felled by his sling, now he weighs these larger problems in the plan of existence.

In Hester Wallin, Benecia's aunt, Solon's children find a powerful advocate for the greater freedom for which they yearn. Hester is a frequent guest at Thornbrough. Under her influence, Isobel is sent to Llewellyn, a modern Quaker college; Orville, scheming to marry money, takes employment with American Potteries, bringing himself into a desired intimacy with the Stoddards—wealthy, lax Quakers.

In due time, Dorothea follows Isobel to Llewellyn. Unlike Isobel, whose shyness is a natural defense against extremism, Dorothea feels she can no longer keep to her father's standards. Then Etta, the youngest daughter, who also longs for a fuller life than her father envisaged, is sent to Chadd's Ford, a progressive Quaker boarding school. There she catches glimpses of "the spinning modern world beyond," of "venturesome bicycling parties," of an amorous cyclist who "leaped lightly from his bicycle" to kiss his fair companion while Etta, unseen, stood "motionless" watching them; and she is awakened wholly to the flux of Nature. At Chadd's Ford an aggressive girl, Volida La Porte (a name connoting flight and liberation) brings Etta under worshipful domination. Solon, meantime, is a stranger to the real moods of his children. He supposes the misfortunes befalling others illustrate "the sins of the fathers visited upon the children." He rejoices that "by constant counsel with the Inner Light he had been able to guard the actions of his own children." After Hester Wallin's death, the liberation of the Barnes children enters its final phase. Her funeral brings Dorothea and Stewart into contact with cousin Rhoda, who has forsaken Quakerism for an active role as a society hostess. Rhoda soon contrives to receive Dorothea as a guest in her home. She sees to it that Dorothea dresses attractively and learns to dance. Under the spell of the dance, Dorothea is caught up in "the rush and swing and spirit of the time." The following summer, Etta runs away from home to attend the University of Wisconsin summer school. In anticipation of a legacy left her by Aunt Hester, she finances her rebellion by pawning family heirlooms.

The immediate cause of Etta's flight had been a quarrel with her father over her clandestine reading. Logically enough, she had moved on from the forbidden fairy tales to other forbidden books— Balzac's *La Cousine Bette,* Flaubert's *Madame Bovary,* Daudet's *Sappho.* Solon can no more understand what moves her now than he had understood her needs as a child. On a train trip to Wisconsin, in an unsuccessful attempt to bring her home, his separateness from the flux of Nature is distinguished in his neglectful response to the world of Nature visible from the train as it hurtles along. Unable to persuade Etta to return home, Solon returns alone, to be plunged into a new crisis. Justus Wallin has died in Solon's absence, and in the readjustment that follows three new directors are brought into the bank: Wilkerson, a man without religious or social ties; Baker, a man whose prosperity is built on backroom deals with politicians and promoters; and Seay, a man outwardly gracious, but inwardly savage. Solon wonders if, after all, he may be out of step with the times. He half decides to liberalize his viewpoint. Never were his principles in greater danger.

From Wisconsin, Etta, who has had enough of "repression and religion," goes to New York. There she becomes the mistress of Willard Kane, a Yankee artist from her native state of Maine who "got tired of painting New England types. . . ." Dreiser does not condone Etta's behavior; yet he comprehends it. It is the inevitable consequence of the unnatural repression of her former life.

Part Two ends with Dorothea's wedding, at Thornbrough. The conditions hinted at in the introductory wedding scene, that then scarcely touched Solon and Benecia, now weigh on them fully. If serenity dominates Part One of *The Bulwark*, unrest keynotes Part Two. Part Three seems to promise chaos or acceptance. In fact, it will provide both.

The same autumn Etta went to New York, Stewart enrolled at Franklin Hall, a Quaker school. He is excited by the clothes his wealthy classmates wear, by the cars some of them have access to. At the same time he is provoked because his own allowance is so meager. Then cousin Rhoda visits him at school and genially confides that all the Barneses and Wallins have "hung onto their Quakerism until they're almost extinct as human beings. . . ." Self-appointed deus ex machina that she is, she provides him with money and cover stories which enable him to go joy riding with his friends. Under her dubious aegis he learns to dance, "vibrating to that rhythm of sex and beauty which can only be fully understood by youth." He steals small sums of money from his family and even from his classmates. Then, suddenly, events hurry forward to a tragic climax. Joy riding with two classmates, he ravishes a girl, Psyche Tanzer, who had been drugged by one of his companions to make her more compliant. The girl dies. The account of Stewart copulating with the expiring "Psyche," by the seashore, suggests the futility of his desire to ally himself with the flux of Nature. Of Solon's children, Stewart alone had felt remorse when he displeased his parents. Arrested, he fatally stabs himself in his jail cell.

While the events leading to Stewart's death were building to their conclusion, events at the Traders and Builders moved toward yet another climax. Ignoring offers of preferment from his codirectors, Solon has invested his own money conservatively and encouraged consideration for the small investor. When he finds out that the bank is insolvent due to behind-the-scenes manipulations of his colleagues, the way of duty is clear. He invites the Treasury Department to do a little plain speaking to his fellow directors. Although the offenders can guess who has informed on them, they choose not to antagonize him—his respectability is a "bulwark" for them to hide behind.

While Orville and Dorothea view Stewart's fate as a social disaster, the event induces Solon to re-examine his own behavior. He recalls that Quakerism's Book of Discipline warns that riches accumulated by parents often bring irreparable harm to their children. His failure, then, had begun with his rationalizations about materialism. Dreiser implies, with characteristic irony, that he has lost Stewart to his stewardship. Now: "cold, profit-seeking business seemed to him utterly corrupting and destructive of normal human life. He had been no less guilty than those others: sitting beside them as director and furthering their schemes for the lunatic accumulation of wealth; money that meant only such unnecessary luxuries and pleasures as had been flaunted before the eyes of Stewart and had finally destroyed him." Over the years, religion and money-making had merged in Solon's mind. He had seen the bank: ". . . as almost partaking of the nature of a church. . . . To accumulate or manage money in order to achieve a good, or needed services, was a worthy and moral principle. . . . And since all Christian principles were of God, one also worshiped God by accumulating property and taking care of it in the best and most frugal and helpful way. . . . great institutions were necessary in the service and care of money and property, and therefore those who served in them were more or less high priests of the people." In his innocency Solon had reactivated the American Dream in all its original purity, but the society that sustained it originally no longer existed. The task was too much for one man alone. Sensing the sophistries of his position, Solon presents himself at the bank. Calmly he declares his role in the reform instituted by the Treasury Department. He concedes there is little he can do to combat the greed of the modern world, but he can at least dissociate himself from it. With his resignation, separated from material ambition and shaken in his rigid understanding of his faith, Solon is available at last to the flux of Nature.

Dreiser now picks up Etta's story again. She who had quested Nature through beauty is forsaken by her lover. The fatal outcome of Stewart's quest of Nature, coming at the time of her own sorrow, stirs her compassion, and she returns home to nurse her mother, lately bedridden with a stroke. To Etta's astonishment, Solon receives her with charity and understanding; his new perceptions have transformed him. When Benecia dies, Etta becomes her father's mainstay. Finding a closeness to Nature at Thornbrough, she is able to think of it at last as her true home.

Throughout *The Bulwark,* Solon is thrust often into the world of Nature but seems indifferent to it. His father had restored the gardens of Thornbrough to their prelapsarian splendor, but Solon never seemed to have leisure to enjoy them. Benecia and he had declared their love for one another there, following a minnow chase, but even then, he was unaware of Nature's contributing effect. Nature beckoned again, on his June wedding day, a tranquil scene spread before the meeting house windows—"wide fields . . . blue-green hills . . . and over all the twittering birds"—but Solon had no eye for it." The first days of his marriage found him looking through a window at a peaceful expanse of Nature, complete with "hopping birds." Yet it is not this scene that he pondered, but his new affluence. One day, after moving to Thornbrough, he found Stewart and Etta, then mere toddlers, frolicking nude by a stream, in a spontaneous salutation to Nature; to him it seemed a gross carnal offense. Following Aunt Hester's death, on his drive from the station with Isobel, she sighed at the beauty of the springtime but Solon was unresponsive: "He looked about him but did not answer, his eyes and senses rather dulled to the finer suggestions and whisperings of the hour." On his journey to Wisconsin, troubling thoughts distracted him from the agreeable view of the passing landscape. When he reached the university he interviewed Etta by the lakeside: "And see what a beautiful place this is!" Etta had said. But Solon ignored her remark, to talk on issues. Presently, however, a view of Nature through a window —"The calm and beauty of the June evening, the grass and trees of the campus, and the lake beyond"—eased "the dark trouble in his mind" sufficiently for him to agree to Etta's terms. Mrs. Harris says this scene gave Dreiser particular difficulty and that its resolution came to him one night in a dream. But true kinship with Nature still evades Solon. Finally, after Benecia's death, impelled by the thought that Thornbrough's garden "should mean as much to him" as it did to her, Solon opens his heart to Nature. Walking in the garden one day he comes upon an exquisite fly devouring a bud which otherwise would have opened into a noble blossom. He considers the scene around him—fish, birds, butterflies, blades of grass, a climbing vine: "Surely there must be a Creative Divinity, and so a purpose, behind all of this variety and beauty and tragedy of life. For see how tragedy had descended upon him and still he had faith, and would have." At last, he was confronted by what he had avoided since, as

a child, he had killed the catbird and orphaned its squabs. Then, he
had built a wall between himself and Nature; afraid of the problem
of the origin of evil, he had been afraid of the Nature which had
brought that problem to his notice. Now he finds in Nature an answer to the question he had found there before. For Solon, the fly-bud
incident opens the way at last to participation in the flux of Nature.

Nature holds yet a further revelation for Solon. One day he meets
a harmless puff adder in his garden. The snake at first seeks to men-
ace him, but when he speaks to it calmly, it approaches him and
cross the toe of his shoe. In 1938, at Iroki, Dreiser himself had
had a similar encounter with a puff adder. Recounting the incident
to Elias, Dreiser intimated it had brought him into new understanding with Nature and the Creative Force. The incident offers an ex-
cellent illustration of the way Dreiser could transmute personal experiences into the substance of literature. Not only does Solon's encounter with the puff adder invert Genesis by making the serpent an
agent of rapprochement rather than estrangement, but it catches also
the essence of a crucial episode in Coleridge's "The Rime of the Ancient Mariner." When Coleridge's afflicted mariner, like Solon, estranged from Nature because he has killed a bird, makes a gesture
of love toward the water snakes, the curse that had weighed on him
is miraculously lifted and he is restored to grace. Dreiser's interest
in this poem was recorded just a few years earlier, in his eulogy of
Sherwood Anderson: "Whenever I think of him, I think of that wondrous line out of 'The Ancient Mariner,' 'He prayeth best who loveth
best, all things, both great and small.'" Solon's experience here has
much the same effect on him. It takes him beyond rigorous Quakerism and tainted materiality to a true understanding of man's part in
Nature.

While writing *The Bulwark*, Dreiser felt a resurgence of his creative powers. He was able to sustain this power by turning frequently
to Nature, interrupting the work for short intervals while he moved
about the grounds surrounding Mrs. Harris' cottage, examining the
flowers and seeking the company of a genial bluebird who, much to
his delight, seemed at home in his presence. Solon and Dreiser re-
discovered Nature together. Of his experience with the puff adder,
Solon told Etta:

> Good intent is of itself a universal language, and if our intention is
> good, all creatures in their particular way understand, and so it was
> that this puff adder understood me just as I understood it. It had no
> ill intent, but was only afraid. And then, my intent being not only

IN GRASP OF THE INFINITE (ABOUT 1945)

good but loving, it understood me and had no fear. . . . And now I
thank God for this revelation of His universal presence and His good
intent toward all things—all of His created world. For otherwise how
would it understand me, and I it, if we were not both a part of Himself?

At this point Etta asks, "Father, has thee always felt this way about
Nature?" Solon answers:

Daughter, until recently I have not thought as I think now. Many
things which I thought I understood, I did not understand at all. God
has taught me humility—and, in His loving charity, awakened me to
many things that I had not seen before. One is the need of love toward all created things.

Solon, the law-giver, at last humbly receives the wisdom of Nature.
While Solon is thought to have been modeled by Dreiser on his own
father, Dreiser is not vicariously submitting himself here to his
father's judgment. Rather is the father shown relinquishing his own
severe code to adopt his child's faith in Nature. Dreiser's concession
comes in recognizing now, and formally acknowledging, a spiritual
goal in Nature.

Etta soon reflects Solon's new found perceptions. Even the discovery that he has cancer does not alter her faith. Woolman's *Journal* teaches her that Quakerism is ideally adapted to a faith in Nature: "John Woolman and her father were helping her to understand
. . . the love and peace involved in the consideration of others. . . .
In this love and unity with all nature . . . there was nothing fitful
or changing or disappointing. . . . This love was rather as constant
as nature itself. . . . an intimate relation to the very heart of being." Etta now feels this greater love herself, and is disposed at last
to respond to it.

One day Etta read to Solon Woolman's account of the conviction he had had, in serious illness, that an angel said "John Woolman is dead." Upon his recovery, Woolman understood that the
angel spoke not of his physical death but of the death of his will.
Woolman concluded: "I am crucified with Christ, nevertheless I
live, yet not I but Christ liveth in me. And the life which I now live
in the flesh I live by the faith of the son of God, who loved me and
gave himself for me." Later, in the final phase of his illness, Solon
asks Etta what has become of the poor old man who had been dying of cancer—a query that shows that he, like Woolman, had van-
quished his will. But Etta, not yet vouchsafed his state of acceptance,

ascribes his query to delirium. Truly he is at one with Nature. The last afternoon of Solon's life finds him offering mingled lamentations on banking institutions, and averring: "Men must be honest with God and with themselves,"—his last thoughts, a further abjuration of materialism. Then—a last query for Etta—"If thee does not turn to the Inner Light, where will thee go?" and he expires.

At Solon's funeral Orville insolently asks Etta why she, who had been the start of Solon's troubles, cries now. She answers gently, "Oh, I am not crying for myself, or for Father—I am crying for *life*." As yet she does not know "the life" lived "by the faith of the son of God," which Solon partook of in his last illness. The "life" she laments is that which society proffers man. Yet something of Woolman's spirit has penetrated her own. She has begun to understand. She has suffered; even her father, a good man, has suffered. It is something to weep over, but something to be borne. Even without understanding she must trust its intent.

The concluding third of *The Bulwark* may well be Dreiser's last testament. It states coherently his final views on man's role in the universe. An old man, sick and impelled, he hews to the main lines of his lifelong search with perfect consistency. Solon rejects materialism and religious formalism to uphold unity in all Nature under the guidance of the Creative Divinity. Berenice Fleming will see it as union with Brahman, but it is the same. The true faith is as Woolman saw it: "a principle placed in the human mind, which in different places and ages hath had different names; it is, however, pure and proceeds from God. It is deep and inward, confined to no forms of religion nor excluded from any, when the heart stands in perfect sincerity."

Attaining "this true faith," man, the cosmic waif, comes at length into "intimate relation to the very heart of being," into the final, all-sheltering embrace of the Creative Force which Dreiser, at last, spoke of as God.

SELECTED BIBLIOGRAPHY

DREISER'S CHIEF WORKS

NOVELS

Sister Carrie. New York: Doubleday & Company, Inc., 1900. (P)*
Jennie Gerhardt. New York: Harper & Row Publishers, 1911. (P)
The Financier. New York: Harper & Row Publishers, 1912. Revised edition, New York: Liveright Publishing Corporation, 1927. (P)
The Titan. London: John Lane, The Bodley Head, Ltd., 1914. (P)
The 'Genius'. London: John Lane, The Bodley Head, Ltd., 1915. (P)
An American Tragedy. New York: Liveright Publishing Corporation, 1925. 2 vols. (P)
The Bulwark. New York: Doubleday & Company, Inc., 1946.
The Stoic. New York: Doubleday & Company, Inc., 1947.

COLLECTED SHORT STORIES

Free, and Other Stories. New York: Liveright Publishing Corporation, 1918.
Chains. New York: Liveright Publishing Corporation, 1927.
Fine Furniture. New York: Random House, Inc., 1930. A single story brought out in a separate edition.
The Best Short Stories of Theodore Dreiser, ed. Howard Fast. Cleveland: The World Publishing Company, 1947.
The Best Short Stories of Theodore Dreiser, ed. James T. Farrell. Cleveland: The World Publishing Company, 1956. (P)

AUTOBIOGRAPHY

A Traveler at Forty. New York: Appleton-Century, 1913.
A Hoosier Holiday. New York: John Lane, The Bodley Head, Ltd., 1916.

* (P) indicates works available in paperbound edition.

A Book About Myself. New York: Liveright Publishing Corporation, 1922. With 8th edition, retitled *Newspaper Days.* (P)

Dawn. New York: Liveright Publishing Corporation, 1931. (P)

OTHER NONFICTION

Twelve Men. New York: Liveright Publishing Corporation, 1919. (P)

Hey, Rub-A-Dub-Dub: A Book of the Mystery and Wonder and Terror of Life. New York: Liveright Publishing Corporation, 1920.

The Color of a Great City. New York: Liveright Publishing Corporation, 1923.

Dreiser Looks at Russia. New York: Liveright Publishing Corporation, 1928.

A Gallery of Women. New York: Liveright Publishing Corporation. 1929. (P)

"What I Believe," *Forum* (November 1929), 279–281.

Tragic America. New York: Liveright Publishing Corporation, 1931.

"The Early Adventures of Sister Carrie," a foreword to *Sister Carrie.* New York: Random House, Inc., 1932. Pp. v–vii.

"The Myth of Individuality," *American Mercury,* XXXI (March 1934), 337–342.

"You, the Phantom," *Esquire,* II (November 1934), 25–26.

The Living Thoughts of Thoreau, ed. Theodore Dreiser. New York: David McKay Company, Inc., 1939. Thirty-two page introduction, "Presenting Thoreau." (P)

America Is Worth Saving. New York: Modern Age Books, 1941.

Poetry

Moods, Cadenced and Declaimed. New York: Liveright Publishing Corporation, 1928. Revised edition, New York: Simon and Schuster, Inc., 1935.

Drama

Plays of the Natural and Supernatural. London: John Lane, The Bodley Head, Ltd., 1916.

The Hand of the Potter. New York: Liveright Publishing Corporation, 1918.

Letters

Letters of Theodore Dreiser, ed. Robert H. Elias. Philadelphia: University of Pennsylvania Press, 1959. 3 vols.
Letters to Louise, ed. Louise Campbell. Philadelphia: University of Pennsylvania Press, 1959.

Bibliography

Birss, J. H. "Records of Theodore Dreiser: A Bibliographical Note," *Notes & Queries,* 165 (September 30, 1933), 226.
Lange, W. W. "Theodore Dreiser, Bibliographical Checklist," *Publishers' Weekly* (December 22, 1923), 1925.
McDonald, Edward D. *A Bibliography of the Writings of Theodore Dreiser.* Philadelphia: The Centaur Book Shop, 1928. Contains a foreword by Dreiser.
Miller, Ralph N. *A Preliminary Checklist of Books and Articles on Theodore Dreiser.* Kalamazoo: Western Michigan College Library, 1947.
Orton, Vrest. *Dreiserana: A Book About His Books.* New York: The Chocurua Bibliographies, 1929.

Biography

Dreiser, Helen. *My Life with Dreiser.* Cleveland: The World Publishing Company, 1951.
Dudley, Dorothy. *Forgotten Frontiers: Dreiser and the Land of the Free.* New York: Harrison Smith & Robert Haas, 1932.
Elias, Robert H. *Theodore Dreiser: Apostle of Nature.* Philadelphia: University of Pennsylvania Press, 1949.
Gerber, Philip L. *Theodore Dreiser.* New York: Twayne Publishers, Inc., 1964. (P)
Matthiessen, F. O. *Theodore Dreiser.* New York: William Sloane Associates, 1951. (P)
Mordell, Albert. *My Relations with Theodore Dreiser.* Girard, Kansas: Haldeman-Julius, 1951. Pp. 1–17 of a paperback volume which also includes two essays on free thought.
Rascoe, Burton. *Theodore Dreiser.* New York: Robert M. McBride Company, Inc., 1926.
Shapiro, Charles. *Theodore Dreiser: Our Bitter Patriot.* Carbondale, Illinois: Southern Illinois University Press, 1962.
Swanberg, William A. *Dreiser.* New York: Charles Scribner's Sons, 1965. (P)

Tjader, Marguerite. *Theodore Dreiser: A New Dimension*. Norwalk, Connecticut: Silvermine Publishers, 1965.

BIOGRAPHICAL CRITICISM

Haley, Carmel O'Neill. "The Dreisers," *Commonweal* (July 7, 1933), 265–267.
Huth, J. F. "Theodore Dreiser: 'The Prophet,'" *American Literature*, IX (May 1937), 208–217.
———. "Theodore Dreiser, Success Monger," *Colophon* (Winter 1938), 120–133; (Autumn 1938), 406–410.
Josephson, Matthew. "Dreiser, Reluctant, in the Films," *New Republic*, 68 (August 19, 1931), 21–22.
Sebestyen, Karl. "Theodore Dreiser at Home," *Living Age*, 339 (December 1930), 375–378.

Anthology of Critical Studies

The Stature of Theodore Dreiser, ed. Alfred Kazin and Charles Shapiro. Bloomington, Ind.: Indiana University Press, 1955. (P)

SELECTED CRITICISM: 1907–1950

Anderson, Sherwood. "Introduction" to Dreiser's *Free and Other Stories*, New York: Modern Library, Inc., 1925.
Arnavon, Cyrille. "Theodore Dreiser and Painting," *American Literature*, 17 (May 1945), 113–126.
Church, Richard. "The American Balzac," *Spectator* (July 25, 1931), 133–134.
Elias, Robert H. "The Library's Dreiser Collection," *University of Pennsylvania Library Chronicle*, XVII (Fall 1950), 78–80.
Farrell, James T. "Theodore Dreiser: In Memoriam," *Saturday Review of Literature* (January 12, 1946), 16–17, 27–28.
Gilkes, Martin. "Discovering Dreiser," *New Adelphi* (December 2, 1928), 178–181.
Hazlitt, Henry. "Our Greatest Authors: How Great Are They?," *Forum* (October 1932), 245–250.
Krieg, Louis W. "The Dreisers," *Commonweal* (July 28, 1933), 330.
Krutch, Joseph Wood. "Dreiser Simplified," *The Nation* (April 1, 1936), 427–429.
Lewis, Sinclair. "The Literary Zoo," *Life* (October 10, 1907), 414.
Lord, David. "Dreiser Today," *Prairie Schooner* (Winter 1941), 230–239.

Norris, Charles G. "My Favorite Character in Fiction: Hurstwood,"
    Bookman, 62 (December 1925), 410–411.
Sherman, Stuart P. "The [Barbaric] Naturalism of Mr. Dreiser," *The
    Nation* (December 2, 1915), 648–650. Reprinted in *The Stature of
    Theodore Dreiser,* henceforth cited as STD.
Smith, Edward H. "Dreiser—After Twenty Years," *Bookman,* 53 (March
    1921), 27–39.
Spiller, Robert E. "Dreiser as Master Craftsman," *Saturday Review of
    Literature* (March 23, 1946), 23.
Taylor, G. R. S. "The United States as Seen by an American Writer," *The
    Nineteenth Century,* 100 (December 1926), 803–815.
Van Doren, Carl. "Contemporary American Novelists: Theodore Dreiser,"
    The Nation (March 16, 1921), 400–401.
Vivas, Eliseo. "Dreiser, an Inconsistent Mechanist," *Ethics,* XLVIII (July
    1938), 498–508. Revised for STD.
Walcutt, Charles C. "The Three Stages of Theodore Dreiser's Natural-
    ism," *Proceedings of the Modern Language Association,* LV (March
    1940), 266–289. Revised for STD.

SELECTED CRITICISM: 1951 TO THE PRESENT

Ahnebrink, Lars. "Dreiser's *Sister Carrie* and Balzac," *Symposium,* VII
    (November 1953), 306–322.
Bellow, Saul. "Dreiser and the Triumph of Art," *Commentary* (May
    1951), 502–503. Reprinted in STD.
Bernard, Kenneth. "The Flight of Dreiser," *University of Kansas City
    Review,* XXVI (Summer 1960), 251–259.
Berryman, John in *Highlights of Modern Literature,* ed. Francis Brown,
    New York: New American Library, 1954. Reprinted in STD.
Blackstock, Walter. "Dreiser's Dramatization of Art, the Artist, and the
    Beautiful in American Life," *Southern Quarterly,* I (October 1962),
    63–86.
Butler, Gerald J. "The Quality of Emotional Greatness," *Paunch,* No. 25
    (February 1966), 5–17.
Cohen, Lester. "Theodore Dreiser: A Personal Memoir," *Discovery,* No.
    4 (September 1954), 99–126.
Davis, David Brion. "A Reappraisal of Early Naturalism in America," in
    STD, pp. 225–236.
Dudding, Griffith. "A Note concerning Theodore Dreiser's Philosophy,"
    University of Pennsylvania Library Chronicle, XXX (Winter 1964),
    36–37.

Flint, R. W. "Dreiser: The Press of Life," *The Nation* (April 27, 1957), 371–373.

Freedman, William A. "A Look at Dreiser as Artist: The Motif of Circularity in *Sister Carrie*," *Modern Fiction Studies*, VIII (Winter 1962), 384–392.

Grebstein, Sheldon N. "Dreiser's Victorian Vamp," *Midcontinent American Studies Journal*, IV (Spring 1963), 3–11.

Hakutani, Yoshinobu. "Dreiser and French Realism," *Texas Studies in Literature and Language*, VI (Summer 1964), 200–212.

Handy, William J. "*Sister Carrie* Reexamined," *Texas Studies in Literature and Language*, I (Autumn 1959), 380–393.

Heuston, Dustin. "Theodore Dreiser, Naturalist or Theist?," *Brigham Young University Studies*, III (Winter 1961), 41–49.

Hoffman, Frederick. "The Scene of Violence: Dostoievsky and Dreiser," *Modern Fiction Studies*, VI (Summer 1960), 91–105.

Howe, Irving. "Dreiser and the Tragedy," *New Republic*, CLI (July 25, 1964), 25–28.

Kern, Alexander. "Dreiser's Difficult Beauty," *Western Review* (Winter 1952), 129–136. Reprinted in STD.

Krim, Seymour. "Theodore Dreiser," *Hudson Review*, IV (Autumn 1951), 474–477.

———. "Dreiser and His Critics," *Commonweal* (June 1, 1956), 229–231.

Kwiat, Joseph J. "Dreiser and the Graphic Artist," *American Quarterly*, III (Summer 1951), 127–141.

———. "Dreiser's *The 'Genius'* and Everett Shinn the 'Ash Can' Painter," *PMLA*, LXVII (March 1952), 15–31.

Lane, Lauriat, Jr. "The Double in *An American Tragedy*," *Modern Fiction Studies*, XII (Summer 1966), 213–220.

Leaver, Florence. "Theodore Dreiser: Beyond Naturalism," *Mark Twain Quarterly*, IX (Winter 1951), 5–9.

Lydenberg, John. "Theodore Dreiser: Ishmael in the Jungle," *Monthly Review*, VII (August 1955), 124–136.

Markels, Julian. "Dreiser and the Plotting of Inarticulate Experience," *Massachusetts Review*, II (Spring 1961), 1–48.

Millgate, Michael. "Theodore Dreiser and the American Financier," *Studi Americani*, VII (1961), 133–145.

Mizener, Arthur. "The Innocence of Dreiser," *New Statesman and Nation*, LVIII (July 4, 1959), 20.

Moers, Ellen. "The Finesse of Dreiser," *American Scholar*, XXXIII (Winter 1963), 109–114.

Nathan, George Jean. "Memories of Fitzgerald, Lewis, and Dreiser," *Esquire*, L (October 1958), 148–154.

Phillips, William L. "The Imagery of Dreiser's Novels," *PMLA*, LXXVIII (December 1963), 572–585.

Richman, Sidney. "Theodore Dreiser's *The Bulwark:* A Final Resolution," *American Literature*, XXXIV (May 1962), 229–245.

Simpson, Claude. "*Sister Carrie* Reconsidered," *Southwest Review*, XLIV (Winter 1959) 44–53.

Steinbrecher, George, Jr. "Inaccurate Accounts of Sister Carrie," *American Literature*, XXIII (January 1952), 490–493.

Thomas, J. D. "The Natural Supernaturalism of Dreiser's Novels," *Rice Institute Pamphlet*, XLIV (April 1958), 112–125.

Wagner, Vern. "The Maligned Style of Theodore Dreiser," *Western Humanities Review*, XIX (Spring 1965), 175–184.

Westlake, Neda. "Theodore Dreiser's *Notes on Life*," *University of Pennsylvania Library Chronicle*, XX (Summer 1954), 69–75.

Willen, Gerald. "Dreiser's Moral Seriousness," *University of Kansas City Review*, XXIII (March 1957), 181–187.

GENERAL STUDIES

Aaron, Daniel. *Writers on the Left: Episodes in American Literary Communism*. New York: Harcourt, Brace & World, Inc., 1961.

Blankenship, Russell. *American Literature as an Expression of the National Mind*. New York: Holt, Rinehart and Winston, Inc., 1958.

Boyd, Ernest. *Portraits: Real and Imaginary*. New York: Doubleday & Company, Inc., 1924.

Cleaton, Allen and Irene. *Books and Battles: American Literature, 1920–1930*. Boston: Houghton Mifflin Company, 1937.

Contemporary American Authors, ed. John Collings Squire. New York: Holt, Rinehart and Winston, Inc., 1928.

Dahlberg, Edward. *Alms for Oblivion*. Minneapolis: University of Minnesota Press, 1964.

Duggan, Margaret. "An Interpretive Study of *The 'Genius'*. Unpub, disser., Boston College, 1966.

Fiedler, Leslie A. *Love and Death in the American Novel*. New York: Criterion Books, Inc., 1960.

Geismar, Maxwell. *American Moderns: from Rebellion to Conformity*. New York: Hill & Wang, Inc., 1958.

———. *Rebels and Ancestors: The American Novel, 1890–1915*. Boston: Houghton Mifflin Company, 1953.

Gelfant, Blanche H. *The American City Novel*. Norman, Okla.: University of Oklahoma Press, 1954.

Goodfellow, Don M. "Theodore Dreiser and the American Dream," *Carnegie Series in English,* 5 (1959), 53–66.

Haight, Anne (Lyon). *Banned Books.* New York: R. R. Bowker Company, 1935.

Hatcher, Harlan H. *Creating the Modern American Novel.* New York: Holt, Rinehart and Winston, Inc., 1935.

Hicks, Granville. *The Great Tradition.* New York: Crowell-Collier and Macmillan, Inc., 1933.

Kazin, Alfred. *On Native Grounds.* New York: Reynal & Hitchcock, Inc., 1942.

Kramer, Dale. *Chicago Renaissance.* New York: Appleton-Century, 1966.

Lewisohn, Ludwig. *Expression in America.* New York: Harper & Row Publishers, 1932.

Lynn, Kenneth. *The Dream of Success: A Study of the Modern American Imagination.* Boston: Little, Brown & Company, 1955.

McCole, Camille John. *Lucifer at Large.* London: Longmans, Green & Co., Inc., 1937.

Mencken, H. L. *A Book of Prefaces.* New York: Alfred A. Knopf, Inc., 1917.

———. *Prejudices: Fourth Series.* New York: Alfred A. Knopf, Inc., 1924.

Michaud, Regis. *The American Novel Today.* Boston: Little, Brown & Company, 1928.

More, Paul Elmer. *The Demon of the Absolute.* Princeton: Princeton University Press, 1928.

Morris, Lloyd R. *Postscript to Yesterday.* New York: Random House, Inc., 1947.

Noble, David W. "Dreiser and Veblen and the Literature of Cultural Change," in *Studies in American Culture: Dominant Ideas and Images,* ed. Joseph J. Kwiat and Mary C. Turpie. Minneapolis: University of Minnesota Press, 1960.

Pattee, F. J. *The New American Literature, 1890–1930.* New York: Appleton-Century, 1930.

Rahv, Philip. *Image and Idea.* New York: New Directions, 1949.

Rideout, Walter B. *The Radical Novel in the United States, 1900–1954.* Cambridge, Mass.: Harvard University Press, 1956.

Snell, George. *The Shapers of American Fiction: 1798–1947.* New York: E. P. Dutton & Co., Inc., 1947.

Stepanchev, Stephen. *Dreiser Among the Critics: An Abridgment* (dissertation abstract, New York University). New York: New York University Press, 1950.

Stewart, Randall. *American Literature and Christian Doctrine*. Baton Rouge: University of Louisiana Press, 1958.

Trilling, Lionel. *The Liberal Imagination*. New York: Doubleday & Company, Inc., 1954.

Wagenknecht, Edward. *Cavalcade of the American Novel*. New York: Holt, Rinehart and Winston, Inc., 1952.

Whipple, Thomas K. *Spokesmen: Modern Writers and American Life*. New York: Appleton-Century, 1928. Reprinted in STD.

Ziff, Larzer. *The American 1890's*. New York: The Viking Press, Inc., 1966.

INDEX

Note: Characters and other fictional subjects encountered in Dreiser's works are entered in small capital letters.

171